Preparing and Sustaining
Social Justice Educators

Preparing and Sustaining Social Justice Educators

Annamarie Francois and
Karen Hunter Quartz

HARVARD EDUCATION PRESS
CAMBRIDGE, MASSACHUSETTS

Paperback ISBN 978-1-68253-652-0
Library Edition ISBN 978-1-68253-653-7

Library of Congress Cataloging-in-Publication Data is on file.

Published by Harvard Education Press,
an imprint of the Harvard Education Publishing Group
Harvard Education Press
8 Story Street
Cambridge, MA 02138

Cover Design: Endpaper Studio
Cover Image: DrAfter123/DigitalVision Vectors via Getty Images

The typefaces in this book are Sabon and ITC Stone Sans.

To our beloved Center X community
(past, present, and future),
allies in the struggle for human rights,
racial justice, and healing
#PowerWith

Contents

Introduction   1
Annamarie Francois and Karen Hunter Quartz

PART I
Preparing Educators to Transform Teaching and Learning

CHAPTER 1   Making the Rhetoric Real   11
Jeannie Oakes

CHAPTER 2   Learning to Become a Community Teacher   31
Annamarie M. Francois and Jarod Kawasaki

CHAPTER 3   Framing Preservice Teacher Learning and Accountability   49
Jaime J. Park, Imelda L. Nava, and Melissa S. Arias

PART II
Sustaining Educators to Deepen Praxis and Continue the Struggle

CHAPTER 4   Reciprocal Learning Partnerships for Equity: Supporting Educators to Critically Reflect, Disrupt, and Take Action   75
Tonikiaa Orange and Jo Ann Isken

CHAPTER 5   Beyond Teacher Education: Creating Opportunities
             for Continued Learning   91
             Jody Z. Priselac and Megan L. Franke

CHAPTER 6   Equity-Oriented Science Professional Development   105
             Lynn Kim-John, William A. Sandoval, Jarod N. Kawasaki,
             Leticia Perez, Jon Kovach, and Heather F. Clark

CHAPTER 7   "It's a Circle": UCLA's Principal Leadership Institute
             and the Practice of Social Justice Leadership   125
             John Rogers and Nancy Parachini

PART III
Transforming Public Schools

CHAPTER 8   A Transformative Partnership: Theodore Roosevelt
             Senior High School and the University of California,
             Los Angeles, Teacher Education Program   143
             Emma Hipólito and Ben Gertner

CHAPTER 9   UCLA Community School: Creating a Workplace
             Culture that Sustains Social Justice Educators   163
             Karen Hunter Quartz, Leyda Garcia, Queena Kim,
             and Marisa Saunders

CHAPTER 10   Mann UCLA Community School: Reimagining
             and Restoring a Neighborhood Public School   179
             Carrie Usui Johnson, Orlando Johnson, Ung-Sang Lee,
             Christine Shen, and Carla Estes

CHAPTER 11   We Asked for Trouble   199
             Jeannie Oakes

             Notes   219
             About the Editors   233
             About the Contributors   235
             Index   243

Introduction

Annamarie Francois and
Karen Hunter Quartz

CICELY'S KINDERGARTEN STUDENTS squirm in front of their Zoom screens. She is teaching students how to write a shopping list, using words and drawings. Later in the day, Cicely joins an online research seminar at the University of California, Los Angeles (UCLA), as part of her PhD program in Urban Schooling. During the check-in, she shares the shopping list and the joy she experienced seeing her students' faces light up: "You can't get a clearer perspective on life than through the eyes of a kindergartner."

Cicely began her teaching career twenty-four years ago, in a school not far from where she grew up. During her first year of student teaching, she was robbed at gunpoint—a terrifying incident that clarified what she calls "a mission to help children see the range of possibilities for their lives so that they don't see crime or this type of behavior as their only option." She still lives and works in the same community, buying her groceries alongside her students' parents. As a fifth-year teacher—when so many lose hope and leave the profession—Cicely said she was "too angry to leave." After ten years, she reflected on what it means to stay in the same community: "Consistency is important, the kids see that people are committed to them." Today, Cicely also mentors student teachers, organizes parent activists, conducts research, and leads professional learning. This book is about the community that supports and sustains educators like Cicely as they transform our public schools to create a more just, equitable, and humane society.

Schools are the moral, political, and social centers of our democracy. When we work to change schools, we are working to change society. In times when our nation's core values are being challenged and our social contract grows ever more tenuous, we look to public schools for a brighter future. In response to the global pandemic and racial violence that erupted in 2020, we saw schools step up to feed families, deliver health care, provide technology, and help young people unpack race, racism, and police violence. We witnessed teachers holding space during precious instructional time to take care of confused, frustrated, traumatized, and righteously angry young people. As they have for decades, educators like Cicely inspire the next generation to believe in democracy, the importance of their own voice, and the power of coming together in community to imagine a better future.

This book brings to life the challenging work of preparing and sustaining educators to disrupt educational inequality in urban communities. It is not a how-to guide. Nor is it a celebration of best practices. Rather, through grounded stories and examples from thirty years of collective work in Los Angeles, we illustrate the kind of professional activity you find in communities that view teaching and leading as progressive political acts of love guided by an antiracist, social justice agenda. You will find pedagogical approaches that honor and draw upon the rich racial, cultural, and linguistic diversity of families and communities to make learning more accessible, culturally relevant, and sustaining. You will find deliberate activity intended to provoke deeper learning, engaged clinical practice and induction, and sustained professional development from "cradle to grave." Activity that ensures educational quality and equity. You will find robust school-university partnerships that work hard to center depth of knowledge, powerful pedagogies, and transformative school cultures. We share these stories knowing that they are part of a much larger narrative about the role of public education in disrupting pernicious inequalities in our society—a story line rooted in particular values, politics, and practices.

A BELOVED COMMUNITY

The UCLA campus is anchored by Royce Hall, named after Josiah Royce, a teacher whose students included W. E. B. Du Bois and T. S. Eliot. Royce was also a philosopher who stated, "My life means nothing, either theoretically or practically, unless I am a member of a community."[1] Royce developed the concept of "the beloved community" that shaped the civil rights work of Dr. Martin Luther King Jr., who believed "our ultimate end must be the creation of the beloved community."[2] Many educators take up this idea, such as bell hooks, who explains, "Beloved community is formed not by the eradication of difference but by its affirmation, by each of us claiming the identities and cultural legacies that shape who we are and how we live in the world."[3] Center X is one of many beloved communities of educators across the globe. As a movement, we share the values of inclusion, respect, and love. We unite around a common set of beliefs about the importance of culture, identity, and justice.

A POLITICAL COMMUNITY

We also unite in political struggle. We ask for trouble. Center X was created in response to the civil unrest and racial uprisings that followed the 1992 Rodney King verdict, and now, almost thirty years later, we continue the fight for racial justice in the wake of the murders of George Floyd, Breonna Taylor, and too many others. We are indebted to Black Lives Matter's cofounder Patrisse Cullors, who, like Royce, anchors the work of our university. A celebrated alumna, Cullors makes her political stance clear: "While other people are trying to subjugate human beings, there's a whole other group of people trying to liberate them, and I'm on that side of history."[4] So is the Center X community. Teacher leaders, school principals, teacher educators, professional development experts, program directors, and researchers are committed to making schools and classrooms liberatory spaces of belonging, connection, and learning, particularly for young people whose lives have been shaped by poverty, racial violence and injustice, and trauma. A community that exists because we've seen firsthand how the multiple faces of bias, discrimination, and oppression affect the lives of our beloved students.

A LEARNING COMMUNITY

We are also a professional community of educators who understand teaching and learning practice. We know (and at times have unconsciously contributed to) classroom and leadership practices that present barriers to social and academic growth, as well as student agency. Dismantling these barriers is slow and steady work. Teachers and school leaders must prepare students to meet academic content standards, develop important socioemotional skills, and become critical thinkers and creative problem-solvers. Skills they will need to actively and productively contribute to what has become an increasingly fragile democracy. Skills they will need to solve the very complex problems their parents and teachers and principals are grappling with today.

OUR HOPE FOR THIS BOOK

Over the years, we have been criticized for being too value-driven, too political, and too radical in the classroom. To be sure, this work is contested by many and runs counter to policies that support fast-track teacher preparation, scripted curricula, high-stakes standardized testing, and other efforts that deskill teachers and constrain their capacity to educate students. As the authors in this book attest, the work to push against the grain is tough intellectual work that is often hard and exhausting. We share Center X's thirty years of experience in hopes that it ignites your imagination about what is possible in your own spheres of influence. We hope it provides other urban teacher educators with an opportunity to reflect on and perhaps reimagine their curriculum and instruction. We hope that teacher education deans and directors, as well as school and district leaders, will find this book a valuable tool for creating authentic, community-dedicated, praxis-focused, and justice-oriented school-university partnerships. And, ultimately, we hope that policy makers at all levels of our educational system will use Center X's experience to create programs and put forward legislation that increases public commitment to the education of our most vulnerable students.

A STORY IN THREE PARTS

Twenty-eight Center Xers came together to write this book to ensure we captured multiple perspectives on a rich thirty-year history of work together. Part I of the story contains three chapters that set the stage. Chapter 1, our origin story, was published in 1996 by Jeannie Oakes, whom we affectionately think of as the mother of Center X. Oakes sets forth a bold vision to make the rhetoric of social justice real by fundamentally changing the way the university prepares and supports educators. In this chapter, you'll learn about the center's seven guiding principles and the historic context that brought them to life. Chapter 2 picks up these principles in its portrayal of the current work of UCLA's Teacher Education Program (TEP). Center X Executive Director Annamarie M. Francois and teacher education researcher Jarod Kawasaki draw on the rich tradition and experiences of *community teachers* to propose a set of abolitionist practices within teacher preparation. These practices bring together the lived experiences of aspiring teachers and K–12 students, as well as an understanding of sociopolitical context, to construct and enact an antiracist pedagogy. Chapter 3 takes up the pressing policy issue of measuring and evaluating teacher quality. Veteran teacher educators Jaime J. Park, Imelda L. Nava, and Melissa S. Arias describe the development and use of a social justice classroom observation rubric designed to extend and deepen teacher learning.

In part II, we transition to the work of sustaining community teachers through ongoing professional learning partnerships. Chapter 4 describes an alternative approach to coaching that reframes the achievement gap as an equity gap that results from the unexamined explicit and implicit biases educators carry with them into the classroom and perpetuate in their practice. Coaching experts Tonikiaa Orange and Jo Ann Isken detail how school and classroom culture, structures, and pedagogies are often culturally oppressive and exacerbate inequalities, and they explore the need for educators to engage in critical conversations and self-reflection seldom found in conventional coaching models. Chapter 5 champions equity-guided, content-focused professional learning "cradle-to-grave" opportunities for educators working for social justice. Longtime Center X leaders Jody Z. Priselac and Megan L. Franke explore two research-practice partnerships grounded in a common vision of public schooling and transformative relationships. In chapter 6, a team of researchers, content and professional development experts, and graduate student researchers look inside a research-practice partnership and describe how it deepened and sustained practice that centers students and leads to increased student agency. Chapter 7 turns to the process of preparing educational leaders for justice and the need for continued support and inquiry. John Rogers and Nancy Parachini, co-directors of the UCLA Principal Leadership Institute, amplify the voices and experiences of new and seasoned school leaders within and beyond their ongoing community of practice.

Part III introduces you to three beloved school communities. You'll hear from the principals of these schools and the partners they work alongside. In chapter 8, Principal Ben Gertner teams up with TEP Director Emma Hipólito to tell the story of Roosevelt High School, a historic neighborhood school in the East Los Angeles community of Boyle Heights. They detail how the university has supported social justice work at the school over the past thirty years. In chapter 9, Principal Leyda Garcia and Assistant Principal Queena Kim partner with UCLA researchers Karen Hunter Quartz and Marisa Saunders to tell the UCLA Community School's story, focusing on how this decade-old partnership in Los Angeles's Koreatown community has created a democratic workplace culture where teachers want to work and stay. And in chapter 10, Principal Orlando Johnson and Assistant

Principal Carla Estes join Center Xers Carrie Usui Johnson, Ung-Sang Lee, and Christine Shen in reporting on the Mann UCLA Community School—a new partnership with a South Los Angeles school slated for closure—contributing to the debate about how best to address the epidemic of school closures in neighborhoods of color.

In full circle, the book concludes with a powerful chapter by Jeannie Oakes, who reflects on what it now means to make the rhetoric of social justice real. In this very personal essay, Oakes reflects on the words she wrote in 1996 when Center X was "asking for trouble." She lifts up the words and legacy of congressman and civil rights icon John Lewis to frame the book's themes, using reflections from the authors about what it means to make "good trouble, necessary trouble." As they did more than twenty years ago, Oakes's thoughtful words and critical analysis will inspire Center X's journey forward.

Marian Wright Edelman reminds us, "We must always refill and ensure there is a critical mass of leaders and activists committed to nonviolence and racial and economic justice who will keep seeding and building transforming movements."[5] Center X remains committed to recruiting, developing, and retaining teachers and school leaders who are transforming public schools. We persist in this work because while we can identify urban schools that support the learning of their most vulnerable students well, high-quality public schooling remains elusive for far too many others. As it was in 1992, the recent racial violence and resulting civil unrest reminds us that the time is always now—and high-quality teaching and leading continues to be our most powerful lever for change and justice. This is a lifetime of work. We invite you to join us—in beloved community—to make some good and necessary trouble.

PART I

Preparing Educators to Transform Teaching and Learning

CHAPTER 1

Making the Rhetoric Real

Jeannie Oakes

ON A THURSDAY AFTERNOON in April of 1992, the faculty of the Graduate School of Education and Information Studies at UCLA sat squabbling in its usual fashion over its agenda of bureaucratic minutiae at its regular faculty meeting. Because our building—historic Moore Hall at the center of the campus—was undergoing seismic renovation, faculty had relocated to the seventeenth floor of a high rise at the busy commercial intersection of Westwood and Wilshire Boulevards. A spacious corner office, formerly occupied by a megacorporation CEO, now enhanced faculty meetings with its spectacular, sweeping view of the city. As we met that Thursday, someone noticed the first fire—a small bright spot to the south and east—and then another, and another, and another. We sat stunned as we watched our city's tenuous

Originally published in *Multicultural Education* 4, no. 2 (Winter 1996).
Reprint permission from Caddo Gap Press.

social contract go up in smoke just hours after the jury delivered its not guilty verdict in the Rodney King beating trial. Then we rushed to our cars and crawled slowly through the traffic toward our homes that were mostly far from the trouble.

I will not claim that we changed dramatically after that Thursday, but some things have not been quite the same. It has not been so comfortable since then for some of us to look past our city as we focus our educational research nationally and internationally. It has not been so easy to claim that our research and teaching interests rightfully claim a larger purview than schooling in our hometown. Some of us started feeling a bit foolish as we boarded planes for Washington, New York, Chicago, and elsewhere to struggle with issues of race, poverty, and inequality in schools. Some of us began to consider how we might bring our work closer to home.

In a very real sense, then, Center X (Where Research and Practice Intersect for Urban School Professionals) at UCLA actually began on that Thursday afternoon in April 1992. But, of course, we didn't know it then. And it wasn't until three years later in the fall of 1995 that we welcomed our first cohort of teacher candidates who had signed on to our teacher education program expressly committed to social and educational justice for low-income children of color in urban Los Angeles.

Our discussions about what we might do in the months following the Rodney King verdict were premised on our understanding that, typically, the structures, cultures, and pedagogies practiced in schools (and rarely challenged or disrupted by university research and teaching) work to exacerbate the inequalities in the rest of our society. With seemingly neutral, sometimes even scientific, technology and language, schools compound the disadvantages of children who have less outside of school. Many with meager economic prospects, often racially diverse and bilingual and limited-English proficient students, are judged to be disabled, "not ready," lacking social capital, or, most pernicious, simply not as intelligent as their most advantaged peers. The upshot is that even though it's disappointing when children don't achieve, it's not really unexpected in urban schools. Everybody says that "all children can learn," but few really believe it. Too often, the one institution that low-income, racially diverse, bilingual, and limited-English proficient and immigrant families count on for access to a better life simply helps perpetuate the cycle of discrimination, poverty, and hopelessness.

This paper skips over the three years of reading, thinking, worrying, arguing, hesitating, persuading, waiting, and hoping that led to Center X—our effort to reshape UCLA's professional education programs in ways that could acknowledge and perhaps even confront these conditions. Suffice it to say that we gobbled up Jim Banks, Jim Cummins, Antonia Darder, Carl Grant, Gloria Ladson-Billings, Marilyn Cochran-Smith, Christie Sleeter, and Ken Zeichner to get a handle on linking teacher education, social justice, and multiculturalism. We wrestled with the ideas of Henry Giroux, bell hooks, and our own Peter McLaren about helping teachers become critical pedagogues. We sought counsel from Luis Moll, Roland Tharp, and our own Ron Gallimore and Kris Gutierrez to better understand the implications of Vygotskyian sociocultural learning theory for diverse Los Angeles schools. We looked to Nel Noddings, our own Lynn Beck, and to the Macdonalds' work to help us struggle with helping teachers become caring advocates for students without reducing them to dependent clients. We kept in mind my tracking work as we thought about the power of structures to shape expectations and limit opportunities. And we considered the ideas of Saul Alinsky and his intellectual/ activist descendants regarding the power of person-to-person organizing. We reread John Dewey. Suffice it to say that we wrote lots of proposals and attended lots of meetings.

What I'd like to do here is to describe what we're actually trying to do in teacher education at UCLA to make our rhetoric about social justice and multiculturalism real.

CENTER X: THE POWER OF MANY

Center X brings together under one mission and organizational umbrella a number of programs that were formerly quite separate, and it has dramatically changed the nature of those activities. Center X is UCLA's Teacher Education Program (formerly the Teacher Education

Laboratory) that grants California CLAD/BCLAD (Cross-cultural Language and Academic Development / Bilingual Cross-cultural Language and Academic Development) elementary and secondary teaching credentials and MEd degrees. It is also six of the state-sponsored California Subject Matter Projects, the UCLA Principals' Center, and other professional development projects for practicing educators. It is also the Graduate School of Education's EdD program in Education Leadership.

We thought that by building on the synergy of these enterprises and developing long-term, positive, interdependent connections with schools and districts, Center X could integrate preservice teacher education, teachers' induction into the profession, and the continuing development of seasoned professionals. We also thought that we could blend our programs for professional educators with the training of our aspiring PhDs. Finally, we thought that by bringing all these people together, Center X might also itself be able to become what we want schools to be—caring, ethical, racially harmonious, and socially just.

Actually, we're a pretty motley crew. Some of us are faculty with programs of research and teaching to be attended to—both junior- and senior-ladder faculty, as well as visiting faculty and postdoctoral scholars. Some of us are what we call "clinical faculty" (although only the medical school is allowed to use this job title officially) with doctorates, who teach courses in the MEd program for our teacher candidates, provide non-degree, professional development activities for practicing educators, and administer our credentialing process. Some of us are practicing K–12 professionals who lead Center X programs and courses on campus or in schools and district offices. Some of us are graduate students hoping to use UCLA educations to launch careers as teacher educators, researchers, or educational leaders. Some of us are teacher candidates with ambitious goals for ourselves in urban schools and high hopes that the Center X teacher educators won't lead us into waters deeper than we can swim. We are Anglo, African American, Latino, and Asian. Some of us speak only English, but many of us also speak Spanish, Korean, Vietnamese, Tagalog, Armenian, and other languages. We are old, young, and in-between; male and female; gay and straight; and who knows what else.

SOME NON-NEGOTIABLES

We knew that many forces would conspire against our ambitious social and educational agenda. Not the least, we'd be pressed to be reasonable, to use our common sense, to be a bit less idealistic. We worried that unless we established a solid, principled grounding for our new Center, we'd soon find ourselves on the slippery slopes of efficiency and expediency. So, when we were ready to go public with Center X, we began with a set of "non-negotiables"—things about which we would not compromise. These are our core values, and these would be the measuring stick by which we would measure our progress:

1. *Embody a social justice agenda.* The racial, cultural, and linguistic diversity of our Los Angeles community is its strongest asset, and we will act on this by constructing extraordinarily high-quality education for all children and particularly for low-income children of color in Los Angeles's schools. We seek to turn policymakers' attention, educational resources, and teachers' talents toward those in our city who have the least outside of school.

2. *Treat professional education "cradle-to-grave."* Education is a seamless process that connects efforts to attract young people into teaching, with learning experiences for teacher candidates, with learning experiences for novice teachers, and with learning experiences for seasoned professionals. Further, it is a process that is focused on serving students—of all ages—and their families and communities.

3. *Collaborate across institutions and communities.* Collaborative efforts provide the best means to address the entire ecology of settings and institutions that contribute to children's education. Center X is committed to develop and sustain long-term, positive, interdependent connections and equal status partnerships among K–12 schools and community colleges, UCLA, and the diverse communities of Los Angeles.

4. *Focus simultaneously on professional education, school reform, and reinventing the university's role in K–12 schooling.* Center X must help new and experienced educators acquire the knowledge and skills necessary for social justice and educational quality in

urban schools. At the same time, the Center's work must press schools to develop cultures that encourage and support putting new knowledge and skills into practice. Moreover, UCLA itself will need to change as it crafts new roles and responsibilities for the university in these collaborative research/practice efforts. We all have much to learn.

5. *Blend research and practice.* Center X will combine opportunities to acquire new knowledge and skills with research aimed at creating new knowledge and the practical application of that knowledge in schools. UCLA scholars must formulate and conduct their research and teaching in ways that reflect the realities of children, educators, schools, and communities. School professionals, in turn, must guide their practice by a process of critical inquiry, reflection, and social responsibility.

6. *Bring together educators' and students' need for depth of content knowledge, powerful pedagogies, and school cultures that enable serious and sustained engagement in teaching and learning.* We view these three domains of teaching and learning as inextricably connected. Our core work is to better understand this complex relationship and promote reform efforts that approach all three domains.

7. *Remain self-renewing.* View change and problems as "normal" conditions that require a flexible, responsive, non-static, learning organization. Center X must resist efforts to shape its activities into a traditional, control-oriented, bureaucratic organization. Rather, it must remain a commitment-driven entity whose structures organize people around important problems, interests, and goals.

A NEW CULTURE OF TEACHER EDUCATION

Once we'd gone public with these principles, we decided that we'd better get a bit more concrete. We were going to educate our novice teachers in schools where most students are poor and non-White. We were going to send them into neighborhoods they may have only seen before on the nightly news. We knew that no matter how committed to our ideals they might be, we knew that being committed wouldn't be enough. We needed to develop and deliver a curriculum that would help them withstand their own and their families' anxieties—as well as their friends' puzzlement—about what they'd chosen to do. We needed to deliver on our promise to educate teachers who could transform urban schools and classrooms. To do this, we'd need to translate our "non-negotiable" principles into a pretty specific set of knowledge, skills, and experiences that would allow our novice teachers to see themselves as grounded and prepared, as well as committed.

Following Henry Giroux's notion of the "transformative intellectual," we wanted them to have "the courage to take risks, to look into the future, and to imagine a world that could be as opposed to simply what is."[1] But we also wanted them to have the capacity and confidence to act on what they could imagine.

How have we attempted to translate our principles into a teacher education program? We identified our four interrelated roles that we thought students should learn to be transformative and efficacious urban teachers, and everything we do with our students—our curriculum—aims at their developing these roles. These are what we help Center X teachers become:

- Caring Advocates for All Students
- Reflective, Inquiry-Based Practitioners
- Community Builders
- Generative Change Agents

Caring Advocates

We knew we'd get no argument from our novice teachers when we shared James B. Macdonald and Susan Colberg Macdonald's view of the importance of educators having a fundamental commitment to a just and caring society: "Human life is experienced in the way we live our everyday lives, our relationships to ourselves and others, our sense of personal belonging in society and the cosmos. We believe this demands a human condition characterized by freedom, justice, equality, and love."[2] But we also expected that our mostly middle-class novices would have had little experience with acting on such sentiments, particularly when they were confronted with the staggering increases in the numbers of Los Angeles children growing up in the physically, medically, and emotionally hazardous conditions that increasingly prevail in our inner city.

Frankly, we were worried that, like so many bright, idealistic, middle-class young people, they would approach this ethic of care with a missionary-like zeal for rescuing people whom they saw as unable to rescue themselves. We had seen in our research too many well-intentioned educators who, because they felt such sympathy, tried to make schools safe and comfortable places that didn't add to their disadvantaged students' burdens. As such, they expected very little of them.

Rather, we wanted to foster an ethic in which care would be expressed as high expectations, confidence in students' capacity, and support for persistence and high achievement. This meant, we believed, that our novice teachers must rethink such fundamental notions as "intelligence," "motivation," "a value for education," "parent support," and "sense of responsibility," that have acquired common-sense meanings that work against those who aren't white and middle class (or, at least, don't act like they are).

We also believed that caring advocacy meant that our teachers needed to learn to use the racial, cultural, and linguistic diversity of their students as a resource for constructing rich and meaningful learning opportunities. We also decided that new teachers must have opportunities to approach learning, teaching, and curriculum from constructivist perspectives that reflect the diversity of our society in all its aspects: gender; race; cultural, linguistic, and ethnic identification; multiple intelligences; socioeconomic status; family structure; and others. We also decided that they needed to learn about sociocultural approaches that could promote literacy and make content knowledge accessible to students from a range of ethnic and linguistic backgrounds, particularly those who have limited English proficiency.

In addition, we thought they should connect with emerging research in the area of cultural congruence and culturally democratic pedagogy that suggests the importance of connecting students' school

experiences to their home culture—in effect, making them congru-
ent. Furthermore, this ethic of caring meant that all our teachers
must learn bilingual and primary language instructional strategies
and have a great deal of practice using them. It also meant that they
needed to become familiar with the social supports that are available
in Los Angeles communities and they must learn how to help children
and their families—not out of kindness alone, but because such supports enable learning and persistence.

Teachers as Reflective, Inquiry-Based Practitioners

We decided that we needed to enable our novice teachers to be questioning and reflective about everything—even the wisdom we thought
we were imparting. It would do little good, we decided, if they simply
"learned" a new set of things that we thought were important in place
of the old conventions. In particular we wanted them to become ever
mindful of how our culture and institutions seem to easily distort
well-meant ideas and actions in ways that perpetuate discrimination
and inequality. During this time at Center X, we decided the teacher
candidates must engage in an ongoing process of reflection and critical inquiry that connects theory, current research findings, scholarship, and practice. So we decided to make inquiry our own primary
pedagogical tool—and, importantly, to model teachers-as-inquirers
with regular "inquiry sessions" of faculty and staff where no "business" could be conducted, only a serious consideration of the meaning
of our enterprise, and a careful scrutiny of the beliefs, values, and assumptions that inform our decisions.

We also decided that reflective Center X teachers must remain actively engaged in the disciplines they teach, as well as learn about teaching. Writing teachers should write, history teachers should conduct
original inquiries into historical topics, science teachers should do scientific investigations, and art teachers should perform. That way, they
could learn how their disciplines create knowledge, have opportunities
to reflect on the equitable dimensions of that knowledge, and more
effectively understand the school and classroom contexts that permit
teachers and learners to engage in creating discipline-based knowledge.

We charged the Directors and Teacher Leaders of the UCLA Subject Matter professional projects with this task, and they have completely reconstructed our "methods" courses, and engage the novices in professional development in the content areas with the Los Angeles Basin's most talented teachers.

Teachers as Community Builders

We knew that our teachers' knowledge, skills, and dispositions must not only extend beyond the classroom walls, but also beyond the schoolyard. Children grow up in the ecology of institutions and activities that educate—for good or for ill. While schools may be the "official" and most formal of these educational agents, they are not necessarily the most powerful or influential. Particularly in low-income, racially, culturally, and linguistically diverse neighborhoods, the influence of teachers and schools may pale in the face of countervailing informal educational agents, such as alienated peer groups and discouraged families. Consequently, we decided that Center X novice teachers must engage with the communities they serve, not so much to "educate" parents in the conventional meaning of the term, but rather to connect what children do in school to their experiences in the community. By engaging children and their families in finding and solving real problems that matter to them outside school, we thought that they could help make schoolwork less abstract and detached (and thereby more likely to be learned) and that they could enhance the power and well-being of the larger educational ecology for children.[3]

Furthermore, we wanted our teachers to know how to include parents and other community members in adult-centered inquiry into school practice and beliefs. We wanted them to learn that community members can inform discussion around curriculum and extracurricular issues and in this process develop more democratic relationships with the professional staff. Working with a range of community resources, such as public health, social welfare, and psychological support systems, we wanted our teachers to support programs that deal more comprehensively with the range of issues facing low-income urban children and schools. Toward this end, we knew that Center X teacher candidates must participate in community projects and connect with neighborhood organizations and Head Start programs, and engage parents in inquiry and discussion about their children's schooling. Some have mounted Social Justice Community Nights in their school communities.

Teachers as Generative Change Agents

Finally, we realized that even exceedingly well-prepared teachers are not likely, through classroom practice alone, to counteract the impact of the deadening structures and cultures of most urban schools. Given this grim reality, we thought that we must prepare our Center X teachers to develop the commitment, capacity, and resilience to participate effectively in efforts to fundamentally reconceptualize, change, and renew urban schools. And we agreed with much of the current educational reform movement that suggests that fundamental change will require teachers who are willing and able to engage in continuous examination of every aspect of their structures and activities.

Consequently, we decided that novice teachers in Center X must undertake an activist role in school reform that goes beyond the familiar search for "what works" to make conventional school practice "more effective" and "just" and even "visionary." Our program must engage prospective professionals in generative processes for implementing change that fundamentally challenges, reconceptualizes, and transforms now decaying urban schools into places of hope and opportunity for all students.

Furthermore, our teachers must be prepared to view change and problems as "normal" conditions that require flexible, generative responses. They must have a lifelong commitment to professional growth as part of their ongoing commitment to reaching the needs of all students. Toward these ends, we decided that Center X teachers must have the opportunity to work collaboratively in teams to initiate change projects in their school and/or communities, and to see this work as a "normal" part of the job of teaching.

A NEW STRUCTURE OF TEACHER EDUCATION

Our first bold step toward a structure that had a prayer of helping novice teachers learn these four teaching roles was to announce that the standard UCLA fifteen-month teaching credential and master's program was insufficient and that we were adding another year of scaffolded coursework and field experiences. (Remember, we're in California, where teacher education doesn't begin until graduate school.) To our surprise, nearly everyone agreed! Where we thought we'd have battles, there were none. Even the California Teacher Credentialing Commission supported our application for "experimental" status to allow us to waive the state regulation that teacher education programs must permit students to become credentialed within one year.

We needed the extra year to accommodate three essential program components. The first is the MEd core curriculum that integrates research-based methodologies with classroom practice by providing advanced study in such areas as multicultural foundations, instructional decision-making, and curriculum development. The second is the course sequence that guides students toward the development of instructional strategies and pedagogical skills needed to satisfy the state's credentialing requirements. The third component of the program prepares candidates to develop their knowledge and skills in methods and strategies of teaching students from diverse cultural and language backgrounds. This third component prepares teachers to provide (a) instruction for English language development and (b) specially designed academic content instruction delivered in English.

It also qualifies our teachers for the state's CLAD (Cross-cultural, Language, and Academic Development) Emphasis credential. The bilingual emphasis (BCLAD) that many of our students also complete provides students with methodology for primary language and content instruction delivered in Spanish and Korean. A two-year Center X program, we argued, would permit students to complete all three components and provide enough time for them to see themselves as Center X teachers.

During their first year, our students complete a program integrating theory and practice to fulfill the requirements for a basic credential. In addition to their coursework, during the fall of their first year, each team of novice teachers has a range of opportunities to observe schools and classrooms in a variety of urban settings that have racially, culturally, and linguistically diverse students. Throughout this period of observation and initial participation, students analyze effective strategies for achieving learning for all students, including constructivist instruction, sociocultural approaches, cultural congruence, and educational technology. A key component of this phase is the students' active engagement in reflection on issues in the schools they are observing.

In the winter and spring of the first year, students are assigned to an urban school site with a racially, culturally, and linguistically diverse student population for "student teaching." Throughout the student teaching period, novice teachers will plan, implement, and assess daily lessons and units with the assistance of a mentor teacher. Key components of student teaching are the novice teachers' active engagement in reflection on issues in the schools in which they are teaching and their involvement with the larger school community.

During their school year, students take jobs in school districts to teach as teaching residents in school sites with low-income, and racially, culturally, and linguistically diverse student populations. During this time, they attend weekly seminars at UCLA, meet with fellow residents and Center X faculty at their school sites, and work in cooperative teams to initiate a Change Project in their local school and/ or its community and complete a case study on the project. These teaching residencies continue the scaffolded university-field residency during the critical induction into teaching, as well as allowing the second-year "residents" additional time to complete their final CLAD/ BCLAD-Emphasis credential requirements and Master's degree in education. At the end of this second year, students complete a portfolio assessment process that synthesizes their theoretical and practical experiences and defend it for their MEd at the end of the second year.

Cohorts

The Center X program is collegially based so that the students move through the combined academic and field work program in a cohort. Each year, a total of ninety first-year students are admitted to the program and assigned to teams determined by either an elementary or secondary focus. Each team is composed of approximately fifteen first-year students and fifteen second-year students. These teams are coordinated by team leaders who are both ladder and clinical faculty members. Because the university curriculum and field component are comprehensively and sequentially designed, students must complete the entire program as fulltime UCLA students.

Some of our friends and probably lots of others predicted that we'd never get students to sign on to such an ambitious program. Our Office of Student Services was convinced that we wouldn't attract a large enough applicant pool to fill our enrollment targets. Frankly, we were a bit nervous ourselves, even though we thumbed our noses at the skeptics. In fact, we received as many applications as we had in years before with our high-status conventional fifteen-month program, and we had more than four applicants for every available slot. The applicants had grades, scores, and letters that matched any in previous years. But they were also different in important ways. Many wrote passionately about their commitment to social and educational justice in Los Angeles; many had significant experiences working with diverse groups of low-income children in the past. We chose carefully, sifting through this embarrassment of riches, and wound up with a cohort that was about half students of color, and nearly a third bi- or trilingual. This first cohort is now working as teaching residents in Los Angeles urban schools. Our second cohort—every bit as talented and committed as the first—has begun its novice year.

Partnerships

Because we are committed to integration of theory and practice, Center X has worked hard to develop a novice-mentor model of student teaching within university-school partnerships. These partnerships with local urban districts provide candidates with a rich and varied set of novice teaching experiences in racially, culturally, and linguistically diverse school sites, especially in classrooms with bilingual and limited-English-proficient students. Each student begins his or her induction into the profession as a "novice teacher," rather than a student teacher, and each teacher in the field primarily responsible for working with a novice teacher assumes the role of "mentor teacher," rather than the traditional role of master or supervising teacher. The mentor teachers responsible for mentoring novice teachers work closely with other teachers at their schools, administrators, and clinical and

ladder faculty members to redefine their roles in this new collaborative relationship. Through university-school partnerships, we work
to operationalize the idea that "It takes a whole school to educate a
teacher." Center X works with school site personnel to develop site-
based approaches for mentoring novice teachers that will encourage
them to become part of the larger school community. As part of these
partnerships, Center X provides clinical and ladder faculty support
for novice teachers in the field. Expert practitioners serve as UCLA
lecturers in curriculum and methods courses. I teach my multicultural
foundations course in a classroom at a partner middle school.

Of course, these partnerships are difficult to initiate and sustain.
While most local school systems are enamored by the idea of partnering with UCLA, the details of working together are not so glamorous.
Much has been written about the problems of bridging the cultures of
schools and universities. Our efforts are no different. Moreover, because we won't negotiate away our commitment to schools with low-
income children of color, we may have lost as many partners as we've
won. We have war stories of attacks by angry school administrators
convinced that we were insulting them and abandoning our commitment to "all children" by not placing our students in their whiter and
wealthier schools.

CENTER X: A PROGRAM OF RESEARCH

The need for teachers with the commitment, knowledge, and skills we
claim to be fostering is well established, and Center X believes that its
program design will enable students to develop them. However, we actually have little empirical evidence about the impact of efforts such as
ours. Consequently, we have designed a strategy to document the implementation and test the efficacy of our work over the next five years.

The research component of our work examines the extent to
which the Center X Program actually does prepare teachers to have
the commitment, capacity, and resilience to provide depth of content knowledge, literacy, powerful pedagogies, and engaging school
cultures for all students, especially those from racially, culturally,
and linguistically diverse backgrounds. It investigates the extent to
which our teachers actually assume the four interrelated core values

of transformative professionals described earlier: 1) a caring advocate for all students, 2) a reflective, inquiry-based practitioner, 3) a community builder, and 4) a generative change agent, to serve students from racially, culturally, and linguistically diverse communities. This research is being carried out by ladder faculty, clinical faculty, and graduate students, in collaboration with educators in our partner schools.

Our Questions

For the research side of our work, we're trying to answer the following hard questions:

1. How does our Center X program—oriented as it is toward issues of social justice, caring, and instructional equity—nurture and sustain novice teachers' commitment to become transformative professionals? Or does it?

2. How does our Center X approach to teacher education that more closely connects students' coursework and field experiences with racially, culturally, and linguistically diverse students and communities help connect theory to their own practice? Or does it?

3. How does participation of novice teachers in collaborative and responsible learning communities both in the university and in the field that construct, use, and share knowledge build program graduates' commitment and capacity to work with communities to effect change in urban schools? Or does it?

4. How does the Center X–supported residency in an urban school during the second year build teachers' efficacy and commitment to low-income, racially, culturally, and linguistically diverse children and prepare teachers who will choose to teach in those children's schools? Or does it?

5. How does the Center X focus on the challenges and rewards of teaching low-income, racially, culturally, and linguistically diverse students enhance new teachers' commitment, capacity, and resilience to teach in those children's schools? Or does it?

6. How does students' sustained engagement with the Center X program ease their transition into teaching, including an ongoing

commitment to change in professional development and renewal in the urban teaching profession? Or does it?

Our Design and Methods

Our study began with a baseline year of data collection in 1994–1995, before we instituted our two-year program, and it will extend over the next five years. In alignment with Center X's commitment to social justice and caring, the study is socially responsive research within the paradigm of critical inquiry.[4] As critical inquiry, our data analysis and interpretation will be continuously subjected to reflection, discussion, and debate within the Center X community and serve as the basis for ongoing changes and renewal of the program. The study design is a longitudinal, multi-method research design based on qualitative and quantitative data. It attempts to understand the dynamics of the teacher education process in context and its impact on students.

We are following four two-year cohorts of teacher education credential and MEd candidates, who have entered or will join the program respectively in 1995, 1996, 1997, and 1998. A series of interconnected data collection and analysis strategies will enable Center X to track novice teachers' development: initial surveys of incoming students and follow-up surveys (both paper and pencil and interviews) of graduates, evaluation of key program elements through portfolios and portfolio defenses, and targeted case studies.

The first two strategies involve the entire cohort of each entering class, and the last one focuses on a sub-sample of students from each entering cohort. The first two strategies aim to tell us what we've accomplished; the latter can help us understand how and why, and where we have rethinking to do.

Surveys

We began our data collection with a survey adapted from the instrument developed by John Goodlad for his national Study of the Education of Educators, and we administer annual follow-up surveys. These surveys provide longitudinal data on novice teachers' socialization into teaching. To get greater depth of understanding of what our students mean by their responses to the survey questions, we supplement this paper-and-pencil survey with interviews about how students conceptualize teaching and social justice for children in central city schools.

Portfolios and Portfolio Defenses

The impact of our program elements will be assessed through the students' MEd portfolios, which include components that specifically address CLAD/BCLAD credential and our MEd requirements. The portfolio, based on student work, is a product that provides rich, in-depth data to determine the efficacy of the program. The portfolio is based on an integration of academic course work and field-based experiences and will focus on how each credential/MEd candidate integrates his or her philosophy of teaching, theories of teaching, learning, language acquisition, culture, inquiry, community, change, and classroom practice. The portfolio will include three components: Theory to Practice, Practice to Theory, and Philosophical Perspective. In the Theory to Practice component, students will include a case study of a Change Project they implemented in their resident year in a racially, culturally, and linguistically diverse school or its community. The credential/MEd candidate sits for a defense of his or her portfolio before a panel, consisting of academic, clinical, community, and student members. At the end of the defense, each candidate has the opportunity to assess the Teacher Education Program's strengths and weaknesses. A recorder will provide a record of each portfolio and defense, based on an established rubric.

Targeted Case Studies

Targeted in-depth initial and exit interviews and case studies of select teaching students will provide rich, explanatory narratives of the context in which our students have learned to become teachers.

Importantly, our primary research goal is not to document and "prove" that we've figured out how to produce teachers who can make center city schools rich, rigorous, socially just, and caring learning communities where all children learn extraordinarily well. We know that we haven't figured it out and that maybe we never will. Our research goal, rather, is to document the struggle of teacher educators and novice teachers who've decided that they can't not try.

ASKING FOR TROUBLE

Using our powerful symbolism of the university and the extraordinary talent of the educators in the university and the schools, the staff at Center X have committed to the view—however idealistic—that schools and teaching for low-income racially, culturally, and linguistically diverse children can change. We've also asked for a whole lot of trouble, and in fact, we've gotten lots. As I read what I've written here, I realize that sentences and paragraphs strung together make our efforts sound far tidier than they are. We're struggling to do something we really don't know how to do. We're asking questions we don't know how to answer. We frustrate many of our partnering educators who want more clarity and definition of our program than we can provide. We worry some of our colleagues who think we're too ideological. We anger some of our students when we won't give them a safety net of classroom management strategies and structured lesson-planning procedures that we think will create more problems than they will solve. We ask everyone to tolerate our ambiguity. We're not being realistic. We work too hard. We work our students too hard. We expect too much.

Frankly, we wouldn't have it any other way. We don't expect to stop the fires from coming again to Los Angeles. But next time, we'll know that we tried.

CHAPTER 2

Learning to Become a Community Teacher

Annamarie M. Francois and Jarod Kawasaki

ON SUNDAY, FEBRUARY 23, 2020, twenty-five-year-old Ahmaud Arbery was shot to death as he jogged near his home in Brunswick, Georgia.

On Friday, March 13, 2020, twenty-six-year-old Breonna Taylor, an emergency medical technician in Louisville, Kentucky, was shot to death while asleep in her small apartment.

On Monday, May 25, 2020, in Minneapolis, Minnesota, George Floyd died after a police officer knelt on his neck for 9 minutes and 29 seconds as he lay face-down in the street, handcuffed and gasping for air. He called out for his mama before going motionless.

Three days later, protests against police violence and racial injustice erupted across Los Angeles County—protests painfully reminiscent of the 1992 Los Angeles uprisings that prompted the creation

---

The authors contributed equally to this essay.

of Center X. In this moment, we are critically aware that our core mission, values, guiding principles, signature practices, and ways of being are more relevant now than ever before. After almost thirty years of advancing social justice through high-quality, critical teacher preparation and professional learning, we come back to our essential question: How do we prepare and support teachers with the pedagogical knowledge, critical dispositions, and tools to disrupt and dismantle traditional norms of schooling to effectively teach students from working-class communities of color? Teachers who engage in antiracist teaching as a revolutionary political act. Teachers who are committed to teaching in working-class neighborhoods of color as members of the community within and beyond the schoolhouse doors. Teachers who draw upon a richly contextualized knowledge of identity, culture, community, and activism to design academically rigorous, culturally relevant and sustaining, liberatory learning environments for their students. Community teachers.

Learning to become a community teacher raises several questions: What does it mean to be a community teacher? What values and beliefs about schooling drive community teachers? How do their values, knowledge, skills, and dispositions come together to promote student learning and social justice? Answering these questions allows us to then ask, How do we prepare aspiring social justice teachers to become community teachers and sustain them throughout their careers? Our responses are informed by activists and scholars such as Jeannie Oakes, John Dewey, Paulo Freire, Peter Murrell, and Tara Yosso. We captured the distinct qualities of community teachers through interviews with exemplary Black teachers recognized as much for their community solidarity as for their culturally relevant and sustaining care and pedagogy.[1] At their core, these teachers embrace teaching as an act of love for their students and their community, as a way to provide critical hope in a time and place where the educational system acts against them,[2] and as a praxis deliberated on personal and communal liberation.[3] Ms. Walker, a fourth-grade community teacher, depicts these ideals in an interview excerpt in which she describes who she sees when her African American students walk into her class on the first day of school:

They walk in and I'm like here they come, a whole different person, a whole different mind. They come with everyone in their lives—every mom, dad, grandma, sister, brother, and neighbor. They come into my classroom with all of them, all of their love, all of their hopes and dreams. Do you know what I like to imagine? This is the crazy part. That when my students walk in, their ancestors and village are following, they're right behind them.

REFRAMING TEACHER EDUCATION AS A TRANSFORMATIVE RESPONSE TO RACIAL INJUSTICE

In 1992, the University of California, Los Angeles (UCLA), Teacher Education Lab began the long and aspirational journey of transforming itself from a conventional teacher preparation program that emphasized constructivism and teacher reflection to an urban-focused experimental program committed to social justice. In keeping with the nonnegotiable guiding principles of Center X, this meant enacting a teacher education program that embodied a social justice agenda and nurtured long-term, positive, interdependent connections and equal-status partnerships with K–12 schools in working-class communities of color. This transformed teacher education program prioritized teacher learning at the intersection of education research, practice, and social justice through a process of critical inquiry, reflection, and social responsibility.

In chapter 1 of this book, "Making the Rhetoric Real," first published as an article in 1996, Oakes articulates the collective visioning and fundamental ideas that would ground Center X so each aspiring social justice teacher might become "1) a caring advocate for all students, 2) a reflective, inquiry-based practitioner, 3) a community builder, and 4) a generative change agent" in schools serving working-class families of color.[4] These roles have endured over the past three decades, even as our country's sociopolitical climate has changed and school policies have followed suit. The field of critical teacher preparation for schools in working-class communities of color has rapidly evolved too. As a learning organization, this means that we are always in a state of reflection and inquiry about how we operationalize our beliefs. Our language and practice have become more refined, textured, and nuanced over the years, informed by the research of critical scholars and the work of critical practitioners.

Peter Murrell put forth a model of social justice teacher preparation in his 2001 book *The Community Teacher: A New Framework for Effective Urban Teaching.*[5] His ideas about the centrality of community knowledge and communities of practice resonated with how we thought about preparing and sustaining social justice educators. In 2010, we launched our first teacher-residency program, Inspiring Minds through a Professional Alliance of Community Teachers (IMPACT). A primary goal of IMPACT was to innovate science, technology, engineering, and mathematics (STEM) teacher preparation through deep school and community collaboration and humanizing STEM pedagogies and dispositions. And now, a decade later, as racial injustice once again compels us to lean into antiracism with renewed intent, we think about our work preparing community teachers through the lens of abolitionist teaching.[6]

In this chapter, we share our vision for how to prepare and sustain community teachers through four enduring antiracist, abolitionist practices embedded in our teacher-preparation program: reflecting on positionality, developing cultural knowledge, engaging in critical inquiry, and acquiring critical pedagogical knowledge and skills. We bring these practices to life through examples of key activities and assignments from our teacher education program and share excerpts from teacher interviews to illustrate how these dispositions result from and are reflected in the lived experience of community teachers. To provide useful context, we begin with a brief description of how the UCLA Teacher Education Program (TEP) is structured.

ORGANIZING TEACHER PREPARATION TO SUPPORT THE DEVELOPMENT OF COMMUNITY TEACHERS

Pursuing and enacting a vision for community teacher development requires the creation of organizational structures that support it. University-based teacher preparation tends to embrace tradition, stifling the imagination and creativity that ignite innovation. Designing teacher preparation for social justice requires developing intentional structures, from recruitment through licensure, to support this vision.

First and foremost, Center X has a clear theory of action and an enduring set of guiding principles, which are summarized in "Making the Rhetoric Real" (ch. 1). All of our community teacher development work is explicitly measured against these guiding principles.

Novice recruitment and selection processes are critical entry points in our community teacher development work. In addition to traditional admission requirements (for example, credential exam scores, grade point average, and transcripts), novices must also demonstrate experience in working-class communities of color, experience with school-aged children, and a commitment to issues of social justice. These signature criteria are evaluated through written statements of intent, life and work experience, academic and professional references, and engagement in a small-group interview process. During the small-group interview, applicants read a critical social justice text, engage with five to seven other applicants in a Socratic dialogue provoked by the text, and provide individual reflections on content and process. Using signature criteria in the application process helps us to identify novices whose values and commitments align with our teacher education program—novices with the greatest potential for growth and success.

The UCLA TEP program is organized around a ten-month sequence of foundations, methods, clinical practice, and seminar experiences that lead to state licensure—all of which are grounded in sociocultural theory, critical race theory, and critical pedagogy. Once accepted, our novices are immersed in public schools serving working-class communities of color and supported by experienced antiracist, social justice educators in their university coursework and clinical practice. Our faculty and staff are predominately practitioner-scholars of color, most of whom are full-time clinical faculty and all of whom have deep K–12 teaching experience. Our diverse pool of K–12 mentors teach in the very schools where most of our students will be hired during their first year of teaching. Many attended these schools as K–12 students themselves or are UCLA TEP alumni. Our community partners, including local school districts, community-based organizations, and education advocacy groups, all share our belief in the power of community teachers to change the world for our most vulnerable students.

REFLECTING ON POSITIONALITY

The first essential practice for developing community teachers is the idea of being reflective about one's own knowledge, assumptions, and past experiences (that is, positionality). We refer to this reflection as a recognition that all of us have multiple and unique experiences that shape the way we view and understand the world around us.[7] For teachers, this is deeply influenced by the way they learned in school and shapes the way they view learning for their students. Recognizing one's own positionality allows teachers to examine alternative approaches to teaching and learning that they might be blind to, given their limited lived experiences.

A community teacher uses their lived experiences to help shape their practice, especially those that support their pursuit of social justice. Ms. Ali, a Black teacher who teaches at a school that serves predominately African American students, had this to say about a racist experience in college that, today, motivates her to teach her students to recognize and combat racism they may encounter in their own lives:

> There have been numerous times when I have found myself to be the only Black and/or person of color in a classroom and have had to navigate racial bias, micro/macro aggression, and being made to feel as if I were invisible. By the time I got to college, my junior year, I wrote a paper for English class about apartheid in which my premise was that the Black people should rise up and kill all the White people in South Africa. The professor called me to her office and accused me of plagiarism. I had not plagiarized the paper. The truth was she did not like nor agree with my premise and that was fine. But to accuse me of plagiarism was insulting and infuriating. All I could do was think how I could beat her ass and get to my car before the campus police got to me. But I had a child, I needed to graduate from college because I was now responsible for her. Therefore, I believe we need to teach children that there are things they can do to combat racism, so it does not fester within them.

This excerpt exemplifies Ms. Walker's oppositional consciousness, one that prioritizes the cultural values and social practices of Black discourse and history and is in direct opposition to traditional American or Eurocentric values.[8]

UCLA TEP gives teacher candidates (novices) many opportunities to be reflective about their own past experiences and how those lived experiences shape the ways they view teaching and learning for their students. Key among these are signature assignments that challenge students to grapple with the complexities of identity, power, and privilege in schooling spaces. For example, all novices take a year-long signature series that asks them to critically examine their beliefs, assumptions, and experiences about working-class communities of color to develop their critical consciousness and surface ways in which community and family knowledge might influence and inform their developing praxis. In the fall quarter, novices investigate values and biases in relationship to their teaching and the sociocultural contexts in which their clinical practice occurs. In the winter, novices examine their assumptions and beliefs regarding race, class, culture, gender, religion, sexual orientation, and other dimensions of their complex identities. These issues are analyzed within the context of their professional learning in schools serving working-class students of color. Finally, in the spring, novices explore options for becoming allies with families and community members.

Each of the three courses in this series examines the relationships among self, community, and families and high-quality pedagogy. This structure highlights the importance of self-awareness and examination, and the interdependent relationships among students, teachers, and community members. This course series is integral to preparing antiracist, social justice educators, as it challenges novices to be reflective and thoughtful about the teaching approaches and strategies they use in the classroom, where those strategies come from, why they think the strategies will work, and how those strategies align with the goals of antiracist, equity-focused teacher preparation.

DEVELOPING CULTURAL KNOWLEDGE

Murrell defines a teacher's cultural knowledge as deeply contextualized and indispensable to the creation of core practices for diverse learners.[9] Cultural knowledge can come from being a community member or immersing oneself in the community to better understand and experience the community's vibrancy, strengths, and needs.

Community teachers view this cultural knowledge through an assets-based lens and seek to show students how their histories, knowledge, and experiences can be leveraged to challenge dominant schooling through culturally specific ways of thinking, being, and teaching.[10] Ms. Joy, a community teacher who for the past thirty-two years has taught in the neighborhood she grew up in, continues to prioritize the development of her cultural knowledge from the first day of each school year:

> I always design intentional activities that build our classroom community as a team. I have to know my students, how they think, what they bring to the table, what makes them shine, what hurts them, their strengths and their needs. It's also important for me to share my stories too. In the beginning of the school year, we paint self-portraits, write poems about ourselves, make slide presentations about our families, and spend time collaborating and creating our space to make it ours. Something else that has helped me learn more about my students and their families is at the beginning of the year, I ask parents to write me a letter telling me all about their child and family, and what I can do to help them bring out the best in their children. These letters come in handy throughout the year. Sometimes I forget that a child is one of three or four and that the parent works nights. That letter reminds me.

Ms. Joy reminds us that the process of developing one's cultural knowledge is an active, persistent, and careful process of learning and unlearning.

Throughout their teacher preparation program, UCLA TEP novices immerse themselves in activity intended to expand and deepen their cultural knowledge experientially. The Community Inquiry Project and Parent, Family, and Caregiver Engagement Project are examples of embedded signature assignments novices complete during their preservice year. The Community Inquiry Project asks novices to become familiar with the diverse perspectives of the community that surrounds their schools, the community's assets, and the issues and challenges it faces. The purpose of this assignment is for teachers to develop rich understandings of their students as individuals and members of a community with a unique history and rhythm that influences the dynamics of local schooling. Novices engage in online research, conduct walking tours, and interview local community members. They capture images of community life as they conduct their walking tours. The images reveal the strengths, hidden opportunities, and challenges they notice. Novices have ethnographic conversations with community members to learn about the history of the community, the current issues within the community, and the relevant resources that are available to address these issues. The multimedia data novices collect become instructional artifacts that they can use during their student teaching and inform the development and implementation of a sustained community-engagement activity. Finally, novices make their learning public by sharing their work with the school community.

The Parent, Family, and Caregiver Engagement Project invites novices to explore interrelationships among families, communities, and school systems. Novices are asked to be in dialogue with parents, caregivers, students, and school personnel to develop a plan for working with families once they become teachers of record for their own classrooms. These conversations inform and influence how novices will introduce themselves, their intentions, and their expectations to parents, family members, and caregivers during their first year of teaching.

Developing cultural knowledge can be a tricky endeavor. Love reminds us that a culture's "traditions and ways of being are intentionally created and crafted because culture reflects the educational, social, economic, political, and spiritual conditions of people."[11] In our early years we asked each novice to take a Culture of Emphasis class, the emphases being Asian American, African American, and Latinx cultures. We allowed students to choose which course to take, hoping some would select an emphasis to learn more about their own cultural histories while others would choose based on their desire to learn about those who were different from them. What sounded good at the time quickly went in the direction of segregated spaces where culture was essentialized rather than studied in all its complexity.

Today, we embed ethnic studies content and pedagogies into our core classes and offer an ethnic studies pathway for novices working toward a secondary social science or English credential. This move from culture of emphasis to ethnic studies opens opportunities for our novices to explore ways to center the knowledge and perspectives of minoritized groups in their practice, without essentializing their histories and experiences. At its core, ethnic studies is about empowerment, liberation, and valuing the lived experiences, narratives, and knowledge of communities of color.[12] In ethnic studies, novices engage with ideas around abolitionist pedagogy, decolonizing curriculum, critical hope, and other transformative ways of knowing and being.[13]

ENGAGING IN CRITICAL INQUIRY

Murrell writes that "the extent to which candidates can critically develop their own positionality determines how central or peripheral a role they play in the development and academic achievement of children, youth, and families in diverse urban communities."[14] In UCLA TEP, critical inquiry happens as novices reflect on the intersection of their history, identity, lived experiences, and positionality. We regularly support teachers to critically examine how these factors influence their teaching practice through a cycle of inquiry that examines student learning relative to these intersecting factors. Ms. Montgomery illustrates this idea by describing how the consequences of a common classroom-management practice she learned in her own schooling and preparation led her to face her assumptions about differentiated discipline:

> Early in my career, I tried to use a reward system to promote positive behavior for a few students to "earn" the opportunity to participate in a field trip. One parent challenged me and let me know [her son] considered himself one of the "bad" kids and that was why he had to earn his way. From that day on, I approach students differently and do not differentiate discipline in that way anymore. I was grateful the parents let me know rather than be resentful or go to the principal. My intention was so far from what happened! My assumptions were so wrong and I learned to ask questions and be more thoughtful in how I approach my position. It also taught me to trust my gut because I was following others in using that strategy.

Like all community teachers, Ms. Montgomery has learned to regularly interrogate her assumptions about students and learning as a way to revise and refine her practice to be more equitable and just. She also sees parents as valuable sources of knowledge, actively listening to them with humility and gratitude.

Developing a critical inquiry stance is fundamental, so it is braided throughout our teacher preparation coursework, fieldwork, and signature assignments/assessments. While novices are engaged in the community inquiry described in the previous section, they take a course titled Social Foundations and Cultural Diversity in American Schools. This course focuses on the historical, social, political, and economic contexts of schooling in the United States, California, and the local area. Novices examine the purpose and nature of their work within these larger contexts in order to develop dispositions toward analyzing, challenging, and dismantling educational and systemic inequities. They then articulate how they might challenge inequities in their classrooms and through the curriculum. This course specifically calls on novices to critically examine sociopolitical inequities in education and formal schooling and how they can design learning environments intended to disrupt these inequities. Taken together, the Community Inquiry Project and social foundations course prepare aspiring antiracist teachers to do the difficult work of examining their emerging practice at the intersection of sociopolitical context, positionality, and practice.

The Master's Inquiry Project is UCLA TEP's culminating assignment. It is an opportunity for our students, now full-time teachers of record (residents), to continue their development as reflective, antiracist educators, and it gives them an opportunity to participate in a systematic, intentional study of their own professional practice. Envisioned as both inquiry and action research, the project is an iterative process of observing, researching, reflecting, evaluating, planning, and action. The process and the insights that residents gain enhance their professional growth as teacher-scholars working to transform their schools into communities of engaged teaching and learning.

The yearlong Master's Inquiry Project contains three interrelated sections. The first asks residents to describe their positionality by revisiting life and schooling experiences and to consider how those experiences have affected their first few months of teaching. Residents also reflect on their classroom, school, and community context in order to develop a set of emerging questions they might consider for their action-oriented research project. In the second section, residents dive into the research literature to better understand their proposed topic, refine their research question, and design an action plan that includes a social justice theory of change to justify their plan. Their inquiry research is conducted for eight weeks and includes collecting multiple artifacts as data sources (for example, student work, interviews, surveys, ethnographic notes). In the final section, residents analyze their data, write up their findings, and discuss the implications of their findings for their teaching practice. The entire project is meant to provide residents with experience in conducting a cycle of inquiry that critically examines factors around student learning within their classroom from a social justice perspective. Resident scholarship is made public through community presentations and archived as resources for future novices to follow.

ACQUIRING CRITICAL PEDAGOGICAL KNOWLEDGE AND SKILLS

Traditional approaches to teaching treat equity, antiracism, and cultural relevance as supplemental to content knowledge and pedagogical skills. We consider them as critically interdependent and as lenses through which we view all facets of teaching and learning. This nuanced view is grounded in our humanizing and asset-based perspective on teaching, learning, and being together in schools.[15] Therefore, teacher education programs must help novices to problematize conventional curricular and instructional decisions in ways that acknowledge who their students are, meet them where they are, and make the learning experience both academically rigorous and personally meaningful.

Ms. Joy describes how she blends rigorous teaching with meeting state standards through a project-based learning (PBL) activity rooted in the lives and experiences of the Black children in her classroom:

My students completed a civic leadership and literacy PBL unit on art, activism, and resistance. Students worked in collaborative groups to research why movements matter for social justice and equity. They studied various activists, such as Mari Copeny (Little Miss Flint), César Chavez, Malcolm X, and Michelle Obama. Then they looked deeply at specific movements to get a better understanding of how and why movements matter. They researched Black Lives Matter, March for Our Lives, and other movements. Then they looked for art that represented activism. The culminating project was a website showcasing students' original art pieces, slideshows about activists and movements, and video announcements like PSAs to get the public's support for their movements.

Community teachers like Ms. Joy design learning environments that provide space for discourse about disrupting racially based achievement gaps and deficit perspectives. They also incorporate instructional models that use historical and philosophical frames of reference meant to sustain the positive and powerful identities of the Black students in their classrooms.[16]

TEP courses and pathways are intentionally designed to provide novices with opportunities to learn and enact critical pedagogical knowledge and skills that promote student learning and agency. This work begins with a common teaching and learning framework that is grounded in social justice frameworks and pedagogies and used in every content area and grade level. (Chapter 3 describes in detail the development and use of the math and science frameworks.) Each framework contains four core dimensions of teaching quality: designing cognitively demanding tasks and content, engaging students in content discourse, scaffolding and differentiation for equitable access to content, and developing and maintaining a positive classroom ecology for learning. We have found that a common framework allows teacher educators to clearly and concretely articulate to both teacher candidates and mentor teachers the program's vision of social justice teaching. The articulation of a subset of core teaching practices, aligned to each dimension and relative to social justice values, makes these practices visible in teachers' classrooms, especially for experienced teachers (that is, mentor teachers). The framework also enables teacher educators to provide clear and focused formative feedback to support teacher candidates.

In addition, novices take traditional methods courses, such as the state-mandated technology course, and reframe them through a critical lens. Grounded in cultural studies, our Critical Media Literacy course uses the tools of technology to encourage novices to examine, analyze, and reflect on their relationship with media, technology, and popular culture. Critical media literacy provides novices with a framework to dissect representations in print, broadcast, outdoor, and internet media.[17] Novices engage with digital storytelling, multimedia creation, and lesson planning with an eye toward creating more inclusive representations that challenge dominant and traditional normative notions of being and living.

BECOMING AN AGENT FOR RADICAL CHANGE

Oakes calls for teacher preparation programs to develop teachers with the "commitment, capacity, and resilience" to fundamentally change the systemically oppressive structures and cultures within schools.[18] We view this mandate as a fundamental responsibility of a community teacher, one that explicitly seeks to dismantle and disrupt systems of oppression through transformative pedagogies, deep relationships with students and their families, and collective action for and with the most vulnerable communities. Community teachers use the four abolitionist practices described above to notice the ways in which oppression exists in everyday classroom life and seek to disrupt the systems and structures that perpetuate it. Mr. White describes his desire to critically interrogate and radically change rules related to how students move in school spaces:

> My kids are never in a straight line. They're quiet, they're respectful, they're never in straight lines. And I dare a teacher to tell me something about it, because my kids aren't walking in a straight line. They will walk quietly but not in a straight line. When there is an assembly, they're not in a straight line, but they're respectful and quiet. Your kids are in a straight line, talking loud as shit. So, what are we preparing them for? Now, there will be times in their adult life where they have to be respectful and quiet of other people. There is never a

time [where they need to be in a straight line], unless you're sending these kids to the jailhouse or to the military.

Ms. Ali speaks to this point a bit differently, casting attention to how community teachers create conditions that empower students to combat the oppressive systems that they may encounter in their lives:

> My priority is for you to be a critical thinker, for you to be able to question authority in a manner from a point of knowledge, not just to be talking back and smack but because somebody has said something to you that is wrong. There's some injustice. Be able to point out injustice, be able to point out bias, and to be able to come up with a solution to change it. You can only do that if you've worked yourself to a point where you can think, you can speak, and you're not bogged down with a whole bunch of life [stuff] that you're too young to really be dealing with. So that's my priority as a teacher.

Teachers with a disposition toward being an agent of radical change pursue a liberatory pedagogy, one that seeks to free the oppressed from their oppressors or develop students' critical consciousness, or *conscientização*.[19]

Becoming an agent for radical change takes these four dimensions and deploys them into all facets of teaching and being a community teacher. For example, for his Master's Inquiry Project, one high school biology teacher developed a secondary science unit that combined students' study of the integumentary system and the social phenomenon of colorism (that is, an ideology in which hierarchies are created within groups of people based primarily on the phenotypic color of the skin).[20] Students learned about the role that melanin plays in ultraviolet light protection in the skin and applied that knowledge to affirmations of their own skin tone (almost all the students were Black or Brown). These affirmations were written on individual whiteboards, and then pictures of all the students in the class holding their whiteboards were assembled into a collage and hung in the hallway of the school. This project is an example of using science knowledge and public display as a way to give students agency and voice to critique popular media's depiction of light skin tones as preferable and affirm the skin tones and identities of their fellow Black and Latinx schoolmates.

FINAL THOUGHTS

The four abolitionist practices described above reflect where we came from, who we are as a transformative teacher education program, and how we see our work as allies in the broader struggle for social justice. We believe the activities are good for novices to learn about, collaborate on, and practice as they develop their teacher identities. Our hope is that these practices will sustain novices over time as they struggle to replace oppressive schooling practices with those that are more joyful, loving, equitable, and just. That said, these practices are not without their tensions and struggles. Teachers need to constantly reflect on the ways they use cultural knowledge to avoid appropriating and essentializing students' histories, knowledge, and experiences. Providing multiple perspectives on core subjects such as history, science, and literature—that is, ethnic studies—especially those perspectives that have been ignored and silenced, requires teachers to intimately know where in their content standards study of multiple perspectives will deepen and broaden their students' worldview, in the event that they are accused of straying from the content standards. Teachers need to learn to build safe and positive classroom ecologies so that students are willing and able to participate in difficult discussions around racial equity and social justice. Yet we believe that the rewards outweigh the risks. We believe in the potential of these four practices to bring about radical change to our education system and classrooms.

We know that we ask too much of novices in the short time between orientation and their first day of teaching. We ask too much of our faculty, who are on the front lines of transformative teacher preparation and do not get half the credit they deserve. We ask too much of our mentor teachers, who protect and care for their students, even as we ask them to protect and care for the next generation of teachers. Yet too much is always what is asked of those engaged in righteous protest—whether in the streets or in classrooms. We envisioned and continue to envision our work as a revolutionary act of resistance to *transform public schooling to create a more just, equitable, and humane society.* Onward.

ACKNOWLEDGMENTS

We would like to thank Tunette Powell and Alison Munzer for their research contributions to this work. The research described in this essay was supported by the Teacher Quality Partnership program of the US Department of Education under award number U336S140049. The views and opinions expressed herein are those of the authors only and do not represent official views and opinions of the US Department of Education.

CHAPTER 3

Framing Preservice Teacher Learning and Accountability

Jaime J. Park, Imelda L. Nava,
and Melissa S. Arias

INTRODUCTION

As teacher educators, we are often asked what advice we might give to aspiring teachers. There is no shortage of advice for teachers these days. We could respond by suggesting research-based teaching practices, building relationships with students and families, or joining a coalition of like-minded educators, but if at the heart of this question is the desire to know what it takes to be successful, we must first ask teachers to define *success*. If teachers do not determine for themselves what it means to be successful and then proactively measure their own effectiveness, they will allow others to decide whether they are effective.

Our society continues to measure teacher effectiveness by focusing on students' test scores, but as Jeff Duncan-Andrade explains, "positive self-identity, sense of purpose, and hope are critical pre-requisites for [student] achievement" and should be prioritized as measures of effective teaching. Including such measures encourages teachers to get to know their students and use this knowledge to empower, challenge, and support them.[1]

In this chapter we share the IMPACT Classroom Observation Rubric and how we use it to frame preservice teacher learning and accountability. We see this rubric as one of many measurements for formative assessment and evaluation that align with our values. We use this tool to provide feedback to our preservice teachers and prompt reflection and goal setting. Our hope is that our preservice teachers will confidently use data to inform their practice and draw from a variety of measures of teacher effectiveness rather than rely on others to determine whether they are successful.

CONTEXT: TEACHER RESIDENCIES AND THE PRESS TO MEASURE TEACHER QUALITY

In 2009, residency models were emerging as alternative ways to support teacher development. A few universities were already engaging in residency models, and the federal government was newly supporting the residency model as an innovation in teacher preparation. At the same time, the federal Race to the Top policy was focusing on teacher evaluation, which propelled research to accurately measure teacher quality. The evaluation of teachers based on one measure—the value they added to their students' standardized test scores—emerged as a political flashpoint. For instance, on August 14, 2010, the *Los Angeles Times* published controversial value-added measures for teachers in Los Angeles schools. It was a very public display of teacher ratings based on a singular measure of teacher quality over time, one that is highly correlated to student socioeconomic status. The *Los Angeles Times*'s misguided action animated our effort to capture teaching quality using multiple measures in the context of the new Inspiring Minds through a Professional Alliance of Community Teachers

(IMPACT) residency program at the University of California, Los Angeles (UCLA).[2]

Capturing the complexity of teaching quality involves using more than one measure. Yet what measures we use and how we use them is a contentious area of education policy research. Much of the policy debate centers on one measure—value-added student achievement data—in high-stakes district evaluations of practicing teachers. The Measures of Effective Teaching (MET) project, for example, is a large-scale study that analyzed observation data, student surveys, and teachers' pedagogical content knowledge to understand whether and how these measures are predictive of students' test score growth.[3] This approach has been criticized because of its central focus on test score growth; however, it has informed state and district teacher evaluation systems because of pressure from the policy community to select research-based measures of teacher effectiveness.[4]

The teacher education community faces similar pressure, given the policy debate surrounding the value of university-based preservice preparation and the heightened scrutiny of the effects of these programs, especially through organizations like the National Council on Teacher Quality. Residencies are an ideal context for exploring different measurement tools. They provide opportunities to capture teacher development through sustained placements in school sites over an entire academic year. Residents (preservice teachers) work alongside mentor teachers, but they are not subject to the school's evaluation process, and their status as a learner is protected by the university. Although residency programs confer a professional credential, the learner-focused evaluation context stands in stark contrast to the high-stakes evaluation context many practicing teachers face in their schools and districts. In addition, opportunities to collect data are integrated into teacher-education programs—not scheduled in as special, often high-stress, evaluation events. Teacher educators and mentors conduct regular observations of preservice teachers and collect preservice teachers' reflections on practice, as well as artifacts of their teaching, as part of their coursework. Programs also have an opportunity to assess preservice teachers' pedagogical content knowledge over time and the extent to which they use particular instructional strategies. In short, the residency context is primed for advancing thoughtful measurement of teaching quality.

After much thought, our research group chose eight measures of teaching quality for evaluating UCLA preservice teacher quality:

- Observation Rubric (OBS)
- Instructional Quality Assessment (IQA)
- Student Discourse Transcripts (DIS)
- Instructional Logs (LOG)
- Value-Added Measures (VAM)
- Pedagogical Content Knowledge Assessments (PCK)
- Surveys of Teacher Attitudes and Beliefs (SUR)
- Performance Assessment for California Teachers (PACT)

These measures capture different types of information about teaching practice and quality and are aligned with UCLA's framework for teacher learning. Guided by core principles of social justice, this framework focuses on content rigor, content discourse, classroom ecology, and equitable access to content. Each measure evaluates preservice teachers on different elements of practice. For instance, with the Observation Rubric, we can determine the use of varied participation structures to promote content discourse in a classroom setting, one that facilitates student reasoning and coconstructed conceptual understanding.[5] In contrast, the Instructional Quality Assessment is an artifact-based measurement that looks at the quality of the assignments preservice teachers give to their students as well as the quality of work these students produce to judge content rigor as well as equitable access to content. And a third measure, Instructional Logs, provides evidence of preservice teachers' ability to use formative assessment strategies as part of their routine classroom instruction.

This framework captures the grounding philosophy of UCLA Center X, one of equity and social justice, and it reflects what is visible in classroom practice through its operationalization into a rubric. UCLA's IMPACT Classroom Observation Rubric is a learning, reflection, and evaluation tool for our preservice teachers, mentors, teacher educators, and partners. It has shaped an ecology for learning and growing on various levels by providing a common language for learning and teacher development.[6]

THE IMPACT CLASSROOM OBSERVATION RUBRIC

Developing the Rubric

The IMPACT Classroom Observation Rubric (ICOR) is a framework that operationalizes what it means to teach content with a focus on equity. We wanted to incorporate the UCLA Teacher Education Program (TEP) mission, California and national content standards, and educational theories to identify elements of teaching that are visible in a classroom setting. We began with secondary mathematics and secondary science observation rubrics and carefully reviewed the Common Core State Standards for mathematics and the Next Generation Science Standards, respectively, to understand what it means to teach mathematics and science for student achievement, with a focus on language development as outlined in the updated California English Language Development Standards.

We also revisited many pedagogical practices for project-based learning and problem-based learning as the state and the local school districts began to shift curriculum and school structures to align more deeply with Linked Learning, an approach integrating technical education, project-based learning, and small learning-themed schools that had additional assessment requirements, such as project presentations and internships. We spent time in our guiding teachers' classrooms, visited schools throughout Southern California, watched videos, and took notes of best practices to make connections to the theories and standards. We met with policy makers, school principals, instructional coaches, and community partners to learn about the shifts in pedagogy deemed necessary for the twenty-first century. We met with community partners to discuss how teachers' engagement in the community would be reflected in the classroom. What technology was available in schools and how was it being used to support student learning? What elective courses were offered? Which industries were involved with schools?

Based on research and several revisions, we proposed four domains to define student-centered, equitable teaching for rigorous content learning aligned to the California Teaching Performance Expectations: Content Rigor, Content Discourse, Access to Equitable Content, and Classroom Ecology. Table 3.1 shows these domains and subdomains.

TABLE 3.1 *ICOR framework and description of the eleven subdomains.*

Content Rigor	Content Discourse	Equitable Access to Content	Classroom Ecology
Engaging in Rigorous Tasks. Students engage in meaningful and cognitively demanding tasks that require critical analyses, application, and generalizations.	**Teacher Questioning.** The teacher uses leveled questions to elicit student thinking and deepen students' understanding of the content.	**Academic Language.** The lesson shows an understanding of the language demands and provides students instruction and feedback on how to read, write, speak, and listen to ideas.	**Classroom Routines.** The teacher and students use observable classroom routines and procedures that allow for safe and intentional interactions between the living and the nonliving (classroom space and materials).
	Facilitation of Participation Structures. The teacher uses differentiated participation structures to equitably engage students in content discourse.	**Content Relevance.** The teacher connects content to real-world contexts and students to make the learning experience humanizing and authentic.	**Community of Learners.** The teacher builds a community of learners and teaches social norms and restorative justice practices to create and maintain empathetic, caring, and respectful relationships.
Checking for Understanding and Feedback. The teacher uses formative assessments to monitor student progress.	**Student Content Discourse.** Student talk builds on the thinking of others to explain concepts and reasoning, using evidence.	**Differentiation.** The teacher shows understanding of students by using differentiation strategies to meet their diverse needs.	**Democratic Classroom.** The teacher incorporates student choice and voice, paying attention to privilege and power in the classroom.

We wanted to develop a framework that would capture the complexity of teaching while supporting teachers to operationalize theories into practice that would help engage all students in a class. While there is no one-size-fits-all approach to teaching, the expectation for the preservice teachers is not to create thirty-two lessons, or a separate lesson for each student in the classroom. We want our preservice teachers to engage in humanizing teaching that prioritizes students as people and to get to know their strengths and needs to better support them in teaching the content. ICOR and the TEP Core Practices discussed in the next section provide entry points for reflection, feedback, and growth.

Ensuring Reliability

ICOR is a reliable measurement tool, according to initial evidence from a generalizability study (G study) conducted by university faculty and researchers.[7] Here reliability means that different raters, classroom observation stakeholders, and field supervisors come up with similar scores for the same scenario. The study investigated two research questions with the intended purpose of applying these understandings toward teacher development and improvement: What are the sources of error variation affecting the scores given by trained, experienced raters? And what is the reliability of average scores under varying scoring scenarios? In sum, this research helped us ensure that the observation rubrics were usable and captured teachers' best practices in their mathematics and science classrooms. After each round of observations, the raters, developers, and researchers discussed sources of error and revisions to make the observational tool more robust.

We learned from the G study that raters with a clearer understanding of instructional classroom strategies for a particular subdomain had higher rates of reliability. To ensure this depth of understanding, we created a list of possible instructional strategies for each subdomain as guides for our raters. These would later become the TEP Core Practices. The raters found this list helpful in scoring the observations, which ultimately resulted in a more accurate scoring and debriefing process. For example, math ratings for Supporting

Academic Language (a subdomain of Equitable Access to Content) had low reliability among the different raters. It was important for the developers and raters to discuss instructional strategies for supporting academic language, detailing teacher and student moves in a mathematics classroom. Once we started to talk about and list specific examples of instructional strategies, the ratings became clearer, and we modified ICOR accordingly. The G study helped us to strengthen the rubric as we engaged in numerous rounds of edits with input from various stakeholders. Table 3.2 shows the revised version of the rubric.

Another major contribution of the G study of ICOR-Math and ICOR-Science to TEP was the development of TEP Core Practices. In *Teaching Core Practices in Teacher Education*, Pam Grossman and

TABLE 3.2 *ICOR domains, subdomains, and TEP Core Practices for math and science.*

Domains	Subdomains Level 1: Not evident Level 2: Emerging Level 3: Applying Level 4: Integrating	TEP Core Practices
Content Rigor	Engaging in Rigorous Tasks	• High-level tasks • Formative assessments
	Checking for Understanding and Feedback	
Content Discourse	Teacher Questioning	• Leveled questions • Think-pair-share • Talk moves
	Facilitation of Participation Structures	
	Student Content Discourse	
Equitable Access to Content	Academic Language	• Word wall • Connecting to experiences • Graphic organizers
	Content Relevancy	
	Differentiation	
Classroom Ecology	Classroom Routines	• Opening closing routines • Community circles
	Community of Learners	
	Democratic Classroom	

her colleagues support a practice-based teacher education approach that identifies "core practices" of teaching, which preservice teachers rehearse with reflection and feedback until they are able to enact them competently.[8] What started out as a list of instructional strategies to help raters with scoring eventually became a starting place for identifying the core practices we wanted our candidates to learn before leaving the program. With the help of other content secondary methods instructors in TEP, we highlighted two or three instructional strategies from the list for each domain and identified them as TEP Core Practices. Identifying the ten core practices was challenging, and not all of us agreed that these were the right ten. However, we agreed on the importance of having a few core practices that we would all commit to teaching in our methods courses. In the next sections, we describe the ICOR domains, ICOR subdomains, and TEP Core Practices in their current form, as shown in table 3.2.

Domain 1: Content Rigor

rig·or

(noun) the quality of being extremely thorough,
exhaustive, or accurate

The first domain of ICOR focuses on content rigor that exists in a classroom. Here, *rigor* refers to expectations and experiences that are academically, intellectually, and personally challenging. Teachers hold the key to unlock students' potential by creating opportunities for students to engage with rich content. Teachers need to not only know the content but also be willing to share it with their students. If students don't have opportunities to engage with rigorous content, then their engagement with the content will remain at surface level, which directly affects their academic achievement. In this section, we elaborate on two subdomains under Content Rigor: Engaging in Rigorous Tasks and Checking for Understanding and Feedback. We also describe the two related TEP Core Practices: high-level tasks and formative assessments.

Engaging in Rigorous Tasks and Checking for Understanding and Feedback. Cognitively rich tasks, such as scientific inquiry labs and problem-solving in mathematics, open up opportunities for students to engage deeply with content by supporting deeper reasoning, language development, and social interactions. Robert Berry, the president of the National Council of Teachers of Mathematics, states, "We must do more to provide students with mathematics tasks that promote cognitive challenge, provide opportunities for reasoning and sensemaking, and deepen mathematical understanding by asking students to translate among multiple representations."[9] This is antithetical to what Martin Haberman describes as the "pedagogy of poverty," which focuses only on rote memory and recalling of facts, which students of low socioeconomic status encounter more often.[10] Lower-level tasks such as those limited to procedures and memorization without connections can reduce meaningful interaction with the content, although they can be foundational to higher-level tasks.[11]

An inquiry-based approach to science allows opportunities for students' inquisitive nature to be validated and come to life, encouraging their own and their peers' intellectual curiosity to go beyond the scope of a science curriculum.[12] Alan H. Schoenfeld explains that mathematically powerful classrooms are those that situate students in learning spaces that foster a positive mathematical identity through rich mathematical tasks that deepen connections between procedural knowledge, conceptual knowledge, problem solving, and reasoning.[13] Students can engage in complex thinking, doing, and meaning building, and develop a deeper understanding of concepts and skills through teachers' navigation and support in selecting content tasks that are open ended, require reasoning and use of evidence, and include appropriate checks for understanding.[14]

The first TEP Core Practice we want our preservice candidates to engage in is the implementation of high-level tasks. Rather than providing straightforward solution strategies, tasks should provide students with multiple entry points, strategies, and processes to reach a solution.[15] High-level tasks encourage students to use a variety of approaches and strategies while maintaining a high level of engagement and cognitive demand. In science, the Next Generation Science Standards entail the use of real-phenomenon story lines to engage students in evidence-based reasoning and authentic science experiences through the use of data from labs or digital lab simulations.[16] Students may interpret these data in multiple ways, which allows them to critique the reasoning of others.

Formative assessments reveal what students understand. While we encourage preservice teachers to engage in multiple forms of formative assessment, we model the Claim, Evidence, Reasoning (CER) strategy and performance tasks to understand students' ability to apply content to reason mathematically and scientifically.[17] Concept maps are another formative assessment we model to assess students' conceptual understanding.[18]

In teaching, we want our candidates to use multiple formative assessment strategies to monitor student progress and use them to inform instruction. How do we know what our students know? Are there multiple ways students can show what they know? What does the teacher do with this information? The candidate might reteach, evaluate, pose more questions, show counterexamples, give more opportunities for students to demonstrate learning, or involve students in feedback. Differentiated feedback is critical in understanding diversity and multidimensionality of student thinking. We model presenting different types of feedback (oral, written, visual) on both process and product to support an intellectually inclusive and dynamic learning environment.[19] During a classroom observation, we look for observable teacher and student moves to constantly affirm and negotiate what it means to teach for excellence, using a variety of strategies to assess and provide immediate and intentional feedback.

Domain 2: Content Discourse

dis·course
(noun) communication in speech or writing

The second domain of ICOR deals with oral content discourse in a classroom. The goal of this domain is to get students to talk about content in productive, rigorous, and equitable ways to deepen their content understanding. By engaging in content oral discourse, students make their thinking public, engage in reasoning, address misconceptions, and learn from each other by building on others' thinking. Under Content Discourse, there are three subdomains: Teacher Questioning, Facilitation of Participation Structures, and Student Content Discourse. Corresponding to these subdomains are three TEP Core Practices: leveled questions, think-pair-share, and talk moves.

Teacher Questioning, Facilitation of Participation Structures, and Student Content Discourse. Beyond the teacher-directed, banking model of education, discourse allows for greater student-focused instruction in which discussion, argument, and critique help students critically analyze the world around them.[20] Promoting productive disciplinary discourse creates more equitable opportunities for student participation and agency.[21] Despite the obvious benefits to student talk, research shows that teachers, especially preservice teachers, have difficulty engaging students in class discussions.[22] Getting students to talk about ideas as readers, writers, mathematicians, and scientists takes careful orchestration of tasks, norms, and fluent facilitation from teachers.[23] Teachers need pedagogical moves to initiate and support, such as arguing from evidence, to facilitate productive content discourse.[24]

Generating effective questions is an art.[25] There is a fine line between a question that elicits student thinking and one that solves the problem for the student. Being able to straddle this fine line comes with reflective practice and knowing who the students are in relation to content.[26] Benjamin Bloom's levels of questioning stress the importance of leveled questions to scaffold and provide access.[27] Using leveled questions, preservice teachers aim to engage their students deeply in the content. For example, the ICOR subdomain Teacher Questioning comprises four levels: level 1, questions that teach students wrong content; level 2, Initiate, Respond, and Evaluate (IRE) low-level recall questions; level 3, *why* and *how* higher-level questions with limited support; and level 4, analysis questions that require deep thinking and connection to content.

Building on leveled questions, teachers can use various forms of participation structures to create greater opportunities for all student voices to be presented and heard. Orchestrating productive content discourse among students requires great depths of understanding and training in content pedagogical knowledge, and research suggests that this task is difficult for most teachers.[28] Teachers must not only select the appropriate task and ask questions but also be able to anticipate student responses, respond to diverse ideas, and evaluate content reasoning, all while facilitating talk to orient students to each other.

The use of a variety of participation structures and talk moves can also help teachers orchestrate content discourse.[29] For example, students can begin working on a task individually, then confer with a partner using think-pair-share, then return to individual work to modify their thinking, and lastly engage in a whole-class discussion to reaffirm or to evaluate misconceptions. Talk moves—namely, re-voicing, elaborating, and evaluating the reasoning of others—further enhance the use of participation structures to share and learn from diverse student thinking. Through attentive listening, teachers can assess students' understanding of further eliciting and orienting.[30]

ICOR allows us to look for and identify evidence of student talk that conveys deep reasoning around mathematical and scientific concepts. Level 4 in Student Content Discourse points to evidence of this. Do students argue with counterexamples? Justify their reasoning with data and representations? Make and test conjectures? Make connections between representations and models? Pose questions? Evaluate their thinking? If observation data show that a few students are engaging in recalling facts discourse, then we can look at level 3 and level 4 criteria and ask ourselves how leveled questions, think-pair-share, and talk moves might be used for a more productive discourse around deep learning and equity.

Berry suggests that teachers examine the context to raise issues of equity in terms of who has the opportunity to talk, whose ideas are valued, and what actions the teacher will take after engaging in a critical reflection.[31] Equitable student discourse results from the interplay of the multiple teaching domains of ICOR. The three core instructional strategies—leveled questions, think-pair-share, and talk moves—provide a starting place for us to begin thinking about ways in which preservice teachers can create opportunities for student discourse. However, our hope in using ICOR is for the preservice teachers to realize its complexity and the interplay of all four domains that influence discourse.

Domain 3: Equitable Access to Content

eq·ui·ta·ble ac·cess
(adjective) fair and impartial
(noun) a means of approaching or entering a place

Promoting equitable access, for us, means constantly checking our explicit and implicit biases to move ourselves away from judgment and assumptions and to move ourselves closer to helping students actualize content mastery. The heart of this domain is getting to know the students in an ongoing manner and grappling with roadblocks that prevent students from intellectually and emotionally entering content fully. This requires teachers to challenge deficit notions about their students and reflect on teaching practices that *can* rather than ones that *can't*. We approach Equitable Access to Content with three subdomains: Academic Language, Content Relevancy, and Differentiation. Along with these subdomains are three TEP Core Practices: word wall, connecting to experiences, and graphic organizers.

Academic Language, Content Relevancy, and Differentiation. In this domain, getting to know students is essential to making content accessible to them. Strong content knowledge is necessary but insufficient in making the content accessible to a diverse student population in any classroom. Equity does not mean that all students engage with content in the same way; rather, it requires that teachers make "reasonable accommodations to promote access and attainment for all students."[32]

Language has served as a gatekeeper to student learning.[33] However, language challenges are often confused with limited cognitive capacity and have hindered access to the appropriate content-level curriculum.[34] Students need opportunities to engage in meaningful interactions with academic language in reading, writing, listening, and speaking in content areas in a variety of processes and products.[35] Therefore, a level 4 in ICOR-Math describes supporting academic language as providing students with opportunities to engage in mathematical reasoning and conceptual explanations with explicit and clear support for using representations, appropriate tools, correct symbols, and syntax for communicating; in contrast, a level 1 entails students copying notes without any other connection to producing language. To support academic language, we encourage the use of a word wall coupled with a graphic organizer to differentiate content, process, and product. Using a word wall to have students copy (level 1) is quite different from engaging students in creating a concept map with linking words from a word wall (level 2), making visual word-association sorting cards using a word wall with examples and counterexamples (level 3), or using a word wall to synthesize ideas and analyze a set of data (level 4).

Teachers who understand theories of language acquisition and who engage in a metacognitive process for how students learn and use language are better able to strengthen their content lessons to meet language demands and as a result provide students with appropriate support. Pauline Gibbons suggests some ways to scaffold and provide support for academic language in the areas of collaborative group work, writing from experience, thinking through active listening, and comprehending readings with a variety of literacy strategies.[36] In addition to these helpful instructional strategies, we must remember that honoring the language that students bring to the classroom every day and creating a safe environment for students to share and engage in deep content is foundational.[37] Jay Park, a preservice science teacher in 2019, nicely captured this asset-based approach: "All languages and cultures will be acknowledged, accepted, and celebrated by allowing students to use them as they see fit within the classroom."

Connecting to experiences is a core practice that uses students' prior knowledge, experiences, interests, and backgrounds to make connections to content. For example, a teacher may elicit prior knowledge by using a Know, Want to Know, Learn (KWL) activity or begin with an experiential task when starting a lesson sequence. Level 1 for Content Relevancy shows no evidence of connecting content to real-world contexts or prior knowledge, whereas Level 4 connects content to real-world contexts deeply. Critical mathematics is an example of a mathematics curriculum that empowers students to read and write about the world using numbers as quantitative evidence for social claims, while the Next Generation Science Standards focus on story lines to connect real phenomena to science concepts to engage students more deeply with the content they are learning.[38]

Domain 4: Classroom Ecology

e·col·o·gy

(noun) the branch of biology that deals with the relations of organisms to one another and to their physical surroundings

The last domain of ICOR focuses on relationships that exist in a classroom. Students interact with each other, the teacher, and the physical space, all the while managing their relationships with academic, social, and emotional learning. Teachers need to help students navigate this complex system to create and maintain positive and intentional relationships. Building a healthy classroom ecology involves positive efforts from diverse stakeholders; however, the teacher presents the foundation and structures to a classroom ecology that might allow humanizing pedagogy to flourish. If students do not feel seen, heard, and understood, then their engagement in the content may not be realized. In this section, we discuss three subdomains under Classroom Ecology: Classroom Routines, Community of Learners, and Democratic Classroom. We also focus on two instructional strategies, opening closing routines and community circles, which support student-centered practices and relationship building.

Classroom Routines, Community of Learners, and Democratic Classroom. Classroom Routines consider thoughtful planning for how physical components, students, and teachers interact with each other. For example, opening closing routines allow teachers multiple opportunities to address norms and to reflect with students on whether these norms help students take care of themselves, take care of each other, and take care of the classroom.[39] In level 1, there are no observable routines, procedures, or social norms, whereas in level 4 there are observable classroom routines, procedures, and social norms practiced by the teacher and the students in meaningful interactions with each other and the physical space.

Furthermore, these relationships can be strengthened when students feel that they are part of a community.[40] Any relationship takes hard work to establish and maintain. Darlene Tieu, a preservice science teacher, wrote, "Before I can expect my students to be open to me, I want to set the example and show my vulnerability to them first." We encourage the preservice teachers to get to know their students and to help their students to get to know them. Many of the teachers share "Where I'm From" poems with their students.[41] The ongoing practice of building a community and restoring relationships gives students agency, accountability, and responsibility and creates an empathetic environment.[42] For example, community circles allow opportunities for students to share, build trust, make connections, reflect, restore relationships, and further negotiate and establish social norms.

Explicit modeling and negotiation of social norms that recognize power and culture in the classroom critically develop and maintain a democratic classroom.[43] Teacher candidates are encouraged to use learning criteria to be transparent with their students about the learning goals. Additionally, clear expectations for learning tasks and assessments have the potential for making student feedback more meaningful.[44] We ask our candidates to consider student input for instructional decision-making. They may do this through community circles or another instructional strategy such as journal writing, voting and polls, or collecting student feedback regularly.

During seminar, preservice teachers have opportunities to reflect on instructional strategies that leverage student voice in their specific context by engaging in a problem of practice—a reflective process with peers to improve relationships—and further, to plan with peers to incorporate TEP Core Practices into their lesson plans. The field supervisors use the observation rubric, ICOR, to collect observational data on Classroom Routines, Community of Learners, and Democratic Classroom for qualitative and quantitative assessment and goal-setting feedback. The question always ends with whether these practices leverage student learning and meet the content learning objectives.

USING ICOR TO SUPPORT TEACHING

My core values as a social justice educator are very simple: scaffold learning content and use it to empower the students' diversity and identities, give them a mentally and physically safe space to learn, and encourage unity to work together and tackle community dilemmas. By working towards these goals, I want to stand in solidarity with my students' strife and be there to celebrate their inevitable and eventual victories.

—Deborah Wang, Chemistry Teacher Candidate, 2017–2018

Supporting our candidates in the development of a social justice teacher identity is at the center of our work. ICOR has helped us support our preservice teachers as they operationalize their working identities into practice by informing our coursework and assignments, serving as a common language among the different stakeholders in the program, and measuring teaching practices for reflection, growth, and learning. Research using ICOR data has helped us improve our coursework. For example, in 2012 Mollie Appelgate found that preservice teachers were not always implementing in their student teaching placements the classroom practices they were learning in TEP courses.[45] In fact, when they did implement TEP Core Practices, the preservice teachers did not always accurately reflect on how well the strategies were implemented and how they supported student learning.

The teaching data from the ICOR measurement tool, used in the G study and the research study by Appelgate, provided evidence that allowed us to more accurately reflect on our practices. The ICOR data gave us insights into how university learning spaces could better align with the TEP Core Practices and into the importance of communicating with all of the TEP stakeholders, including the guiding teachers and the field supervisors. These studies had a profound impact on improving TEP practices, such as creating Methods with Mentors professional development spaces, and on the development of TEP assignments aligned with the ICOR domains. In the next section, we describe three TEP assignments that were developed as a result of teacher data analysis using ICOR in secondary mathematics and secondary science.

The Planning, Instructing, Assessing, and Reflection (PIAR) Assignment

The planning, instructing, assessing, and reflection (PIAR) assignment supports the preservice teachers in learning more deeply about high-level tasks and formative assessments (see table 3.2 under "TEP Core Practices"). In the first quarter of the program, the preservice teachers have to plan a three-day lesson sequence and teach it, focusing on mathematical reasoning and problem-solving or inquiry-based science learning tasks. For example, ICOR-Math describes level 1 tasks as primarily procedural, level 2 as primarily procedural with some connection to concepts, level 3 as conceptual with some connection to procedures and reasoning, and level 4 as performance-based with application of concepts to problem-solving and reasoning tasks such as proofs, conjectures, and generalizations using data and symbolic and graphical representations.

The PIAR assignment emphasizes formative assessments from a differentiated perspective. The preservice teachers are asked to plan multiple forms of formative assessments to use during instruction. In addition, the preservice teachers plan a formal assessment with a rubric. They then analyze student work and provide students both written and oral feedback. Lastly, the assignment ends with the completion of a written reflection from the teacher candidates about their learning process and feedback on their assignment in two ICOR subdomains: Engaging in Rigorous Tasks and Checking for Understanding and Feedback.

Sophisticated teaching that displays deep understandings of content pedagogical knowledge happens when instruction and formative assessment are concurrent, when the transitions between the two are so seamless and fluid that they appear to be one. We encourage our candidates to constantly listen and look for students' demonstration of learning through two of our core instructional strategies, high-level tasks and formative assessments.

The Video Instructional Rounds Cycle (VIRC) Assignment

The Video Instructional Round Cycle (VIRC) assignment is a series of interconnected learning activities using videos, in which the preservice teachers enact a particular discourse practice in their discipline.[46] Through this assignment, the preservice teachers learn more deeply about Content Discourse instructional strategies: leveled questions, think-pair-share, and talk moves. In the second quarter of the program, the preservice teachers engage in VIRC four times, requiring at least one of the focus discourse strategies. For VIRC round 1, the preservice teachers read about leveled questions and content questioning; watch and analyze video clips on questioning; and, finally, carefully craft questions in their lesson plans, aligning them with the reasoning and conceptual understanding components of the learning objective. Then the preservice teachers go into the field and film a 10- to 12-minute clip of themselves teaching the lesson for their first instructional round. The video clip is uploaded to course website and labeled "Teacher Questioning" before class. During class, the preservice teachers are paired to watch and analyze their peers' videos, give feedback, and close with self-reflection.

This cycle is repeated three more times. VIRC round 2 focuses on participation structures; VIRC round 3 focuses on talk moves; and VIRC round 4 focuses on the facilitation of small-group or whole-class discussions that include all three subdomains in the Content Discourse domain: Teacher Questioning, Facilitation of Participation Structures, and Student Content Discourse.

For each cycle, the preservice teachers use ICOR to score their peers on each of the three subdomains. They also time stamp evidence and provide qualitative feedback, including what the teacher did well and what could be improved. The VIRC assignment helps the preservice teachers use ICOR to assess discourse practices concerning students for their peers and themselves, resulting in deep engagement in learning and reflection grounded in praxis. The preservice teachers leave each cycle with a deeper understanding of the ways they are engaging students in content discourse and next steps to improve their practice using the ICOR four-level scale. The levels in each subdomain, coupled with feedback, provide opportunities for growth and support. The goal is for teachers to see learning to teach as an intellectually invigorating and collaborative endeavor.

The Community Science, Technology, Engineering, and Mathematics Project-Based Learning (C-STEM-PBL) Assignment

In the community science, technology, engineering, and mathematics project-based learning (C-STEM-PBL) assignment, preservice teachers design and implement an end-of-the-year project incorporating students' experiences, interests, community, and familial and cultural assets in secondary mathematics and secondary science classrooms.[47] In the third quarter of the program, the preservice teachers incorporate instructional strategies from two ICOR subdomains, Content Relevancy (under Equitable Access to Content) and Democratic Classroom (under Classroom Ecology).

Each teacher candidate designs a project-based learning (PBL) lesson plan using the Buck Institute framework, project welcome letter, time line, check-in points, rubric, and overview graphic organizer. With course readings, guest speakers, and peer feedback, the preservice teachers adjust and finalize their C-STEM-PBL. They collect student work, including their oral presentations to community members, written work, technology-based products, and artifacts. The preservice teachers share these artifacts in the seminar. The assignment ends with reflections on the Content Relevancy and Democratic Classroom ICOR subdomains.

An example of a past C-STEM-PBL is a geometry project in which students used the architectural software Floorplanner to design three-dimensional buildings in their community. The students began with a walking tour of their community and brainstormed assets they wanted to design to support their community members. The students decided to build homeless shelters, Planned Parenthood centers, and centers for young adolescent females, among other community-based organizations. Their presentations included a rationale for their building, a community map showing where they would build, floor plans, the dimensions and calculations for their plans, and a budget for the materials and building.

The preservice teachers receive feedback under the ICOR domains from their peers in the seminar before they implement the project with the students. In level 1, the Democratic Classroom practice is teacher-directed with no student input; level 2 is primarily teacher-directed with little student input; level 3 includes student input; and level 4 fully incorporates student input with attention to equity. The preservice teachers assess each other's C-STEM-PBL in light of opportunity for authentic student choice in content and process, ranging from the inquiry question, project process, presentation audience, and products. The enactment of C-STEM-PBL offers one pedagogical move supporting the Content Relevancy and Democratic Classroom subdomains, both of which our candidates had more difficulty implementing in the classroom, according to our G study using ICOR teaching data.

ICOR MEASUREMENT AND ACCOUNTABILITY

Developing social justice mathematics and science educators is difficult and complex.

Preservice teachers need support in developing an understanding of social justice theories and content pedagogies along with concrete and tractable practices that they can use in their classrooms. ICOR was designed with this in mind—to help preservice teachers develop a robust understanding of what it means to be a social justice mathematics and science educator and provide a set of practical strategies to enact in their classrooms. Specifically, in our methods courses, we have found positive development in our discourse practices, especially when we have preservice teachers practice, film, and engage in peer feedback.

ICOR operationalizes social justice by developing a common language between university faculty and novice teachers and serving as a tool to provide feedback for improvement. It also provides program- and research-aligned expectations for pedagogical practices. However, we must be mindful of providing feedback so preservice teachers have opportunities to iterate practice and improve. While ICOR is a tool for feedback and learning in our program, it is also a tool for evaluation that supports the process of accreditation.

We recognize the tension that exists between evaluation and learning, and ICOR has helped us to navigate that tension, both for our program and for our preservice teachers who encounter evaluative tools in their practice. ICOR provides an opportunity to reimagine these types of evaluative tools as ones that can align to program vision and that can be used for formative feedback and learning. The danger always exists that these tools, intended largely for learning, can be repurposed for teacher evaluation; for example, the learning-focused Danielson framework is widely adapted and used for district-wide evaluation although it was intended for formative purposes.[48] While ICOR exists outside of the district evaluation rubrics, it can be used to complement and extend other frameworks, particularly given its social justice orientation. We need learning tools so we can repurpose and restructure them to advance the work of justice in schools.

This work is layered and complex, and ICOR can be fluid, moving from formative feedback to program evaluation depending on the intention and goals for its use. We believe that teacher candidates should be supported to learn, embrace, and use multiple-measure frameworks such as ICOR. Our advice for aspiring social justice educators is to proactively measure your own effectiveness. And to the teacher educators supporting preparing this next generation, embrace the opportunity to measure good practice and use the data to empower, challenge, and support your students.

PART II

Sustaining Educators to Deepen Praxis
and Continue the Struggle

CHAPTER 4

Reciprocal Learning Partnerships for Equity

Supporting Educators to Critically Reflect, Disrupt, and Take Action

Tonikiaa Orange and Jo Ann Isken

THE JOURNEY BEGINS

As a novice teacher, you are filled with excitement and anxiety about your first day of teaching. Over and over in your mind, you have thought about how best to bond with students and families and how to build a strong working relationship with your mentor teacher. Your heart races at the possibilities of what you will learn and the contributions you can make to the lives of children. You are ready to dive into the rewarding yet challenging teaching profession, knowing you will be soundly prepared by the University of California, Los Angeles, Teacher Education Program (TEP) and confident you will learn from and alongside carefully selected mentor teachers who support the efforts of equity and social justice instilled in you by TEP.

Students who choose to attend TEP often say they do so because of our explicit focus on equity and social justice and because of the program's commitment to serve in urban schools with our most vulnerable populations. This explicit focus on equity and social justice comes with the expectation that field experiences with mentor teachers will mirror that commitment. So some of our novice teachers were surprised when they began their student teaching and observed subtle and obvious instances of inequity on the part of their mentor teachers. Our novices were at times disappointed at what they saw in the classrooms. After all, weren't their mentor teachers experts? Weren't they supposed to promote equity instead of reproducing inequity? Our carefully vetted mentor teachers were seasoned in the profession, dedicated to equity and social justice, and had supported many student teachers. Most had training in one of many models of effective coaching. However, some of our novice teachers were feeling dissonance between what they were observing in field placements and what they were being taught in TEP:

> My partner teacher labels students as "low" and continues to use deficit language when describing a particular group of students.

> There is so much of a focus on rules, everything is controlled, and the students are always being yelled at.

> The behavior management system seems to continue to punish the same group of Black students.

> Why are we still asking kids to line up by gender, boys and girls?

> The way we are presenting this history lesson is just incorrect. It is a misrepresentation of the story of Thanksgiving.

We asked our novice teachers to not make assumptions without raising questions about the practices they were witnessing. We suggested that they problematize their observations with their partner teacher to bring forth new ideas about how to understand and shift classroom practices. However, our suggestions were often met with responses such as "I don't feel comfortable," "They will be evaluating me," "They are the experts," and "I don't know as much as my mentor."

Our mentor teachers' perception of effective coaching centered on guiding novice teachers through lesson design and modeling long-held "best practices," followed by feedback on the reproduction of those practices. The mentor gave advice as an expert teacher whose potentially uninterrogated practices should be adopted as part of the novice's emerging tool kit of practice. This coaching approach tends to silence an equity stance and obfuscate a social justice lens.

This tension between our novice teachers' observations and their mentors' coaching stance motivated us to find a new coaching paradigm, one that envisioned a relationship between novice and mentor as a partnership moving together to take action toward equity.

TRADITIONAL COACHING PARADIGMS IN TEACHER PREPARATION

In urban classrooms, coaching teachers on "research-based best practices" is not closing pervasive achievement gaps or disproportionate discipline challenges faced by learners who are most underserved—students of color, immigrants and linguistically diverse students, students from low-income households, and special-needs students—students who have historically been judged to be deficient, lacking social capital, or simply not as intelligent as their more advantaged peers.[1] As "expert" as mentor teachers may be, they are often unconsciously reproducing practices and attitudes that marginalize students.

As illustrated in the quotes above, novice teachers note when their "expert" mentors might be using curricular, instructional, and classroom ecology practices that reveal deficit notions about students. A typical coaching conversation around the first quote might lead the novice and mentor to a discussion of how to remediate or provide interventions for the "low" students. Although preparing teachers with best practices to differentiate for students is important, these kinds of discussions miss the opportunity to surface and explore root causes that lead to inequitable learning opportunities for students. For example, is the mentor teacher aware that she perceives her students as "low"? What does "low" mean? What does the mentor teacher's conception of "low students" mean as she thinks about her lesson planning, assessment practices, and expectations for student achievement? Failing to attend to hidden biases, values, or beliefs results in pedagogical practices that marginalize students in schools. If coaching conversations between novice and mentor teachers do not provide a forum for raising and discussing these questions, we cannot transform schooling for our most vulnerable students.

This chapter examines a new framework for coaching, Reciprocal Learning Partnerships for Equity (RLP). RLP centers equity and the coconstruction of an equity action. Reconceptualizing coaching shifts traditional coaching paradigms into a professional learning partnership that challenges the notion of an "expert" mentor modeling and transmitting "best practices" to a skill-acquiring novice. This framework is grounded in the development of relational trust, reciprocity, examination of one's identity and positionality, and taking an explicit equity stance. An equity stance moves participants from discussing "best practices" to collaborative analysis of instructional moves that might impede student engagement and success. RLP positions individuals to develop a critical consciousness that allows them to engage in a cycle of inquiry leading to transformative action.

RECONCEPTUALIZING COACHING

Coaching models typically focus on a coach guiding and supporting the mentee through a cycle of ongoing goal setting, data analysis, reflection, and learning of new teaching skills. Instructional coaching models have emerged as a promising practice to improve the quality of instruction and increase student achievement—more so than other professional development and school-based interventions.[2] Coaching can be a metacognitive process, helping teachers gain a deeper awareness and understanding of their instructional decision-making. Good instructional coaches can provide teachers with guidance on research-based strategies to improve and apply to their work.

After observing hundreds of coaching conversations, we noticed the unconscious deficit-oriented perspectives and language repeated time and time again. We needed a lever to deepen coaching conversations to capture the complex and invisible ways deficit thinking shows up in classroom practices. We recognized that interrogating, disrupting, and transforming inequitable practices is required to move the needle toward social justice and equity in the classroom and that both coach and novice teachers must be active participants in the conversation. We needed to develop a common language for discussions about equity and to create a space where mentor and novice teachers' underlying beliefs and assumptions are brought to the fore. In this shared space they could successfully unpack their practice and transform the ways in which they engage our most vulnerable students.

RLP is not a coaching model. Embodying the belief that coach and novice teacher must be partners in a coaching relationship, RLP is an approach to coaching. It is an approach that begins with a mutual understanding that participants come to the table with lived experiences, knowledge, and skills that can be leveraged to improve student outcomes. It provides a framework for dialogue and praxis around issues of equity that lead to active reflection and reflective action.

A traditional coaching conversation privileges the mentor from a position of power: a relationship in which one is an "expert other" guiding the development of a less prepared learner. Novice teachers are often positioned as powerless and voiceless in the relationship or as empty vessels to be filled with "tried and true" (and sometimes evidence-based) teaching practices. Clearly, mentors bring years of teaching experience to the table. Novice teachers too have experience and knowledge relevant to classroom settings and, as aspiring teachers, are positioned to ask critical questions regarding what instructional strategies are best for whom, why, and how culturally diverse students experience those practices. RLP creates a space for aspiring and accomplished teachers to freely question and critique classroom practice and explore ways to address issues of equity. The RLP framework provides a foundation that reshapes the ways urban teachers engage one another in productive dialogue about issues of equity throughout their careers.

THE RECIPROCAL LEARNING PARTNERSHIPS FRAMEWORK: THEORY TO PRACTICE

The development of the RLP framework is grounded in three theories that speak to the ways in which we believe learning occurs and the context in which it takes place in our partnership conversations. First, we believe that learning is a social process and that it occurs through the interaction between people and cultures. Grounded in sociocultural theory, RLP centers the cultural identities, beliefs, and norms of participants, recognizing that culture and experiences influence each person's views, biases, and assumptions and, therefore, the selection and implementation of actions around teaching and learning.[3] Social, cultural, and historical experiences frame the way one views and understands teaching and learning. Both participants bring unique perspectives that influence decisions about practice.

Critical race theory and critical third space theory further inform the framework. Critical race theory considers the cultural knowledge, skills, abilities, and languages of communities of color as powerful and valued assets in the fight for equity. It recognizes that race is central to power and centers communities of color as holding power in their cultural capital. Critical race theory calls for us to nurture and develop educational practices that acknowledge cultural strengths of communities of color to fight for racial and social justice. RLP dialogue centers the voices of those traditionally unempowered. Once this mediated dialogue has occurred, a new strategy for bridging can take place between mentor and novice teacher.[4]

Critical third space is an active space; it calls us to action. Critical third space enables the disruption of cultural contexts and beliefs in multiple directions, whereby each educator may learn to "occupy the subject position of the other, and in doing so create something else, something other than."[5] It is the space where educators interrogate the present and transform their mediated learning into action. It is in this newly created third space that resistance and disruption occur. In RLP the third space is where the partnership engages in inquiry and action.

Language matters. If we truly wanted novice teachers and mentors to have authentic dialogue about the complexity of teaching and learning, we needed a new way to talk about this reconceptualized relationship. We needed to create a lexicon that positioned novices and mentors as learners on an equal footing, learning from one another and making new discoveries together. While using a single title for aspiring and accomplished teachers would have suited our purpose perfectly, data collection and licensure reporting requirements prevented us from doing so. We carefully considered our language in naming the partners in the relationship. We use *partner teacher* to describe accomplished teachers whose classrooms are sites of novice learning. We use *fellow* to name an aspiring teacher of equal relational status, involved in the same activity and allied with their partner teachers. A fellow represents an ally in the work, whose questions, knowledge, and experience are equally important when engaging in the RLP framework.

RECIPROCAL LEARNING PARTNERSHIPS IN ACTION

RLP engages participants in a process of participatory inquiry.[6] The process activates each participant's sense of agency; surfaces and examines participant perspectives, assumptions, and biases; and involves a fluid exchange of ideas that leads to the creation of new knowledge and subsequent equity moves. This is complex work that needed to be made concrete and usable. First we developed the four key principles for participatory inquiry within an RLP approach. We then developed a series of questions that prompt equity-grounded dialogue that leads participants to actionable steps.

Principle 1: Name the equity issue(s). To begin to address classroom policies and practices that impede student success, it is important to identify inequities related to curriculum, instruction, assessment, and classroom ecology.

Principle 2: Engage in reciprocity. In participatory inquiry, there is an expectation of fair exchange of knowledge that is then used to inform shared, coconstructed actions intended to transform biased practices. Reciprocity depends on developing *relational trust to confront bias, stereotypes, and unjust practices.* It is rooted in personal exchanges, respect, personal regard, competence, responsibility, and integrity; and it is developed through interactions, conversations, tension, critical collaboration, and the demonstration of cultural competence and emotional intelligence.[7] Relational trust creates and supports appropriate conditions to tackle inequities in schools and creates a space and the conditions in which change can occur.

In order to build relational trust within an RLP approach, participants examine how identity and positionality interact, influence, and potentially bias their understanding of and outlook on classroom practice.

Principle 3: Take an equity action. The partnerships must explicitly prioritize equity over equality and identity over dominant norms of access and achievement. This asserts that equity centers the dialogue and signals a commitment to privilege "education over schooling, and power/identity over mere access and achievement."[8]

Principle 4: Conduct critical reflection. In critical reflection, learning partners revisit and access changes in practice with a focus on equity efficacy. They also reflect on the process, the strength of the dialogue, their comfort and capacity to engage in the dialogue with honesty and positive intent, and their willingness to acknowledge unexamined biases and assumptions.

The cycling and recycling between action, dialogue, and reflection can yield compelling outcomes for the reciprocal learning partners. Every time the learning partners cycle through a conversation, it strengthens the deep relational trust needed to create the conditions to have courageous conversations about equity. The learning partners are more willing to explore deeply held unconscious biases, and more comfortable in identifying and voicing issues of identity and positionality that may affect their decisions on practice.

FRAMING QUESTIONS THAT PROMPT DIALOGUE

We found the need to use framing questions when engaging in an RLP conversation. Partner teachers and fellows often did not know how to enter into a conversation about equity in a coaching context. They knew how to have equity conversations in large, more anonymous groups. However, RLP positions two individuals to make themselves vulnerable in revealing identity, bias, and positionality that may unconsciously be influencing their teaching decisions. Most importantly, the framing questions preclude partners from recreating traditional "coaching" conversations in which one is the expert with the goal of perfecting a best practice.

The framing questions scaffold the conversation for partners and ensure equity is at the center. The questions act as an entry point by providing the language for partners to begin conversations about issues that they have most likely never spoken about in this context. They provide access points for all, regardless of their comfort and level of sophistication with equity dialogue. The questions leverage conversation and reflection. Finally, the questions mediate the dialogue, allaying some of the fear and discomfort associated with these courageous conversations. The following are examples of framing questions:

- *Equity questions.* How is oppression playing out right here, right now? What will we do about it?
- *Reciprocity questions.* How are we building on one another's knowledge and expertise? What are we both willing to commit to change?
- *Relational trust questions.* How are we modeling effective communication? How are we demonstrating a sense of responsibility, accountability, and flexibility with one another?
- *Identity questions.* How do our students' identities factor into our decision-making around classroom policies and practices? How is our own identity influencing our beliefs about students and learning?

- *Positionality questions.* How does our identity and position as an educator, role, and place in the classroom recognize, honor, or complicate the interactions we have with students, family, and community members?
- *Equity action questions.* What will we do to engage and dismantle inequity and oppression that is playing out in our classrooms and school? What have we done to expand our knowledge and understanding of the diverse cultures in our school? What coconstructed action are we going to take to tackle the equity issues we have named?
- *Critical reflection questions.* Have we demonstrated the effectiveness of the equity action? Does it need to be revised? Changed? What further knowledge or information do we need to take action? How have our identity and positionality influenced our beliefs about students and learning?

PREPARING MENTORS AND NOVICES TO DO EQUITY WORK

Our kids barely got any recess the first week of school! On the first day of school, they got nothing. They got an earful of how they need to behave at snack and how they need to line up. They came into the classroom with somber faces. When I would ask my own son what he did in school, he always shared things that happened on the playground. My son would tell me who he played with, who was mean, who got in trouble. I realized how little recess our kids at this school got that first week of school, and thought of how things would be when I became a veteran teacher. I am not sure what my thoughts on recess are. So, I did some quick research, and the majority of what I found seemed to favor playtime at school while also critiquing how more schools are opting for less recess in exchange for more academic time. One article stated "Furthermore, the period allotted to recess decreases as the child ages and is less abundant among children of lower socioeconomic status and in the urban settings." That struck me, why are more kids not getting more recess time in urban areas? Then after reading some other articles it started to hit me.

Kids in urban areas are portrayed as uncontrollable, lacking, and violent. I would like to discuss shifting things around with my coaching teacher, but do not feel comfortable approaching her. My teacher threatened a kid a few times to take time away from his recess if he didn't behave. Guess what color his skin is? Does this add to her perception of him being a disruptive kid? But how do I approach her without her being threatened?

—Hannah, Center X Student Teaching Fellow,
reflective journal entry

How are the issues presented by this fellow teacher brought into a coaching conversation? In the scenario above, the fellow and partner teacher were just beginning to establish the relational trust necessary to begin to have a critical conversation about race, discipline, and the students affected most by the recess policies. The fellow proposes questions for the partner teacher that may be uncomfortable and is well aware of the potential repercussions of asking them. How is taking away recess an effective form of discipline? What perceived misbehaviors result in a loss of recess? Is this policy applied to all students who exhibit this behavior? Who loses recess the most, and why? Will asking these questions seem threatening or informative? Engaging in dialogue around issues of assumptions, bias, and inequitable practice is not easy and does not come naturally for most teachers. While RLP recognizes the coaching space as fertile ground for these critical conversations to take place, it also assumes the need for teachers to learn and practice the language and skills needed to make the space productive. Two primary spaces were created for partners and fellows to engage in this important work together: a weeklong summer institute and monthly Partners in Practice convenings.

The summer institute had two primary goals. The first goal is to strengthen participants' individual and collective understanding of the historical and racist origins of educational inequity and how social inequities create social, emotional, and academic obstacles for children, and to develop a critical understanding of deficit thinking based on race, ethnicity, gender, and language and how it shows up in teacher practice. Our second goal is for participants to begin to build the relational trust requisite to doing the work together on equity. Participants learned the RLP framework, practiced identifying issues of inequity, and then practiced working together to coconstruct an equity action. We focused on reciprocity, knowing that in order to coconstruct, there has to be a shift and balance of power. Our aim was to make sure the partner teacher and fellow saw one another as partners in this work, both contributing knowledge and information to tackle the hardest circumstances they would encounter in the classroom.

We developed monthly Partners in Practice meetings to provide partner teachers and fellows with the space and tools to engage in productive dialogue about uncomfortable issues and the ways in which they themselves perpetuated inequity in their classroom policies and practice. At every meeting, we reviewed the four RLP agreements that help develop and sustain productive interaction and group dialogue:

- Partner teacher and fellow see each other as partners and work together in the classroom to disrupt inequity—not what "you" or "I" will do, but what "WE" will do together.
- No one is the "expert." As partners, everyone brings something to the table and has expertise and knowledge that can contribute to creating an action toward equity.
- Partner teacher's role is not to be the facilitator of reflective questioning but to be a "coactor" to solve issues of inequity, taking part in the change that happens in the classroom.
- Discussions on relational trust, positionality and identity, and reciprocity must be considered in every dialogue. These discussions are key in order for partner teachers and fellows to address their own biases and beliefs about inequity in the classroom and how they come to the table to coconstruct an action.

Each month learning partners were asked to bring an equity issue to discuss and then coconstruct an equity action to address that issue. The results of their equity action would be the focus of their critical reflection during the next meeting. They engaged in dialogue about how their actions played out and whether inequity and dispro-portionality decreased in their classrooms. Both partners and fellows attended these meetings, ensuring support of the tenets of the RLP framework and the focus on cocreating equity actions that they both addressed in partnership. The meetings were facilitated by RLP fa-cilitators who also supported the work in the field. RLP facilitators visited each partner and fellow partnership to mediate any conflict or address issues that needed facilitator support. Issues authentic to the partners' daily practice grounded the discussion, which focused on self-critique of norms, beliefs, practices, and actions.

Reciprocal Learning Partnerships Example: Revisiting a Coconstructed Equity Action

The following steps are designed to support the conversation between partner and fellow teacher, guiding them toward the coconstruction of an equity action. The questions and statements foster the reflec-tive process between the partner and fellow teacher. Framing the responses using "we" and "our" cues reciprocity and the shared re-sponsibility for equity action. Below is an example of this reflective process used by a partner and fellow teacher.

Step 1: Name the equity issue.
- What are the equity issues impacting the achievement of our students with special needs?
- We need to further understand why students of color identified as special needs are not participating in our class.
- Are we exhibiting the same high standards for our students iden-tified with special needs as for our general education population?

Step 2: Revisit a coconstructed equity action.
- We watched each other to determine how we were inviting all of our students to participate in class.
- We looked at our participation protocols and considered whether certain protocols engaged students of color with special needs more than other protocols.

Step 3: Practice critical reflection.

- How have students benefited from our equity action? There is now a sense of a community being built in our class that includes students of color who are identified as special needs, making all students more collaborative and engaged.
- How did students benefit from our collaboration? Our collaboration with one another allowed us to see through a different perspective and shift our lessons in various ways. One of us had expertise in observation protocols. The other had expertise in culturally responsive practices. As a result of our collaborative efforts, we tried more participation protocols to engage students.

Step 4: Revisit reciprocity.

- How did we build on one another's knowledge? Each partner teacher brought assets to the table. One of us brought new culturally responsive teaching practices to address engagement, and the other infused examples and strategies to make lessons more engaging and rearranged the room setup for more participation and collaboration between all students.
- *Positionality.* In what ways did we resist, disrupt, or change the constructs of our positionality? The teaching partner with more years of teaching experience allowed herself to be open to questions and critique from her fellow. After we both shared our beliefs, without blame or judgment, about the potential participation of special needs students of color in general education classes, we were able to coconstruct a new protocol that centered special needs students of color for successful participation.
- *Identity.* How did our identity affect how we saw the equity issue? Because one of us is a teacher of color, she immediately wondered why students of color who are identified as special needs were not participating in our class. One of us is White and had not noticed a difference in the participation. We challenged ourselves to interrogate the reason, specifically looking at our beliefs about how race affects special education students and our response to challenge structures and our practices to be more intentional and inclusive.

- *Relational trust.* How did we demonstrate a sense of responsibility, accountability, and flexibility? We were willing to try new things, and we did not feel afraid to take action and make mistakes. We both came to the table with new participation protocols and ideas to engage students of color identified as special needs. At the beginning of every conversation, we explicitly worked on trust and understanding that our comments would be shared without blame or judgment.

Step 5: Co-construct a new equity action.
- Provide more scaffolding for collaboration for students of color with special needs to be certain they can access the curriculum.
- Hold one-on-one meetings with students of color with special needs.
- Provide more formative feedback to all students.

There were many potential issues that could have come up during this RLP conversation that would have impeded the movement to action if they were not confronted. Before the RLP framework was established, issues did arise that impeded movement to action. A transgender fellow was challenged in building relational trust with their partner teacher due to religious beliefs. Conflicts in belief systems about behavior management surfaced between a Latina fellow and a Caucasian partner teacher based on the personal experience of the Latina fellow in public schools. Once the partner and fellow began to have a reciprocal dialogue about identity, relational trust, and positionality, they were able to see each other through a different lens to work more cohesively to solve equity issues in their classrooms.

CONCLUSION

To educate our most vulnerable children, it is imperative that we rethink how we support new teachers coming into the field and shift the way we think about coaching for all teachers. RLP reframes how we think about the lived experiences and perspectives of novices as important contributions to their emerging practice and that of their mentors. It also reframes how we think about veteran teachers: from experts by virtue of years of experience to ongoing learners who serve as reflective thought partners for aspiring teachers. In doing so, RLP promotes teacher agency and the ability to work with colleagues to observe, reflect, and coconstruct modifications to practice or novel solutions that center equity as the goal of all discussions.

Our primary focus must be continuously and critically reflecting on "best practices" from professional development sessions and teacher preparation programs through the lens of the impact on our most vulnerable students. In order to do this, we must redefine the purpose and practice of coaching. RLP advocates observing classrooms with the question of which students are benefitting or thriving as a result of the implementation of teacher practices, and more significantly, which students are not.

RLP challenges people to remain open to new ways of "seeing" how they teach and how students learn. It creates intentional space for dialogue about unconscious practices that might marginalize students. Within these partnerships, teachers work together to examine the historical context of school systems and coconstruct the actions they take to redesign teaching and learning for culturally diverse students. Most importantly, this work helps build collective efficacy and helps teachers throughout their careers to center themselves as colearners in a reciprocal dialogue—an ongoing conversation that positions everyone with knowledge and assets as someone who can enhance teaching and learning in the urban classroom.

Positioning all teachers as partners in learning may yield a final long-term benefit. RLP may be a significant contributing factor to the retention of teachers in the profession by meaningfully engaging educators in learning that deepens their practice around issues of equity.

CHAPTER 5

Beyond Teacher Education

Creating Opportunities for
Continued Learning

Jody Z. Priselac and Megan L. Franke

PREPARING TEACHERS FOR SOCIAL JUSTICE is not enough. Idealistic, well-prepared, and justice-oriented novices far too often find themselves assigned to urban schools where pedagogies of poverty are the norm.[1] To resist the undertow and create transformative spaces where students engage in inquiry, construct knowledge, and solve problems in their communities and the world, social justice educators must engage in sustained ongoing learning that helps them create equitable spaces for deeper learning.[2] Creating ongoing opportunities for professional learning becomes essential for supporting urban teachers and their students.[3] The challenge, then, is to create ongoing learning for teacher education students that centers social justice and a view of learning that is transformative.

Our experience in creating ongoing learning for teacher education students comes from twenty-five years working in the Teacher Education Program at the University of California, Los Angeles (UCLA). Commitment to ongoing learning is a central component of the program's mission, which was first articulated in Jeannie Oakes's 1996 article "Making the Rhetoric Real" (reprinted as chapter 1 of this volume).[4] As Oakes outlines in that article, the Teacher Education Program is housed in UCLA's Center X, along with the Principal Leadership Institute and other professional development programs that are long-standing, content-based, and part of a statewide network. The programs within Center X share the same goals: they work together to challenge the status quo and prepare educators focused on issues of social justice, and they carry out that work in partnership with local schools, districts, and communities.

Ongoing learning is an underlying assumption of Center X. Center X was founded in response to racial inequality and based on a theory of learning that centers relationships. Together these two ideas—the importance of ongoing learning and centering relationships—continue to shape what and how we learn. We recognize that the learning we are working to support will never be complete because the people, contexts, and societal structures involved in that work are all actors that shape what happens and for whom. Ongoing learning is about collective work that challenges the status quo in ways that take up our social justice agenda. It is about the relationships we create and sustain, the constant negotiating about what matters, and opening spaces for others to participate.

We consider learning to be situated where cultural histories and experiences shape how one engages in any setting and where one's experiences and histories have been shaped by political, economic, and social structures.[5] Positing knowing and coming to know as inseparable focuses on the relationships among individuals and the roles, positions, and patterns of activity that are made available to them as they participate in the practices of various communities.[6] Learning occurs as people participate together, as their rich histories shape how they participate together, where the structures of schooling and society shape how they participate together.

Learning defined as such drives Center X's teacher education work and our partnership work with local communities. We design for it; we evaluate it; and we adapt based on it. We have learned that positioning people in relation to each other, projects in relation to each other, and district efforts in relation to the center's efforts is required for the kinds of learning we are hoping for—learning that challenges inequality. We have found that it is about collective action. Collective action requires working across the siloed spaces in universities and districts in ways that create new relationships, new ways of working together, new work to do together.[7]

Too often, ongoing learning for teacher education focuses on a set of activities: alumni network events, ongoing affinity group meetings, or workshops. While these activities exist in Center X, they are the artifacts of an approach to ongoing learning that considers what we are doing together, why and how we are doing it together and with whom, and how this approach is situated within a larger system of work. Focusing only on the activities offered to teacher education alumni makes it too easy to separate people and work. Separating people and work leads to isolated efforts and silos that make it difficult to consistently address inequality. Silos often result from and add to the ways schooling structures and higher education systems lead to inequality. Part of our work to create ongoing learning for teacher education alumni around social justice is to work together across schools and higher education to challenge and change the silos.

To tell the story of ongoing learning for our Teacher Education Program (TEP) students, we begin by looking back at an early and significant partnership that enabled the forging of new relationships and the cocreation of new work with a focus on inequality. We then turn to a more recent partnership that emerged from long-standing relationships with our TEP students and the district. These two examples illuminate the ways Center X creates ongoing learning opportunities for teachers by leveraging and building relationships, developing collective work, and consistently renegotiating how work is accomplished across structures.

A SCHOOL-UNIVERSITY PARTNERSHIP

In 2001, Center X and the Los Angeles Unified School District (LAUSD) Local District 7 partnered to disrupt the inequities that exist in the high schools attended by our city's most vulnerable students—students of poverty and of color. The partnership restructured relationships within the center itself and between the center and LAUSD, while opening up space for our TEP students to learn while in the program and as alumni. The collective work centered on literacy in the content areas and asked participants to challenge their assumptions of young people, reimagine classroom practice, and consider the conceptions and structures that were shaping students' opportunities.

The partnership's main goal was to work with the district to increase student access to learning through strengthening teachers' instructional practices around teaching literacy. The underlying goal was to work with teachers and administrators to figure out how to adapt engagement with students around content in ways that centered students' ideas and enabled all those working in schools to see the students' competence. The partnership was also a way to help teachers to see their collective work and to reimagine some of the structures of schooling that prevent students from fully participating in learning.

Local District 7 at that time was one of the eight local districts in LAUSD, serving ninety-two schools and over eighty thousand students living in the communities adjacent to and just south of downtown Los Angeles. In 2001, the ten thousand students enrolled at the partnership's three high schools were nearly 78 percent Latino and 21 percent African American. Also, 49 percent of all students were English language learners. Nearly 100 percent were on free or reduced-priced lunch. Local District 7 had an average graduation rate of less than 60 percent, and student academic performance on standardized testing was at the lowest levels. The district superintendent's vision provided the impetus for partnering Local District 7 with UCLA Center X. A longtime social justice advocate, she was determined to break this cycle and provide students with access to the quality education they deserved. She turned to Center X because of our commitment to social justice and our guiding frameworks for professional development. She invited us to collaborate in designing and implementing a program that engaged and supported teachers at their own schools during their professional day, creating school-wide, systemic approaches to foster secondary literacy. The primary focus of the partnership was engaging the 254 teachers of mathematics, sciences, social science, and language arts at the three Local District 7 high schools to recognize and strengthen their roles as the most effective teachers of literacy within their content areas through teacher professional development and coaching. The work of the partnership was guided by the notion that by improving practices in the teaching of content literacy, student access to learning increases. During the six years of the partnership, we saw changes in teacher practice that demonstrated teachers' understanding of the importance of engaging students with text. These changes paralleled a steady rise in student achievement in literacy scores on standardized tests, high school exit exams, and the schools' academic performance index.[8]

Lesson Learned: Relationships Matter

The Local District 7 superintendent turned to Center X when seeking a partner to transform the schools in her district because she had engaged with our center on previous projects before she became the district superintendent. She had developed a close relationship with our faculty in teacher education and supported our TEP students in her previous school. She had hired many TEP graduates to teach in the schools in her district. She brought Center X professional development support to her school. She knew firsthand of our commitment to social justice. This relationship was key to the success of the partnership—not only in the beginning but in challenging moments.[9] This isn't to say that we had the same notions about what guided the work, but rather that the strength of our relationship enabled us to trust and respect each other's motivations.

At the inception of this partnership, teachers in all four content areas overwhelmingly questioned the purpose and value of professional development that focused on content-specific literacy. Teachers in other content domains believed that it was not their responsibility to teach literacy, and they could not understand why they were being required to now do the job of the English teachers. English teachers who understood the importance of literacy tended to believe that they already knew how to teach it and didn't need any additional professional development. We had to find ways to engage teachers in the learning without losing the cross-department literacy focus. Teachers and coaches began developing a relationship and shared understandings by doing work together. They read and discussed articles related to the importance of content literacy. They exchanged ideas about instructional practices that would engage students. While we had a set of shared literacy tools that informed our discussion, we also honored input from teachers. We started to notice a change in attitude when teachers began implementing strategies with the support of coaches and then seeing changes in student participation. While developing this relationship took longer than we had anticipated, it was key to moving the work forward. It was important that we remained committed to the goals of the partnership while acknowledging teachers' concerns.

Staff turnover in the schools, district, and university was a significant challenge. High-poverty schools typically have an annual turnover rate of 20 percent, and that was the case with the three Local District 7 high schools. In addition to losing teachers, at the end of the first year of the partnership two of the three principals left. We had to begin again to develop relationships and support principals' participation in the work. Because these schools are so big and have so many programs, it was difficult to gain their attention and commitment to the partnership. One of the principals did not support pulling teachers out of the classroom for professional development and made it extremely difficult for us to provide professional development. He believed that students would lose too much instructional time because substitutes would not be able to reach the students. We developed a cadre of substitutes who committed to coming regularly. We also provided professional development for them on the literacy strategies so that students would have continuity in instruction. And while we lost much of the ground we had gained in developing relationships, we began to build it back so that we were able to continue the work around literacy and teacher practice. In the second year of the partnership, we lost all three principals, several assistant principals, the local district literacy coordinator, and several of the university coaches. We were continually challenged to bring new teachers into the work while honoring the work that other teachers were already doing. Our coaches worked hard to strengthen relationships and build community in departments, creating places where teachers felt connected and supported to improve teacher retention.

Lesson Learned: Bridging K–12 and University Cultures

As a result of this partnership we learned that there is a need to address more closely the disconnect between K–12 and university cultures. In the beginning teachers believed that the partnership would not be around very long—especially since it was connected to a university. Their experience with universities was that faculty came to schools just long enough to collect data for research and then left. We worked hard to help all at the schools see we were trying to create different kinds of relationships and that we were there to stay. The Center X partnership coaches became a part of the fabric of the schools. We encouraged teachers to have an equal voice in how we would do this work together. We weren't there to tell them what and how to teach but to provide structures and resources for them to examine and use to strengthen their own practice. Our goal was for teachers to see this as ongoing learning and not as a one-time workshop. We learned that in order to develop collaborative relationships, partners need to be mindful of the cultural differences that exist and engage in open discussions about how to work toward common goals.[10]

Early on it became apparent that the partnership needed a person who could build a bridge between the district and the university and whose main focus was to facilitate the work. This person became the liaison between the two institutions. She spent as much time at schools as she did at the university and district office. This made it possible for her to develop relationships and understand the different points of view so she could handle challenges as they arose. The liaison played a vital role in developing structures for continuous and open communication. Access to timely information is extremely important, as schools are very busy and complex institutions. The liaison helped establish and build relationships. Without her, the partnership would have struggled. The liaison kept us all connected—a critical component in the success of the partnership.

The Local District 7 high schools became important sites of learning for our preservice teachers. We prepared our TEP students with the same content-based literacy strategies and placed them for field experiences in the classrooms of the teachers in the partnership high schools. TEP faculty also taught seminars to preservice teachers at the high schools and included the mentor teachers in the classes. The high schools committed to hiring our graduates, who had developed relationships with teachers and students. The TEP became an important tool in bridging the K–12 and university cultures. In addition, the partnership was an important lesson about how the preparation of novice teachers needs to be deeply integrated into the communities they will teach in.[11]

Reflecting on the Partnership

We began our work by creating structures that would allow us to develop relationships, build trust, share ideas, and value what each institution brings to the discussion. University faculty and staff and school teachers and administrators met regularly to craft the work. We built in time for reflection and change. We did all of this work in the district, and we committed to being a part of the work for the long haul. As a result of this partnership, we have learned the importance of genuine collaboration. We are two very different institutions with different cultures and different ways of working. We could not have done this without spending time developing relationships.

Our Local District 7 partnership created a new set of relationships by building on existing ones and opened opportunities for new forms of learning and participation by those in Center X and our TEP students. Our work together in the center takes many forms, develops relationships with various partners, and is initiated in different ways by different people. Many years after our Local District 7 work, we established another LAUSD partnership that focuses on mathematics in preK–5, developed from methods courses and professional development work. This project created additional opportunities for our TEP alumni to play an important leadership role.

A COLLECTIVE LEARNING PROJECT: COGNITIVELY GUIDED INSTRUCTION (CGI)

The ongoing learning opportunities for our TEP students sometimes start with the students themselves. As TEP students complete their preservice teacher education program and move into full-time teaching in our local communities, they take with them experiences, relationships, and a set of knowledge, skills, and stances developed within the program. They as individuals and as a collective are assets that promote the development of ideas and work across Center X and schools and communities. Our TEP students develop ongoing learning opportunities that serve a broader community of teachers, schools, and TEP alumni. The emergence of the cognitively guided instruction (CGI)–LAUSD partnerships is an example of the opportunity and ongoing learning that our students support and benefit from.

As a part of their elementary mathematics methods course, TEP students learn about CGI. CGI is a research-based approach to the teaching and learning of mathematics that helps teachers make sense of the development of students' mathematical thinking and how to center students' ideas in creating opportunities for mathematical learning.[12] A focus on CGI in the methods course helped the preservice teachers develop expertise in attending to the details of students' mathematical ideas, seeing the mathematics capabilities of each student, and learning how to take up their students' ideas.

As our preservice teachers take teaching positions in schools and continue to build their practice, they also build coalitions with other teachers using CGI and together look for professional development opportunities. Add to this the UCLA Mathematics Project (UCLAMP) within Center X, which provides CGI professional development opportunities as well as research on CGI conducted by a UCLA faculty member in Center X over a twenty-five-year period. Having teachers in schools already engaged in the work and connected to Center X, school principals, and district leaders helped build a partnership that now involves more than 210 elementary schools and preschools in LAUSD, 150 teacher leaders, and more than 30 professional developers, with TEP alumni in each of these groups.

Relationships Are Key

The CGI–LAUSD partnership came to be because of long-standing relationships, and it continued because of new relationships and openings for participation. These long-standing relationships resulted from people being engaged in work on the ground over many years—this is not a result of just talking together but of working together in ways that create deep understanding of the substance of the work and knowledge of the commitments that we share. These relationships continued to develop, and fortunately turnover rates were lower than in the LAUSD Local District 7 partnership; the key personnel that did leave helped manage their succession.

New relationships also emerged. These relationships were both people connecting with people and people connecting with new tools, ideas, and mathematics. Teachers built new relationships with each other around the teaching of mathematics; teacher leaders built relationships with teachers in a different school; and principals got to know other principals through ongoing work together. Teachers connected in new ways with mathematics, with their students, and with their own thinking about their work. Students built new relationships with mathematics, what it means to do mathematics, and their own ideas of who they are as mathematicians. These relationships matter because they create new openings for participation and learning. This partnership has created new opportunities for our preservice teachers to be in classrooms with teachers taking up a similar approach to the teaching and learning of mathematics—thus providing opportunities for our preservice teachers and their guiding teachers to support each other and learn together.

Challenges as Opportunities

The evolution of the CGI–LAUSD partnership with UCLAMP has been quite successful; it has grown from 12 schools to 120 schools. Teachers and principals ask for continued participation, and the waiting list for participation is growing. There is a clear coalition around a common set of goals for the teaching and learning of mathematics. However, as with any endeavor of this kind, there are many challenges, including variability in opportunity and access, the pressure to move quickly, the need for uniform professional development and practice, and a constant worry about funding.

Establishing and developing relationships with people or new ideas takes time. The structures of districts and universities expect efficiency, turnaround, and compliance—not flexibility and long time frames. Managing the structures that shape the work, navigating around them, and working to change them requires people in different organizations to share the view that policies and practices need to be navigated and changed, as well as people who have the knowledge and skills to make those changes. This is where so much work occurs to challenge the status quo for students. This is the work we want our TEP alumni to participate in. The TEP alumni also bring their knowledge and expertise and their identities as social justice educators that help to craft and shape the work.

Learning Together

The design of the partnership was based on our view of learning rather than control or compliance.[13] Engaging in the work is not about "mastery" or "fidelity." Engaging in the work is about learning together. So as teachers engage together around CGI, they bring their ideas, histories, and expertise. They share that with others, make sense of the ideas of others, and work toward making sense of children's mathematical thinking in the context of their school and practice. This means that there is not a CGI professional development curriculum but a fluid set of big ideas, principles, research, and practice-based evidence about children's thinking that serves as the substance of the engagement. Practitioners are constantly expanding and developing these ideas. This learning approach happens at all levels: with teachers, principals, teacher leaders, and professional developers. Everyone is a designer and learner.

The implication of this approach is that the work LAUSD does on CGI evolves. It can be responsive to new curricula, current issues, and new policies. For example, the partnership took on new meaning as structural racism took center stage in Los Angeles and beyond. Teachers, teacher leaders, professional developers, and the district saw the need to make issues of racism more explicit in the teaching and learning of mathematics. They saw that they could raise their concerns and ideas and work with colleagues to address racism within the CGI work. Our teacher education alumni played a central role in raising and pressing these issues within the partnership.

CLOSING THOUGHTS

Ongoing learning centered in social justice emerges throughout Center X. Project work and partnerships are not all as comprehensive as our early LAUSD Local District 7 partnership or as large as our CGI–LAUSD partnership, but each Center X project enables collective learning. For instance, the Writing Project has created a local network of teachers learning together within a national network. The Science Project is a collaboration with university researchers and districts outside of LAUSD. Each Center X project develops relationships with people, ideas, artifacts, and tools in ways that create synergistic opportunities for learning. These opportunities allow TEP students to find spaces over the course of their career to participate in ways linked to their jobs, their commitments, and their expertise. This ongoing learning comes to life for our TEP students as they, too, participate in creating, advancing, and learning with others in ways that align with the goals and principles of the center.

As Center X engages in these projects, we learn from the starts and stops, from the artifacts that are developed around, from, and with the participants. What always remains are these relationships. The relationships create opportunities for new work, new ideas, new ways of participating together. The relationships include the principals who create environments for our new teachers to learn and the district social science director who is figuring out how to support the new curricular adoption that TEP students and alumni will be using. The relationships include our TEP alumni, who will engage with our new teachers in alumni network activities and in professional development projects. And the relationships will also include the professional developers who will engage with our new teachers in Center X and in districts. These relationships allow for a quick phone call that will lead to new opportunities, for a chance meeting to create new connections, and for an ongoing, constantly negotiated set of shared ideas and values. What the center does is keep social justice salient and racial inequality a focus of learning; it works so that the relationships can evolve, challenging the status quo, asking hard questions, revaluating long-standing and current practice, and sustaining innovation.

CHAPTER 6

Equity-Oriented Science Professional Development

*Lynn Kim-John, William A. Sandoval,
Jarod N. Kawasaki, Leticia Perez,
Jon Kovach, and Heather F. Clark*

SCIENCE EDUCATION IN THIS COUNTRY is mainly oriented toward preparing young people to enter science careers. Equity in science education is therefore most often framed in terms of expanding the pipeline into science careers to include more women and more youth from Black and Brown communities. This career focus often leads science teaching to emphasize the facts and concepts of science in ways that limit young people's understanding of how those facts and concepts are developed and what makes them trustworthy. The contexts in which people encounter science in their everyday lives outside of school makes this understanding of how science works especially important.[1]

We now know that the best science teaching helps students learn both the concepts and practices of science by guiding students through investigating and explaining real phenomena, and this view of student-centered science teaching underlies the latest reform efforts, the Next Generation Science Standards (NGSS).[2] The NGSS, adopted by California in 2015, are a drastic departure from business as usual and require most teachers to radically reorganize their teaching to become student-centered.

Here we tell the story of our work helping a cadre of science teachers in an urban school district learn to teach to the new standards. We, a group of professional developers and educational researchers, were motivated by our understanding that the standards align with ambitious student-centered teaching that helps students learn science and develop productive ideas about how science works and also supports youths' identification with science. We knew that this kind of teaching has always been rare in American schools and believed that if we could help this group of teachers develop a more student-centered practice, they would be giving their students a real chance to learn science in productive ways.

As with most such efforts, there were some significant successes and some more limited. This is the story of what we learned about how to organize science professional development in partnership with a cadre of teachers in an urban school district. It is also the story of what they learned from us—but our main focus here is on what we learned from them and how it has changed our work to create professional development that supports and sustains social justice science educators.

STANDARDS AND EQUITY

The impetus for educational standards, not just in science but in all subjects, is the drive to ensure that all students learn the same concepts equally well regardless of where they live and go to school. Efforts to specify what science students should learn, and how, go back more than a century, to well before the regime of standardized testing of the last couple of decades.[3] Standardized testing has not been a helpful force for equity, as poor test results are often used to take resources away from schools that need them, schools that typically serve the most disadvantaged students. Standards, as specifications of the appropriate or desirable foci for learning in a subject, are potentially a lever for equity to the extent that they support quality learning experiences everywhere. Of course, standards are interpreted and enacted in specific places by specific people, so the extent to which they promote equity is contingent on those interpretations.

We had three reasons to believe the NGSS might provide a lever for improving science teaching and learning and thereby promote more equitable science learning experiences. First, the standards were developed from a framework that synthesized decades of research on science learning to argue for thinking about what it means to learn and know science in a different way. This new framework offers a specific vision of student-centered science instruction. It involves engaging students in legitimate versions of science practice—designing and doing experiments, developing and refining models and explanations, analyzing evidence, making arguments—as the means through which they learn science concepts. It links this approach to the aim of understanding science in order to explain phenomena in the world. For example, most of us learned about cell structure from teacher lectures and carefully scripted experiments designed by the teacher or pulled from a textbook, and then we were asked to make a model, out of dried macaroni or papier-mâché or something, to show that we understood what we had been told. The NGSS approach would pose a question about which kids might be curious, such as, How does your finger heal a cut? Students would then learn about cell structures and their function by iteratively refining a model of that healing process, using readings and experiments as the means to evaluate their models and make them better. We know this helps most students learn the science better than the traditional way.

Second, these student-centered approaches provide students with agency. When students have the responsibility to figure out what experiment to do and how to do it, or what should go into their model and how they should evaluate their model against their peers' models, they have the chance to grapple with and resolve the problems the sciences themselves grapple with. This helps them learn how science really works and what makes scientific methods and explanations credible, including the limits to that credibility. So rather than opening up a unit by front-loading vocabulary terms about a complex concept like photosynthesis, students might be asked to draw a model articulating their understanding of how a redwood tree grows from a tiny seed. Along the way and through small-group and whole-group discussion, students revise their model by adding key terms like *light energy* and *sugar molecules* to articulate key ideas of plant growth. This type of modeling coupled with productive discourse depends on and utilizes student inquiry and talk, thereby increasing students' agency while deepening their understanding of photosynthesis. Agency enables students to become authors of scientific knowledge for themselves, which supports interest and the development of science identities. This sense of agency is a crucial means for inviting into the sciences students who have historically not been welcomed into them.

Finally, the orientation of the NGSS toward real-world phenomena presents meaningful opportunities to integrate culturally relevant pedagogies. If science teaching is going to be oriented out to the world, rather than into the textbook, then teachers and students can identify phenomena to study what they see in their communities and in their everyday lives. Chemistry, for example, is often taught abstractly, through exploring substances and reactions that are often chosen for no reasons that students can discern. Yet understanding chemical state changes, or bonding, is extremely useful for understanding phenomena like urban heat islands or how climate change produces more frequent and extreme wildfires in California. This sort of community orientation to phenomena creates the potential for students in minoritized and disadvantaged communities to see science not just as something they can do themselves but as something that can help them address issues they care about.

SUSTAINING TEACHER PROFESSIONAL LEARNING

The NGSS hence opened up opportunities for our nation to reimagine the way science is experienced in the classroom. The teacher-centered, textbook-driven classroom science that invited only certain students into the classroom community is no more. The NGSS call for student-centered learning, driven by student inquiry in which all student ideas and contributions are valued and encouraged. This new vision was one shared by the University of California, Los Angeles (UCLA) Science Project.

The UCLA Science Project (UCLASP) is a standing group providing professional development to science teachers throughout the metropolitan Los Angeles area. It has been operating continuously since 1990, as part of a broader initiative in California known as the state subject matter projects. For most of its history, the UCLASP mainly provided summer professional development workshops or institutes, with generally minimal follow-up during the school year with teacher participants. As evidence mounted that the best professional development for teachers was sustained over longer periods of time and closely connected to the schools where teachers work, the UCLASP began to develop longer-term partnerships with client school districts in the region.

The arrival of the NGSS provided an opportunity to develop a model of professional development that could be sustained over an entire school year, even multiple years, within a school district while offering possibilities of real changes in teaching. Our own professional development staff had to learn the new standards and the research behind them. We had to create structures and resources that would allow teachers to understand them and to use them as levers for changing their practice to use their students' ideas, histories, and experiences as productive resources for transformative science learning. By looking closely at our first major partnership to provide professional learning around the NGSS, we show how we developed a professional learning structure and process that facilitates deeper learning for science teachers and students in ways that promote equity. Ultimately, we hope the journey of our professional development partnership described in this chapter will give rise to new ways of thinking about supporting social justice educators through sustained, equity-focused, student-centered professional learning.

PARTNERING WITH A FOCUS ON STUDENTS

Faced with the enormity of overhauling science instruction across six intermediate schools (grades 6–8) and four comprehensive high schools (grades 9–12), Xavier Unified School District (not its real name) sought an external partner for assistance. With nearly a third of the district's students classified as English language learners and more than two-thirds qualifying for free or reduced-price lunch, they needed a partner with expertise in urban schooling and a strong track record of helping teachers create effective, accessible, and equitable learning environments that serve all students well. This search eventually led the district to the UCLASP at UCLA's Center X.

The research-practice partnership between the Xavier Unified School District and the UCLASP sought answers to questions that all districts, schools, and teachers across the nation were asking: What does NGSS instruction look and sound like? What professional development experiences will get us to achieve this new vision for the teaching of science? With both organizations rooted in social justice, the opportunity to transform science teaching was here, and the challenge was clear. So we sought to build a sustainable model for science teacher professional learning focused on equitable student-centered teaching, one that would engage students in the practices of science and promote student agency, as well as develop teachers' cultural competence in order to make science meaningful for the students they serve.

Structuring Professional Development for Sustainable Change

It is now well established that supporting meaningful and lasting change to teaching practice requires sustained professional development. Professional development must address the potential tension between teachers' prior ideas about science teaching and the types of science teaching the NGSS envision. We sought to establish a collaborative professional development partnership that could help our participating teachers understand how the NGSS differ from business as usual and support their ongoing efforts to change their practice. At the time our work with the Xavier Unified School District started, in 2015, there were few if any available examples of curricula we could offer our teachers to model what NGSS-aligned teaching might look like. So we developed three years of professional development work to support teachers' efforts to redesign their existing materials and instruction. Describing the broad structure of this work will clarify what we and our teacher partners learned from the effort.

Each year we began with a summer workshop during which teachers worked through model learning experiences that our team developed to try to demonstrate the main instructional focus for the upcoming school year. During each school year, teachers worked in subject- and grade-alike teams (for example, grade 7 physical science or high school chemistry) to revise two common instructional units, one in the fall semester and one in the spring. These cycles of lesson revision occurred over several weeks and culminated in a "research lesson" taught by one or two team members and observed and debriefed by other team members, a professional development facilitator, and a researcher. Each year we spent over sixty hours of time with our teachers.

Our first year was designed to focus on opening up instructional activities to allow for student agency. For example, if one of our teams focused on modeling, we coached the teachers on that team to consider how they could give their students as much responsibility for modeling as possible and to consider how to structure those opportunities. If they focused on experimentation, we prompted them to consider how to structure questions so students could design their own experiments and evaluate the pros and cons of different designs. We expected that students' having responsibility for doing the science would generate a lot of student talk. So in the second year we intended to focus on how to organize that talk productively so that it remained focused on the science concepts and practices. We intended to focus the third year on the kinds of student work our teachers might push their students to do, to help them think about how to assess student learning under this new teaching approach.

Two Challenges to Student-Centered Teaching

As is often the case when you are trying to solve a problem whose features you do not fully understand, we hit an unexpected challenge early in the first year of the project. Actually, we hit two related challenges, which became central to our work from that point forward. Understanding the nature of these challenges and our response to them illustrates the heart of what we learned from our partnership. It's the failure that leads to the success in this story.

One challenge was that our group of teachers thought a lot about what science their students should learn and how to tell whether they understood it, but they did not really consider *why* their students might be interested in science, or not. In our first round of work with the teachers in the first year, it was common to hear one of us ask a group of teachers what they were working on. The high school chemistry team, for example, would answer "reactions." We would then ask, What is it about reactions that is important to understand? The answers we would get back would be framed solely in terms of chemistry concepts. When we would then ask what those concepts helped students to explain out in the world, the response would be silence. Our teachers just were not in the practice of linking their science to phenomena in the world.

A related challenge was that our teachers were unsure of the value of hearing their students' thinking. It is very common in science classrooms for teachers to ask only known-answer questions and to evaluate students' responses only in terms of whether they are right or wrong. Research shows, though, that having students express and compare their thinking with their peers' thinking, whether they are right or not, helps them learn the right answers. Our teachers worried that if they opened up lessons as we suggested, then they would be in danger of letting misconceptions linger and go unanswered. The dual challenge, then, was to convince teachers of the value of orienting instruction toward explaining things in the world while giving students space to say what they think, debate each other, and actually work as scientists to come to the best answer. That first year, we were not very good at it.

Our middle school physical science group, for example, was eager to change their teaching to get their students more engaged. They chose to revise a unit on force and motion because they felt students often struggled to understand the basics of Newtonian mechanics even though they explain many things we see every day. They quickly, that fall, decided they could anchor a more engaging unit to explaining the forces involved in an automobile collision. One of the teachers in the group, Ms. V., volunteered to teach the focal lesson that we videotaped for each teacher team. During her lesson, Ms. V. had her students work in groups to identify and define vocabulary from a common reading. Once they were done, she solicited their answers: "Table 1, what did you learn?" A student from table 1 dutifully reported their findings. Ms. V. then asked table 2 the same question, to which they answered, "We got the same as them." This process repeated itself as she asked the rest of the eight table groups what they had learned from the reading. Students were listless. Many of them didn't even bother to look up when their peers answered. Ms. V. herself seemed inured to the routine, as if the answer hardly mattered. She knew the lesson was not engaging her students, but she did not know how to fix it. It was dispiriting.

During the next two years, Ms. V. and her colleagues returned to that force and motion unit two more times, each time thinking about how each lesson could be more coherently tied to the car collision, how students could be given more open-ended opportunities to explore features of the situation, and how they could use those explorations to build and refine models of the forces in play. The lesson we watched in the first year had changed: student groups were given "tech decks," small toy skateboards that could be used on their tabletops to represent a car, and other materials they could crash the "car" into. They had a lot of leeway to decide what materials to use and how to use them. Their only instruction was to observe what happens when the "car" hits the object and try to explain it. After giving the students time in small groups, Ms. V. transitioned into a whole-group discussion. Whereas in the first year students were in orderly rows of lab tables and could barely be bothered to look up, here they were in pairs at desks, and they all, to a person, oriented themselves to look toward the center of the room. Ms. V. stood off to the side. Discussion and disagreement erupted. Because two students were talking over each other, Ms. V. stepped in (all names are made up):

MS. V.: These are all really good, valid points. You both have really good, valid points. Yes?

TRACY: I'm on Gladys's side but just a different—we used a different tactic. We used the tech decks, but instead of what—another tech deck, we used the bucket as a wall—since a tech deck is a rolling object, of course it's gonna move . . . So, since we used it, we saw that it bounces back.

JONAH: But not all walls are gonna move . . . [inaudible] that ball when it moves.

[cross talk between students]

TRACY: No, but you would probably . . .

[cross talk between students]

TOM: Wait, so, you're saying . . .

MS. V.: Wait. Can we all give him the opportunity to speak?

TOM: He's saying there's a big, fat wall.

MS. V.: There's a big, fat wall, right? And a big, fat car, let's say like a truck, slams into it and not a scratch on the car and not a scratch.

[cross talk between students]

MS. V.: Hold on. One at a time. One at a time.

[cross talk between students]

JONAH: But they're made out of different things.

[cross talk between students]

KELLY: You [inaudible] the type of damage.

SHARON: Yeah, there's always gonna be damage. Even if it's a little damage, there's still damage on it.

There was a lot of chaos, to be sure, and part of the work Ms. V. did as this discussion continued was to corral students toward some consensus interpretations of what they saw. There are several features of this conversation showing Ms. V.'s classroom had become more student-centered, a place where students could author their own understanding of science. First, they were talking to each other, often urgently, not just answering Ms. V.'s questions. They were highly animated and focused. All the students were paying attention to the debate, and sidebar conversations were happening that then prompted new entries into the discussion. Second, students were drawing on their everyday experiences with objects and materials in the world as resources in the discussion, moving easily from a plastic bucket as a simulated wall to real walls and trucks. Third, students were holding themselves accountable for explaining the phenomenon at hand, a crucial feature of productive student dialogue. Finally, Ms. V.'s role in this discussion was to promote that accountability by making sure students heard and responded to each other. She was not merely the "sage on the stage."

Ms. V. had integrated many important features of student-centered teaching into her science classroom. Her practice was now more aligned with the NGSS. She was no longer a "lecture and lab teacher" but committed to structuring opportunities for her students to figure things out for themselves, with her guidance as needed. Not all of Ms. V.'s colleagues made this same transition, but many of them did. Those like Ms. V. became convinced of the value of students talking genuinely to each other rather than through the teacher. They saw that students could engage in legitimately meaningful science work even when they did not necessarily have all the right answers. They saw that such work enabled students to get to the answers and to see what makes an answer scientifically "right."

EQUITY AT THE CENTER OF INSTRUCTION

By the third year of our partnership we noticed shifts in instruction among a number of teachers. Students no longer sat in rows facing the teacher; they sat in groups facing each other. Teacher-initiated questions were replaced by student-initiated discussion, and as a result, the increased level of engagement was palpable. How did Ms. V. and others like her get here?

The UCLASP and Xavier Unified School District came together during a nebulous time for science education. Teachers were faced with a new set of standards that included drastic changes to pedagogy during a time when no curriculum existed and very little could be found to show what the NGSS might look like in the classroom. Teachers felt a great sense of urgency to begin creating and developing NGSS-aligned instructional units. Hence, professional development sessions were largely devoted to unit and lesson development; UCLASP facilitators led teachers through structured activities (for example, identifying anchor phenomena or rehearsing whole-class discussions) and facilitated lesson planning in their content groups.

In our curriculum-development work with teachers, one indicator we looked for was the coherence of the instructional units our teacher teams developed through their work with us. Coherent instruction engages students more deeply since the aims of activities are clearer and make it easier for students to link concepts to their prior understanding. We offered teachers a tool to organize units as story lines in which each lesson aims to help students build more of a story explaining an anchoring phenomenon. As they worked with us, lessons became more overtly linked to one another. We also saw that how well teachers were able to anchor their lessons to a real phenomenon depended upon the quality of the phenomenon they chose to use.

Creating a culture of equity in the classroom means all students have agency in their learning. In order to keep equity at the center of instruction, we coached teachers to open up their instructional activities to give students more opportunity and responsibility to negotiate and enact practices of questioning, experimentation, modeling, data analysis, argument, and so on.

We found that some of our teachers were more successful than others in providing consistent opportunities for their students to meaningfully engage in science practices.[4] Those teachers took up the challenge to create contexts where students had legitimate opportunities to resolve contested aspects of scientific work.[5] We emphasized the centrality of student talk by helping teachers learn strategies for eliciting student talk, listening to students' ideas, and then putting students in dialogue with each other. These are strategies to promote accountability.[6]

Our analysis of our partnership with Xavier has shifted how we think about and organize science teacher professional development to promote agency among students. This partnership opened up the opportunity to study the uptake of NGSS practices by teachers as we iterated professional development plans. With Ms. V. and some of her colleagues, we saw what was possible. We saw student agency.

We saw student-to-student discourse. Yet seeing the uneven success we observed with other teachers, we knew we needed to refine our professional development approach so that we could better support all teachers in learning how to promote agency and student-to-student discourse in their classrooms.

By coupling our growing knowledge of the NGSS with the planning and observational data we collected over three years, we attempted to make the seemingly complex vision of the NGSS and all its supporting documents more tractable and concrete. First, we developed four key points we call the "Four Pillars" of NGSS-aligned science instruction that help articulate our vision for transforming science teaching. We then developed the "NGSS First Five," a sequence of professional learning activities that operationalize the Four Pillars into concrete and actionable steps for teachers to implement in their classrooms. The development of the pillars and NGSS First Five has increased our ability to scale this approach to the NGSS broadly. We now work with districts not only to implement the NGSS but to implement them with the intended vision "science for all."

FOUR PILLARS OF EQUITY-CENTERED NGSS INSTRUCTION

Below are the UCLASP's Four Pillars of NGSS-aligned science instruction. All of our ongoing professional development work aims to help teachers understand and use these pillars in relation to each other. All of the pillars are needed to hold up the structure of instruction.

Pillar 1: Planning for Coherence

Because we understand the importance of creating learning sequences that connect to students' lived experiences, their context, and prior knowledge, we focus on connecting learning to local phenomena. We support teachers as they shift away from isolated or confirmatory activities toward opportunities for students to construct scientific explanations over time. Planning for coherence requires selecting a phenomenon that can anchor units of instruction, and making sure that each lesson in a unit has a clear place in helping students develop and refine an explanation for that phenomenon.

This pillar explores several questions important to teachers as they plan for science sensemaking in their classroom. Guiding questions that drive the design of our professional include these:

- How do we select good anchoring phenomena?
- How can story lines be used to plan for coherence?

What makes some phenomenon in the world good as an anchor for a unit of instruction? There are many, many ways to answer this question, and we firmly believe that any number of phenomena could make a good anchor for any set of science concepts one might want students to learn. The NGSS want students to learn "core" disciplinary ideas, the big ideas of biology, chemistry, physics, and earth sciences. Ideas are core precisely because they can explain a number of different things. When we work with teachers around planning for coherence, our primary aim is to help them think about the kinds of events or questions in the world that their students are likely to find interesting or important. This can range from "How does your body heal a cut?" to "What causes urban heat islands?" to all manner of other questions. The important point is that a big enough question can be asked about something that a good bit of science can be learned trying to answer it.

Story lines are a tool developed to help teachers design coherent units of instruction.[7] Each row in a story line (which we now call a chapter in the story) answers three questions: (1) What question are students trying to answer? (2) What scientific practices do students do to answer the question? and (3) What will students know after they have done that work? The idea is that each chapter of the story line leads to the next, until by the end of the story the overarching question of how to explain the anchor phenomenon has been answered. The tool helps teachers focus together on what scientific work (practices) students will do and how that work will help them answer their questions.

Pillar 2: Framing Clear Aims

Framing refers to the ways a teacher makes the purpose of an instructional activity apparent to students, orienting students to the roles they are expected to play in the activity. Framing tasks around anchoring phenomena is crucial to helping students see the purpose of learning science concepts. Framing toward student agency motivates students to engage in science practices. We support teachers to develop orientations to framing with their students. Guiding questions for this pillar include these:

- How do I connect this lesson to the anchor phenomenon?
- How do I connect this lesson to students' lives?
- What can we do to accomplish our work today?
- What criteria or standards do we need for our work?

We came to the importance of framing by seeing how hard it was for some of our teachers to consistently orient their lessons to anchoring phenomena and students' lives. The work of framing, as we see it, is partially to make the purpose of instructional tasks clear. More importantly, framing communicates what teachers expect from students. When teachers frame the goal of a task as jointly figuring something out and agreeing upon when we have figured it out, rather than getting the right answer, students are positioned very differently in relation to the scientific knowledge they are meant to learn. They become producers rather than passive consumers. This is not only more meaningful; it is a crucial means for developing student agency and identity.

Pillar 3: The Centrality of Talk

Science talk allows students to share their current understanding of concepts and phenomena in the classroom and compare their thinking with that of their peers. After several decades of research focused on student dialogue in learning, the evidence is now squarely that student-to-student dialogue is a key feature of rich learning environments. When students discuss and argue their ideas with each other, they learn better. Teachers are tasked with creating structured talk opportunities that serve several purposes. Science talk presents individual student ideas to the classroom community for the individual, class, and teacher to evaluate and possibly refine. Through small- and large-group dialogue, the variety of students' ideas are revealed, allowing the teacher to highlight the differing mechanisms and reasoning students propose as explanations for a phenomenon. Whole-group discussions surface and define agreement and disagreement and help organize resolution toward consensus. These talk interactions mirror the way scientific knowledge is constructed over time.

As teachers begin to integrate talk opportunities into their NGSS story lines, they must grapple with questions like these:

- How can we plan for talk in our classes?
- How do I support productive conversations?
- How do I prepare students for small-group conversations?

There are a number of approaches in science teaching to promoting productive student dialogue; there is no one best way to do it. We focus our teachers on a few strategies our experience suggests are fairly easy to master. First, students need legitimate things to talk about, meaning open-ended questions that have multiple reasonable answers, or opportunities to disagree about consequential things, such as the best way to do an experiment. Second, teachers can practice two broad strategies to promote productive discussions. One is to press students to elaborate their thinking until what they think is clear to themselves and the rest of the class. A second is to listen for different, even competing, ideas from students and put them into direct dialogue with each other. Our professional development now models and helps teachers rehearse such strategies.

Pillar 4: Developing Disciplinary Ideas Through Practices

Key to understanding science and how it works is developing an understanding of how science concepts are developed through scientific practices of investigation, explanation, argument, and so on.[8] This is a radical way for most teachers to think about their science teaching, and one of the most important lessons we learned in our work with Xavier was how hard this was for teachers to learn. We have developed supports for teachers to organize opportunities for students to make decisions about how to design investigations, how to analyze and represent data, and how to collectively discuss standards for their own work. Guiding questions that drive the design of our professional development include these:

- How do science and engineering practices help students understand how science knowledge is created?
- How can we use modeling to revise our thinking?
- How can we use disagreements to drive learning?

These questions clearly link back to the previous pillars. Our focus with teachers is to help them overcome a common perception: many teachers think that students have to know a particular concept before they can use it in a model or an experiment. Models and experiments, though, are used to derive concepts and test them. We work with teachers to see the possibilities of letting their students grapple with uncertainty, to work through ideas to refine them and make them better. Again, the evidence synthesized in the framework underlying the NGSS shows students learn science better through such work.

NGSS FIRST FIVE

In our work with Xavier Unified School District, we found that the Four Pillars simplify NGSS for teachers. Teachers are visibly less focused on flipping through pages of standards to create curriculum and more focused on pedagogy that keeps students at the center of instruction. In addition to student-centered instruction, the Four Pillars keep science accessible to all students by ensuring that learning is relevant and focused on student sensemaking opportunities such as student-to-student talk and science practices.

The creation and integration of the Four Pillars took us and our partner district three years of intensive professional learning for practice to transfer into classrooms. The reality is that most districts do not have the luxury of time and resources this partnership was afforded. We needed a way to operationalize the Four Pillars into a feasible professional development plan for the eighty-plus school districts in the Los Angeles region.

Based on our work with districts, we knew that five days of professional development was often a reasonable and maximum number of days to which districts were willing to commit—which gave birth to UCLA's NGSS First Five. This professional learning plan outlines the first five days of professional development a teacher might need to begin developing understanding about the NGSS. Each day of the First Five is directly aligned to the Four Pillars. Days one through three introduce teachers to the use of local phenomena as a way to increase relevance for student learning. During these three days, teachers experience what NGSS learning feels like as an adult learner. The talk opportunities that support the development and deepening of science ideas are intentionally woven throughout. As a result of these first few days, teachers understand the importance of framing learning around the world our students experience and live in, as a way to increase access to a traditionally intimidating subject area. The focus on student talk extends into days four and five, increasing in sophistication. Teachers move from understanding how to promote student talk toward how to organize argumentation in ways that promote student agency. Teachers also experience and reflect on the power of a collaborative learning experience that engages learners in the doing of science. At the end of the First Five, teachers have a solid understanding of how to organize their classroom with a critical lens promoting equity and inclusion.

Once teachers have shared experiences with the First Five, partner districts may choose another year of collaboration with the UCLASP to learn to coconstruct their own NGSS story lines. In the second year of professional learning, the responsibility for the development of NGSS curriculum and instruction lies more heavily on the teachers or teacher groups. The continued partnership with the UCLASP provides sustainable coaching and accountability to ensure that equity and social justice continue to be central to student learning.

SCALING SOCIAL JUSTICE SCIENCE TEACHING

Teachers in the Xavier Unified School District spent years learning how to enact the NGSS—and, as with Ms. V., we noticed dramatic shifts in classroom pedagogy. More importantly, teachers learned the outcomes of creating a culture of equity in the classroom. Integration of social justice practices with classroom science served as fertile ground for students to find their voices and increase their confidence. Understanding the relevance of learning science also opened up opportunities for students to connect their lived experiences to science phenomena.

The learning progression for the UCLASP had interesting parallels to that of teachers. We had a great deal of agency to create, reflect on, and iterate professional development plans. It was through these collaborative spaces that we also found our voice in science education—what we want to say—and found our confidence to support more teachers and understand why we must seek social justice in classrooms across more districts. We asked ourselves, "How can we get as many students as possible to learn science through this social justice frame?" The goal of seeing *all* students experience science in the ways we envisioned became our beacon.

Establishing district partnerships was a multistep process that required the commitment of multiple stakeholders: district leaders, school leaders, and teacher leaders. During these initial exploratory conversations, equity and social justice was front and center. The UCLASP presented the nonnegotiable requirement of working with *all* teachers from all grade levels, within a targeted span (K–5, 6–8, or 9–12), in order to move forward with a formal partnership. While this was a risk, we believed in the nature of working with all teachers to increase the probability that all students received NGSS-aligned instruction, and not just a select few. Hence, the decision to partner with the UCLASP came with a hefty commitment of resources: funding and time. Because the stakes were so high, districts involved their boards of education, parents, school and district administrators, and teachers in the decision-making process. On average these exploratory discussions lasted six months and served as an important foundation for the success of each partnership.

Developing the Four Pillars and operationalizing them into the NGSS First Five increased our capacity to scale a socially just version of the NGSS. We shared our work, our mission, and our vision of social justice science teaching broadly. Consequently, the call from other districts for partnerships increased significantly—we moved from serving four or five districts to now partnering with fifteen to twenty districts per year. As the demand for our support has increased, our identity also has shifted from professional development providers to professional learning partners. This shift in identity communicated the importance of coconstructing learning outcomes, codesigning sustainable teacher-learning plans with districts, and continuing to refine our own responsibilities as partners supporting science teacher learning.

This work continues to evolve as our partnerships grow and we learn more about the needs of the students, teachers, schools, and communities we serve. The NGSS cast a new vision for science education that places students at the center of science learning and sensemaking. This framework led to the development and adoption of the NGSS across the nation, creating opportunities for teacher-preparation programs and professional development providers to redesign science education around rigorous science sensemaking that values students' ideas, histories, and experiences as assets for learning. Preparing and sustaining social justice educators has been central to the mission and vision of the UCLASP since its inception. Our partnership work has never been more important than it is now in infusing social justice science teaching into our schools and communities and building toward a more socially just society.

ACKNOWLEDGMENTS

This effort was supported by a grant from the National Science Foundation (award number 1503511). The views expressed herein are the authors' and do not necessarily reflect the views or opinions of the National Science Foundation. This work could not have happened without the teachers who dedicated their time and effort to working together for three years and opened their classrooms to us. We are grateful to Anahid Modrĕk, Alex Kwako, Lilia Rodriguez, Na'im Eggleston, Nathan Cournoyer, and Jody Priselac for their efforts on the project.

CHAPTER 7

"It's a Circle"

UCLA's Principal Leadership Institute and the Practice of Social Justice Leadership

John Rogers and Nancy Parachini

*PLI completely transformed my definition of a leader. . . .
Leading for social justice is about creating community and
capacity—developing leaders at all levels in our schools,
working towards a more just education system for all students.*

—Maria Martinez-Gertner, University of California,
Los Angeles (UCLA), Principal Leadership Institute alum[1]

*PLI empowered me with the language and concepts to name
what I intrinsically recognized as unjust in our educational
system, and provided me with the lens and the tools to
actually work towards effecting change on a systemic level.*

—Dan Thalkar, UCLA Principal Leadership Institute alum

IN MARCH 1999, California's state legislature passed Assembly Bill 2, requesting that the University of California (UC) Regents establish Principal Leadership Institutes at UCLA and UC Berkeley. Asserting that "a strong principal is an essential component in school success," the legislature pointed to "districts around California . . . experiencing a growing shortage" of leaders capable of meeting the demands of this "very challenging career." As these shortages were concentrated in low-income communities of color, the need to expand and enhance the leadership pipeline represented a critical racial and social justice issue. By creating the Principal Leadership Institutes, the legislature hoped to "make a principalship a more attractive and visible option for the most talented individuals to pursue" and, in the process, contribute to educational equity in the state.

Over the past twenty years, the UCLA Principal Leadership Institute (PLI) has responded to the legislature's call. It has developed hundreds of highly skilled and justice-oriented school leaders who serve in communities of color across Los Angeles County. These leaders support culturally responsive and rigorous learning environments that emphasize student inquiry and dialogue. They are adult educators who foster powerful teacher and staff professional development that centers on equity concerns. And they are community leaders who have the knowledge and commitment to forge partnerships with parents, grassroots community groups, civic leaders, and organized labor.

Each year, PLI enrolls thirty-five to forty experienced educators in a program of study that culminates with students receiving an administrative credential and master's degree. The students participate in coursework at UCLA and conduct fieldwork practice at their school sites. Throughout the academic program, students grapple with critical questions of practice facing social justice educators. They begin by examining the historical forces, structural conditions, and ways of thinking that lead to educational and social marginalization. Building on these insights, students then design and implement fieldwork projects that challenge and disrupt those patterns of marginalization.

PLI's strength as a principal preparation program is that PLI is much more than a principal preparation program. Long after they graduate, PLI alumni continue to learn with one another and support the learning of new PLI students. The power of the PLI experience lies in the vital exchanges between principals and aspiring principals and in the larger web of relationships grounded in a shared commitment to social justice leadership.

This chapter examines PLI as a community of practice dedicated to learning about and enacting social justice leadership in greater Los Angeles. The community of practice spans from novices entering the program to alumni who have served as principals for several years. Not only does PLI include emerging and veteran leaders, but it creates space for all of these participants to interact with each other in ways that foster further reflection and growth.

In referring to PLI as a community of practice, we have in mind a site of learning and action in which participants come together around a joint enterprise, and in the process develop a shared repertoire of activities, tools, and ways of speaking and acting.[2] In communities of practice, learning occurs through participation and social interaction. By working with and observing more established members, newcomers forge more knowledgeable and skilled identities. In Jean Lave's words, "Crafting identities is a social process, and becoming more knowledgeably skilled is an aspect of participation in social practice. By such reasoning, who you are becoming shapes crucially and fundamentally what you 'know.'"[3]

We wish to emphasize the dynamic character of PLI. The practice of social justice leadership is always contextual and always changing. This fluidity reflects in part the constant emergence of new threats in the broader sociopolitical environment as well as new opportunities for social justice movements. (Consider, for example, how the COVID-19 pandemic and the Black Lives Matter movement reshaped the landscape of social justice leadership in 2020.) It also reflects contradictions inherent in efforts to promote democratic and egalitarian schools within a society highly stratified by race and social class. Social justice principals must develop strategies for navigating educational and social welfare systems whose structures rarely challenge and too often uphold oppressive social relations. Rather than socializing novices into some static practice, PLI brings together novices and veterans for the purpose of ongoing reinvention.

In the rest of this chapter we describe several dimensions of PLI as a community of practice. We begin with an overview of PLI as a leadership preparation program, presenting the key learning experiences students encounter during each of the five quarters of academic study. In the second section we highlight the various ways that PLI alumni interact with PLI students during the preparation program to deepen reflection and understanding. The third section describes the different sites in which PLI alumni learn from and with one another. In the fourth section, we present a spatial representation of how PLI alumni are distributed across schools in greater Los Angeles. The fifth section presents vignettes of PLI alumni who are enacting social justice leadership as principals of a high school and an elementary school. We close with some thoughts on how to sustain learning within this dynamic community of practice.

PLI AS A LEADERSHIP PREPARATION PROGRAM

Every year, thirty to forty Los Angeles educators join PLI's fourteen-month program. PLI students attend evening and Saturday classes at UCLA while continuing to work with their schools and communities. In coursework, they grapple with how sociocultural learning theory, critical race theory, democratic theory, and improvement science offer analytic tools for understanding and redressing the injustices and constricted learning opportunities in Los Angeles schools. PLI students also work with experienced social justice school leaders who guide them through a series of fieldwork exercises at their schools. At the end of the program, students graduate with a tier-one administrative credential and a master's degree in education.

Serving historically marginalized student populations is the central focus of the UCLA PLI program. This requires that students understand the variety of historical and contemporary forces that shape experiences of marginalization inside and outside schools as well as the ways that educators, students, and community members can join together to challenge such marginalization. PLI coursework engages students in lessons on these topics, and fieldwork activities allow students to investigate and try out new strategies for enhancing inclusion and equity.

The first quarter of the program addresses both the promise of public education for all and historical patterns of exclusion, segregation, and stratification. Students read sociocultural learning theory and the dialogic theories of John Dewey and Paulo Freire and then explore these approaches as they engage with one another in class. Class discussions and problem-based assignments encourage participants to reconsider their own educational histories as students and teachers and to articulate their vision of powerful learning and educational equity.

The second quarter highlights the ways that educational leaders use research to identify and challenge marginalization in their schools. Students tackle critical issues of inequities for specific marginalized groups. The goal is for students to learn to identify patterns of marginalization for a particular group and then take a leadership stance that focuses on creating equitable opportunities. Students typically focus attention on groups such as emergent bilinguals, African American students, foster youth, students with special needs, and LGBTQ+ youth, among others. They explore research about this group, gather data on the experiences of this group at their school, and read about and discuss school-wide strategies for transforming educational beliefs and practices relative to this group. This sustained study leads to the development of a leadership project at their school site that is aimed at transforming the experiences of their focal group.

The third quarter focuses on culturally responsive and sustaining instructional leadership and supervision. PLI students learn about and engage in instructional practices that honor the lives of K–12 students and families and place their experiences and identities at the center of the curriculum. The PLI courses emphasize the role of PLI students as adult educators. The underlying premise is that enhancing learning opportunities for K–12 students requires that leaders establish powerful and affirming learning experiences for the teachers who work with these students.

The fourth quarter examines the legal structures and leadership practices necessary to support inclusive, equitable, and participatory school communities. A law and education course highlights legal cases dealing with vulnerable populations and equal educational rights. Students expand their ongoing research on a particular marginalized group by investigating the legal strategies that have been used to advocate for improved learning opportunities for this group. A second course on democratic leadership examines how and why to engage students, teachers, and community members in collaboratively constructing the work of public schools. Democratic theory, with its commitments to universal capacity building, mutual regard, and shared purpose, provides a compelling counterpoint to marginalization or "othering."

During this quarter, students also are guided in the development of a master's essay that draws upon their previous coursework and fieldwork to reflect on why a particular group has been marginalized and how school leaders can challenge this marginalization. The essay is meant to synthesize and apply the lessons students have encountered throughout the program. It aims to identify root causes of inequities and research-based tools and practices that will effect change. In addition to the essay, students develop a public talk on this subject, which they present to PLI alumni, school and district officials, union and parent leaders, and PLI faculty.

The final quarter deals with the day-to-day management of school operations through a racial justice lens. The students write and share op-ed pieces about an issue of inequity that is present at their school. Traditional operations issues such as discipline and scheduling are viewed through a critical social justice perspective. For example, restorative justice is proposed as an alternative to suspensions for resolving student conflict, and the master schedule is viewed as an opportunity to open up access to students who have previously been denied opportunities.

PLI AS A COMMUNITY OF PRACTICE: ALUMNI PLAY A VITAL ROLE IN EDUCATING NEW LEADERS

Upon graduating from the program, students are told that "the PLI program never lets you go." Alumni are invited—again and again—to join with one another in learning spaces and to contribute to the learning of the next cohort of PLI students. This effort to sustain relationships over time serves a broader purpose than traditional "alumni relations." School leaders advocating for social and racial justice often experience a sense of isolation and aloneness as they advocate for historically underserved students and their communities. Some PLI alumni leaders work at schools or district sites where they are the lone spokesperson for dismantling inequalities for Brown and Black students. The PLI way intentionally pushes against this isolation by nurturing social justice alumni networks that create lasting bonds with PLI colleagues and professors.

Alumni are present from the very first moment prospective students learn about the program. For example, alumni join PLI recruitment sessions at school sites and at UCLA, where they describe their personal experiences with the program. In annual surveys, PLI students consistently report that alumni played the most important role in shaping their decision to apply to the program.

After prospective students apply to PLI, they are invited to participate in a group interview in which they discuss how school leaders can disrupt racial injustice and other forms of marginalization. Alumni serve on the interview panels and gauge the applicants' potential to contribute to the PLI community. After the interview session, applicants have the opportunity to discuss program details with the alumni. Often this is the beginning of a lasting relationship between the current students and the alumni that extends into, throughout, and beyond the program.

PLI alumni are integral to every facet of the program. Alumni volunteer to serve as writing mentors and thought partners who work with students on their assignments. They attend class sessions and participate in course discussions, support study groups, share leadership strategies and protocols, serve as final project assessors, and collaborate with current students to help them design and implement inquiry projects. This joint participation between alumni and current students creates a sense of shared identity and belonging tied to the larger cause of enacting social justice education in Los Angeles.

Consider, for example, the role PLI alumni played during a PLI class on democratic leadership in the spring of 2020. A couple weeks into California's COVID-19 stay-at-home order, six PLI alumni joined the class virtually to discuss the significant challenges they faced as principals in ensuring student well-being and quality learning in the low-income communities they served. Each described distinctive strategies for negotiating dilemmas associated with constrained resources, imperfect information, and one-size-fits-all mandates from district leadership. Yet, even as their stories differed, they articulated a shared commitment to the practice of social justice leadership.

For principal Cynthia Gonzalez, the practice of social justice leadership meant developing guidelines for teaching and learning that were responsive to multiple demands on teachers' time, while providing her students with the "live" instruction they needed and deserved. Rather than wait for the district to post new work rules, Cynthia drew on the reservoir of trust she had built up with her staff to establish a regular schedule for synchronous class sessions. She told her faculty that if students in affluent schools "are getting that type of face-to-face interaction . . . our kids of color deserve that, too."

Mauro Bautista's practice of social justice leadership centered on making sure that, amid the economic destruction unleashed by the pandemic, his school addressed the social welfare needs of its most marginalized students. When many students could not be reached through the school's phone banking, Mauro created a system of home visits to inform families about how to access laptops and free meals. For many staff members, the virus or physical distance from the neighborhood made it difficult or frightening to participate in these visits. Mauro, who lives in the community surrounding his school, conducted many of the home visits himself. "As a principal," he pointed out, "you got to be front and center."

To Jose Navarro, the practice of social justice leadership meant fostering relationships that acknowledged one another's humanity and responded to the physical and emotional strains of the pandemic. Navarro noted that educational systems sometimes respond to crises through top-down directives. When districts send communiqués to principals, principals do the same to their teachers, who in turn mimic this same behavior with their students. Navarro warned that "if we just use coercion—do it or else—we are reaping what we sow." During the pandemic, he started every meeting with a check-in that aimed to "recognize humanity in the room before you jump into business."

By engaging PLI students in dialogue about their emerging practice during the early days of the pandemic, Cynthia, Mauro, and Jose contributed to a dynamic and fertile space for nurturing social justice leadership. Several current PLI students commented that they were "inspired" by the principals. One student drew upon Jose's example to revamp his agenda for the special education faculty meeting he regularly leads as department chair. He split up the department into small groups and created a protocol for teachers to check in on each other and then facilitated a discussion about personal wellness. The PLI student concluded, "Well after COVID-19 is gone, I hope that I will remember to prioritize wellness and lift the humanity of every student/person in need."

Interaction with alumni both grounds the students' theories in practical concerns and broadens their perspective beyond the classroom. As school leaders with experience in efforts to effect change, the alumni are able to share their own struggles to challenge and overcome systems that perpetuate inequality. The presence of the alumni prompts reflection and provides affirmation for the current students. It also invariably motivates the alumni who feel their commitment to social justice rekindled by the energy of the students.

PLI ALUMNI LEARNING OUTSIDE THE PREPARATION PROGRAM

There are other spaces in which PLI alumni are able to reflect and be in dialogue with one another. Eighty alumni meet monthly in small groups over dinner to discuss their efforts to advance social justice in Los Angeles schools. The alumni take responsibility for facilitating these meetings. In each session, one member of the group presents a current professional or personal dilemma. Fellow alumni grapple with this issue together in a confidential and supportive environment. The space allows participants to reflect on their practice and consider possible ways forward, in light of their shared commitments to social justice principles.

In the last two years, we have established an inquiry group for veteran principals to share their work with one another. This group meets with us monthly to discuss the challenges and joys of social justice leadership in a society deeply riven by injustice. These dialogues often explore how school leaders can promote wellness for themselves and the communities that they serve, as high school principal Patricia Hanson explains:

> The time to pause and reflect, it's really given me a much stronger sense of pride in my role. I'm inspired by colleagues that are facing similar circumstances, [and] doing it with grace. [The principals' group] has had a major impact on me, not just in my role as a principal, not just in my relationships with other principals and with colleagues, but also . . . my relationship with myself—how to maintain a healthy, positive dynamic with my work self and my home self. I can't sacrifice my well-being because I feel a sense of accountability to the community—to be the leader that this community needs and deserves.

The principal group also offers PLI alumni a space to think beyond the day-to-day logistics issues that shape most district-led meetings. Elementary principal Letitia Davis feels it "has been beneficial to have a separate space for school leaders that are girded in social justice as a frame." Reflection with fellow PLI alumni isn't limited by "perfunctory and compliance-driven" issues, but rather engages with deep questions about learning, democracy, and freedom. The members of the group, Letitia adds, can explore when and how to push back on "district edicts," knowing "that there is no judgment or someone taking notes" that will be used against them.

PLI ALUMNI LEADING IN THE LOS ANGELES COMMUNITY

There now are over 750 graduates of UCLA's PLI, the vast majority of whom are educators of color who currently work in or with public schools across greater Los Angeles. Roughly one half serve as principals or assistant principals or in district leadership positions. Many others hold formal leadership roles at their schools, as program coordinators, instructional coaches, or department heads. A small number of PLI alumni are teaching or leading programs in higher education, and a handful are either taking time off or working outside education.

Almost all PLI alumni are not only still working as educators, but they are doing so in the low-income communities of color that the program was created to serve. In close to 90 percent of the Los Angeles County schools where PLI alumni lead or teach, the majority of enrolled students qualify for free- or reduced-price lunch. The powerful presence of PLI leadership can be seen in the map (figure 7.1) below. The darker shaded areas of the map show neighborhoods with the highest proportion of children living in families with incomes below the federal poverty line. A PLI alum serves as principal or assistant principal at each of the schools indicated with a white dot. In many of these schools, other PLI alumni also play key leadership roles. In this way, PLI alumni exert influence in local neighborhoods and across the broader educational system.

PLI ALUMNI PRACTICING SOCIAL JUSTICE LEADERSHIP

What characterizes the practice of PLI graduates working in low-income communities of color across greater Los Angeles? As we suggest above, there is no static or singular way of being a PLI graduate. The practice of social justice leadership is both dynamic and situated in particular contexts. Yet graduates of PLI share a set of analytic tools and ways of thinking aimed at identifying and challenging patterns of inequality and transforming prevailing norms about whose knowledge and experiences matters and who is capable of rigorous learning. Practicing social justice leadership means redistributing resources and recasting putative deficits as assets.

FIGURE 7.1 *PLI alumni presence.*

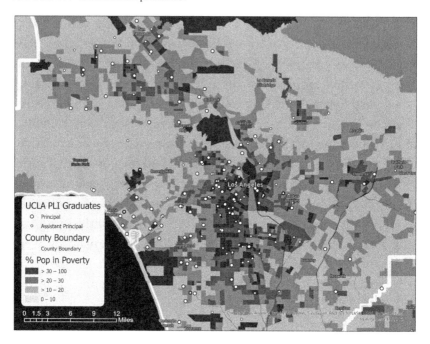

Source: Map and base layer content is the intellectual property of Esri and is used herein with permission. Copyright © 2020 Esri and its licensors. All rights reserved.

A Circle

Mauro Bautista, the principal we introduced earlier who conducted home visits in the early days of the COVID-19 pandemic, lifts up his Los Angeles community as a vital source of strength for his school and his students. He describes his neighborhood of Boyle Heights as having a rich history of political activism. It is the neighborhood he grew up in during the 1980s and early 1990s. Back then, he acknowledges, street violence was "more prevalent, gangs were more visible, [and] drugs were . . . more in your face." While "there was an incredible amount of pride" in the community, many of Mauro's peers talked about moving away from Boyle Heights "the first chance they got." But Mauro always thought about the positive change that could be made in the community. When he left his neighborhood to attend college at UCLA, he did so with the idea that he would "come back and give back." Mauro explains his decision by quoting advice given by an elder to Esperanza in Sandra Cisneros's classic novel, *The House on Mango Street*: "When you leave you must remember to come back for the others. A circle, understand?"

Mauro now has been a teacher and principal in Boyle Heights for twenty years. He identifies as "a social justice educator" who sees it as his "responsibility to be on the lookout for systems that create inequities" and then to "build coalitions that are working together to break the reproduction of . . . [the] systems that reproduce those inequities." Mauro has forged alliances with neighborhood organizations to challenge punitive discipline policies. He also has remade his school into a community school. Not only has it become an inviting place for parents and community members to congregate, but its purpose is to serve the Boyle Heights community: "We want our students . . . to see that they have a responsibility to make the community better."

Mauro's work as a community educator is all the more impactful because he lives in the community. He says he is "blessed" to live in the community he serves and describes his presence in the neighborhood as "an incredibly positive lever":

> When school is over, your students and your families are your neighborhood. You see them everywhere. You see them at the bakery. You see them at the laundromat. You see them at the grocery store. You see them in the post office. You see them in the bank. So, because your interactions with them doesn't end at the school gates . . . there's this conscious effort to consistently and continually be humane and respectful.

These connections have deepened as Mauro and his wife, Claudia—another PLI graduate—have enrolled their own children at Mauro's high school. "Everyone benefits," Mauro explains, "when you're working hard to build a school where you would not have second thoughts about sending your own children." As he interacts with his neighbors who also are parents of his children's classmates, there is "a lot of joy and pride, because [we] have had many positive experiences together."

Connecting Back

PLI alum Dr. Letitia Davis, the elementary principal we introduced earlier, began her fight for racial justice when she was a young child. Raised in the Bay Area, Letitia's parents instilled a sense of pride in her identity as an African American as well as a commitment to activism. Her mother tried to join the Black Panther Party as a teenager but was denied due to her young age. Her father organized a protest against the Ku Klux Klan while an undergraduate in college. The education Letitia received at home was not reflected in her public school experiences: "I remember vividly in first grade, I was thinking to myself, why is it that I don't see anything that looks like me unless it's Martin Luther King's birthday or a little bit in February for Black History Month?" When Letitia came home with assignments from school, her parents encouraged her to reframe them in ways that "connected back to us." Letitia recalls: "My mother had us reading James Baldwin when we were in high school. This is the house that I grew up in."

Like most educators who enroll in PLI, Letitia already had a history of enacting social justice in her daily work in schools before entering the program. PLI deepened those dispositions—her "core pieces"—and provided additional tools and processes to challenge racism and marginalization. "PLI helped to fortify," Letitia notes. But it also afforded space for her to envision leading in her own way—where she "could be unabashedly Letitia."

Letitia's personal experience of the power in education that is "connected back to us" has inspired a lifetime quest to foster culturally responsive learning. Six years ago, Letitia was looking for a school where she could collaborate with like-minded teacher leaders, staff, and parents to create curriculum and instruction based on the cultural and linguistic identities of African Americans and others from the African diaspora. She heard about a traditional elementary school in the Baldwin Hills area of Los Angeles that was considering converting to a "pilot school" where new autonomies from district mandates would make it possible to select the teaching faculty and custom design the school curriculum. "I went to the community meeting before I even applied, and found out that culturally responsive pedagogy was something they wanted to really focus on as one of their instructional areas. I thought, okay, this is a good match."

After six years with Letitia at the helm, Baldwin Hills Elementary School, a school whose enrollment is over 80 percent students of African descent, has become a space for teacher leaders and community members to develop and implement culturally responsive pedagogy. Letitia notes that her experience with PLI encouraged her to join with "social justice and change agents" committed to connecting the school with the culture and experience of the surrounding neighborhood. "It's us there within the community doing the work," she reasons, who have the grounding and desire to "push those agendas." In a recent blog post, Letitia shares what this looks like in practice:[4]

> Culturally responsive pedagogical practices, paired with engaging [student] scholars in 21st century skills and competencies, is the frame upon which we build our curriculum. Our students read texts, explore histories, and see reflections of who they are culturally as their first teaching—and as the foundation upon which all other learning is set. This level of relevance shows the level of value we place on our students, recognizing their worth and value as children of color, and it is a means not just to bring about affirmation and validation but to push the level of rigor.

In early 2020, the state designated Baldwin Hills Elementary a California Distinguished School. Letitia attributes this accomplishment to her teacher leaders, several of whom are also PLI alumni. "We were honored and met the [State] Superintendent . . . in the middle of February and the story aired literally one week before quarantine."

Letitia is proud that students at her school experience powerful and empowering education through a model that mirrors how she learned at home. Baldwin Hills Elementary is a school that connects to and is centered on the lives of the student scholars. Like Mauro, Letitia has forged deep professional and personal ties to her school: "It's a blessing because it is the school where my own children go, and I have faith and confidence [that] what they're getting is what they need. They are nurtured in every way, academically, culturally, socially every day."

Closing the Circle

Throughout this chapter, we have described PLI as a community of practice centered on enacting and reflecting on social justice school leadership. What practice is PLI enacting? First, PLI develops the capabilities of school leaders to expand access to high-quality teaching and learning and to carry forward the principle that all Los Angeles residents are fully deserving of such educational opportunities. Second, PLI fosters community-based educators—many of whom grew up in the neighborhoods where they now teach and lead—who have the skills and commitments to bridge the formal curriculum and the distinctive cultural practices and linguistic capabilities of the communities that they serve. Third, PLI supports democratic leaders who amplify the voices of teachers, students, and families and who themselves adopt a public-facing stance, speaking out on behalf of their students and against injustice.

Ongoing dialogue and reflection are essential to sustaining and deepening this practice. PLI creates multiple sites for emerging and veteran social justice leaders to talk with one another about the meaning and purpose of their work. This occurs from the very first moments that novices encounter the program during the group interview process. Reflective dialogue is infused throughout the program's coursework and fieldwork. And this dialogue about social justice leadership continues after graduation. PLI alumni return again and again to play a role in program activities because this participation deepens their own understanding of and commitment to social justice leadership and because they feel a powerful connection to the PLI community. As Mauro Bautista reminds us, "It is a circle."

PART III

Transforming Public Schools

CHAPTER 8

A Transformative Partnership

*Theodore Roosevelt Senior High School
and the University of California, Los Angeles,
Teacher Education Program*

Emma Hipólito and Ben Gertner

ALMOST THIRTY YEARS AGO, the University of California, Los Angeles (UCLA), Graduate School of Education and Information Studies embarked on a reimagining of its Teacher Education Program (TEP) in response to social unrest in Los Angeles. By transforming the mission, curriculum, and sites of learning, the hope was that UCLA TEP graduates would become caring advocates for all students, reflective inquiry-based practitioners, community builders, and generative change agents.[1] As part of the reimagining and restructuring of the program, UCLA committed to creating partnerships with underserved communities in Los Angeles. Among the first K–12 schools UCLA reached out to was Roosevelt High School in the historic neighborhood of Boyle Heights, just east of downtown Los Angeles. This chapter explores the twenty-five-year partnership between Roosevelt High School and UCLA TEP in order to shed light on how synergistic relationships between universities and urban schools can create powerful sites of learning that prepare and sustain social justice educators.

Partnerships between university-based teacher-education programs and K–12 schools are rarely collaborative.[2] Typically, a preservice teacher is placed with a mentor at a school site with minimal communication and interaction among the two institutions. In these types of partnerships there are few opportunities for university faculty and mentors to interact, much less develop a shared vision for teaching and learning.[3] However, as the roles of field-based activities and clinical practice have gained increasing prominence in teacher-education reform policy, the relationships among school-based mentors, teacher candidates, and university faculty have also grown in significance.[4] As many educators have noted, preservice teachers need to be able to observe powerful teaching. They cannot be simply asked to imagine what they have not seen. Roosevelt High School's partnership with UCLA has created a site for reimagining teaching and learning—one that is powerfully connected to the contexts, collective knowledge, and activist legacies that define many urban communities across the nation and Boyle Heights in particular.

To explore the Roosevelt High School-UCLA partnership, we begin by laying out the context of Boyle Heights and the school community. We then examine UCLA TEP ties to the school and describe the cohort of like-minded educators that has developed over the past three decades. You will meet nine of these educators and hear about their experience enacting transformative practices that are centered on a deep connection with the community, involve a collaborative and creative production of knowledge, and reconceptualize systems and structures of schooling. These practices are changing the educational experiences of area youth as well as the field-based experiences of UCLA TEP teacher candidates.

CONTEXT: ROOSEVELT HIGH SCHOOL AND BOYLE HEIGHTS

Roosevelt High School, situated in the Los Angeles neighborhood of Boyle Heights, has a long and storied history. From its founding in 1923 until the 2009 opening of another public high school, Roosevelt High School was the only comprehensive high school in this section of the city. At one point in its history, it was one of the largest high schools in California, with a student population of over five thousand ninth, tenth, eleventh, and twelfth graders, and a year-round schedule instituted to address severe overcrowding. Today the Roosevelt campus includes both the main campus, known as Roosevelt High School (RHS), and a magnet school, known as the Math, Science, and Technology Magnet Academy at Roosevelt (MSTMA). In the coming pages, Roosevelt High School will be referred to as RHS, and the Math, Science, and Technology Magnet Academy at Roosevelt as MSTMA. When we are referring to both schools, we will use "Roosevelt."

Boyle Heights, located just east of the Los Angeles River and bordering downtown Los Angeles, has drawn diverse groups of Angelenos. This neighborhood has been a port of entry for immigrants and US transplants since its beginnings in 1876, with Jews, Mexicans, Japanese, Russians, and African Americans having made Boyle Heights their home.[5] The Roosevelt campus has long reflected the diversity of Boyle Heights. Old high school yearbooks show a cross-racial and multiethnic mix of students engaged in groups and activities typical of many American high schools, such as the Junior Reserve Officers' Training Corps, football, and the National Honor Society, as well as other activities more unique to Roosevelt, such as Russian tea ceremonies and the building of a Japanese garden.

The school is probably best known for being one of the sites of the 1968 student walkouts, or blowouts, demanding better schooling conditions. These acts of resistance became a turning point in the Chicano Movement in Los Angeles. Many of the students' demands still resonate to this day: smaller classes; bilingual counselors, teachers, and administrators; lessons on Mexican American culture, art, and history. The blowouts at Roosevelt High School and student-led struggle that followed represent years of organizing and speak to Boyle Heights's deep-rooted history of political activism.

From the 1920s through the 1940s, Boyle Heights was a hotbed of labor movement activism; many of the residents worked in the local manufacturing industries and joined unions and other progressive organizations working for social justice.[6] The neighborhood was home to the grassroots Community Service Organization (CSO), founded in 1947 to fight against housing, employment, and education discrimination. CSO held voter registrations and "get out the vote" efforts in East Los Angeles, and it successfully helped propel Edward Roybal, a Roosevelt alumnus, to the Los Angeles City Council and the US House of Representatives in 1962, making him the first Californian of Latinx descent to serve in Congress since 1879.[7]

This spirit of organizing and resistance continues in Boyle Heights. Since 2006, Roosevelt students have walked out in defense of immigrant rights, protested against school overcrowding and punitive discipline policies, and demanded district-wide implementation of an ethnic studies curriculum. This history draws UCLA TEP students to the campus and continues to play a meaningful role in Roosevelt's curriculum and approach to instruction.

THE UCLA TEACHER EDUCATION PROGRAM

UCLA TEP's relationship with Roosevelt dates back to at least the early 1990s. It was and continues to be the type of school TEP seeks to connect with—a school that serves students of color in a traditionally underserved community. To do justice to the long history of the Roosevelt-UCLA partnership, we tapped into the experiences and memories of nine current educators at the Roosevelt campus, all of whom are UCLA TEP alumni and most of whom are teachers of color. These educators have classroom experiences that range from three to twenty-five years, most averaging over a decade of teaching experience. Seven teachers are faculty members in the English and social studies departments. We also spoke to an instructional coach and a mathematics teacher. Six of our teachers work at RHS and three at MSTMA. The educators shared what brought them to the school, the connections to the school community they made in their curriculum, and their connection to UCLA TEP.

Presently nearly half of UCLA TEP's English and social studies preservice candidates complete one of their student teaching placements at either RHS or MSTMA, spending approximately eight months on the Roosevelt campus. There are no preservice math and science teachers placed at either school, as UCLA TEP has few alumni in those departments. The familiarity English and social studies TEP students have with Roosevelt creates a strong draw to the Roosevelt campus; however, the draw to Roosevelt is distinct from other placements. Students are attracted by the historic nature of the school and surrounding community. We heard this repeated by our educators, who used words such as "legacy school" when naming underlying factors that pulled them to the school. Another factor is the resonance with home. Some TEP students grew up on the east side of Los Angeles or in other working-class communities of color in California. Their impetus to teach is to give back to these communities. For example, Rocio, a math teacher who completed her student teaching at RHS, offered, "I was an [English as a second language] student myself so I think that's what kind of captivated me and pulled me in when I worked with that population. . . . I kind of saw myself in them and hoped for a lot of good things."

Three teachers we spoke to had ties to East Los Angeles communities that predated their enrollment in TEP. For example, Lena, an RHS alum and a newer member of the RHS faculty, shared, "I love this community, and I want to see it grow. And so my goal was always to come back." Similarly, Tom, our most experienced educator, who began his teaching career at RHS in 1994, had family in Boyle Heights and cousins who had graduated from the school.

Significantly, for some time RHS and MSTMA had a convergence of educators with connections to UCLA teaching at the school and serving as mentors. While the specific individuals changed over time, there was still a sense that new teachers would be able to connect with other supportive educators at the school. For example, two teachers named an RHS social studies teacher who taught social studies methods courses for TEP and who served as a mentor to new teachers at the school site. Over the years, the trusting relationships developed from these student-teacher interactions created a pipeline to Roosevelt, particularly in social studies and English. Both Sunny and Gabriela, MSTMA English teachers, said that this instructor—and several other RHS educators with TEP connections—influenced their decision to accept a teaching position at Roosevelt. Gabriela added, "It just felt like this instant network," as there were a good number of "solid teachers" at the school.

However, despite this strong network, our more experienced alumni spoke to an initial dissonance between their goals for change and the preparation they received from TEP. We heard words like "disconnect" and "forced" in regard to their own efforts to apply social justice theory to practice. One educator reported feeling "challenged" and "isolated" in her student teaching placement. Thus, although they had completed student teaching placements in urban partnership schools, some alumni reported struggling to enact their social justice goals. Over time, TEP has developed a stronger understanding of the importance of identifying social justice–focused mentors to apprentice preservice teachers and has continued to foster ties with alumni who can serve in this role. Today, as noted by Tom, at Roosevelt there is a closer alignment between TEP students' field-based experiences and the program's coursework and goals: "Lately UCLA has much more focused on social justice and even things like ethnic studies, which wasn't around when I went. . . . So we're coming in with similar philosophy, similar attitudes, similar beliefs about how we can best help the students." TEP alumni at Roosevelt have also built strong connections among themselves. In the next section we describe the impact of those relationships.

COHORT OF LIKE-MINDED EDUCATORS

Teaching can be isolating, as most teachers work alone with their students for most of the day and have little opportunity to collaborate with other adults. Educational research has pointed to the importance of building a community of like-minded educators in retaining teachers in urban schools.[8] Within the last few years, we have seen the amplification of the voices of a group of like-minded educators (many of them TEP alumni) who together have worked to make substantive changes at both RHS and MSTMA. This group has served as a support system that affirms and sustains the criticality of the work Roosevelt teachers are spearheading both within and outside the classroom. Lena, a new teacher, spoke about the importance of this group to her:

> I feel like teaching [can] be a very isolating profession. It's very easy to get into your own little world, and I'm just going to focus on my class, my kids, my curriculum. Sometimes your class, your kids, the curriculum doesn't go as planned. It's good to have folks who have gone through the same programs, read similar readings, done similar training to . . . share strategies and share experiences in a way that makes me feel less alone in this job.

For a new teacher, the connection to alumni fosters a reflective practice and supports growth. We heard something very similar from Alberto, one of the more experienced educators, who added that he continues to feel "passionate" about coming to work because of this group. He went on to explain that he understood teacher burnout to be a result of a lack of community and that community for him means shared "commonalities, not just educator friendships but also commonalities in terms of our educational philosophy and the reasons why we teach and what brought us to teaching." Thus, a concentration of educators with shared beliefs and a shared experience in teacher preparation sustains the work at Roosevelt.

TRANSFORMATIVE PRACTICES

Paramount to TEP's work is a mission focused on the transformation of urban schools. At RHS and MSTMA, TEP alumni and like-minded allies have worked together to bring meaningful change not only to classroom curricula and instruction but to the systems of schooling as well. We define these transformative practices as those that center on a deep connection with the school community, involve a collaborative and creative production of knowledge, and reconceptualize systems and structures of schooling.[9] These were among the goals set forth by TEP during its restructuring and that likewise arose when Roosevelt teachers were asked about their classroom practices and community connections.

DEEP CONNECTIONS TO COMMUNITIES

On Saturday, May 19, 2018, I walked onto campus to help prepare for the 8th Annual Eastside Stories Conference. In my hand was fresh sage from my garden to give to the Aztec dancers who kicked off the event, which this year commemorated the fiftieth anniversary of the East Los Angeles blowouts. The Politics & Pedagogy Collective—Roosevelt educators and students dedicated to raising youth empowerment, social justice in schools, and community through critical pedagogy and activism—were the main organizers of this event. This year Center X and TEP were co-sponsors and a number of TEP students and alumni attended. I briefly reflected on my Jewish identity, a connection to Boyle Heights' Jewish past. Today I am an outsider at a school that is over 99 percent Latinx.

To launch the conference, I headed into the auditorium with students, visitors, and educators to hear a welcome address by students and a keynote by Dr. Shawn Ginwright, professor at San Francisco State. On this day, surrounded by like-minded educators, youth, and community, I envisioned what that freedom might look like at Roosevelt. I reflected on how fortunate I am to be a member of this vibrant community.

—Ben Gertner, RHS Principal

A defining aspect of the Roosevelt teacher practice is the deep expertise teachers have with regard to the school and the Boyle Heights community. Educators speak about the school and the surrounding neighborhood using the lens of "community cultural wealth," defined by Tara J. Yosso as "an array of knowledges, skills, abilities and contacts possessed and used by Communities of Color to survive and resist racism and other forms of oppression."[10] This lens challenges dominant societal narratives, which often focus on the shortcomings of urban communities of color. Despite the efforts of teacher education programs to raise up ideas of multiculturalism and culturally responsive pedagogy, research has shown that deficit notions persist.[11]

Talking with our group of educators, we learned more about the role TEP played in developing this lens of cultural community wealth. Lena, who has "deep family roots" in Boyle Heights, pointed to the community work she did in TEP as having ignited "a little fire" within her and an understanding that to be a "true caring teacher" she needed to know the history of the place as well as parents and students. Juana, who grew up in another East Los Angeles neighborhood, pointed to work she did in TEP that developed her understanding of how to connect to a community: "I was proud of my community. But I think TEP was always really intentional about whether it was through curriculum or whether it was through relationship building that you look at the community through an asset lens." Juana went on to list the ways—readings, activities, connecting with communities—that TEP "showed me what it could look like to work in the community, to honor the community, to build relationships with the community."

Others spoke of becoming grounded in community history once they became RHS educators. Like Lena, Alberto also hoped to work in the community after learning about Roosevelt's history when he was an undergraduate in a Chicana/Chicano studies class. Still, after moving to Boyle Heights, Alberto reported, "I started learning a lot more about the community . . . the folks who were the cultural workers from the neighborhood were already doing the work in the community." Conversely, Gillian did not know a lot about the history of Roosevelt or the local area when she moved to California to enroll in TEP; however, once she was employed at Roosevelt, other teachers taught her about Boyle Heights. She cited this as a powerful experience. She learned about local Japanese American history from Japanese American teachers and about the 1968 walkouts from a student activist of the era.

Research on UCLA TEP has found that its community-focused pedagogy helped preservice candidates work through the deficit thinking of urban communities.[12] Our educators' and our own experience supports this conclusion and takes it to another level. We consistently heard Roosevelt teachers speak about their efforts to connect students with the history of Boyle Heights. For example, Lena shared that the goals for the courses she teaches are to have students "recognize the issues and the systemic oppression that happen in communities of color." She frames her approach so that students also "identify assets and the cultural wealth that they have here because I want them to understand that yes, Boyle Heights is not perfect, but as members of this community, it's our role to fight for it and continue to push back against people trying to push us out." Roosevelt students are learning not only to uplift the assets of the community but also to protect them.

COLLABORATIVE AND CREATIVE PRODUCTION OF KNOWLEDGE

In early summer 2015, a small group of Center X Teacher Educators met to discuss establishing an ethnic studies pathway within the UCLA TEP. We understood the close ties between ethnic studies epistemologies and the pedagogies TEP seeks to foster in its teacher candidates. We also knew that the LAUSD [Los Angeles Unified School District] School Board had recently mandated that every student in the District would take one high school ethnic studies class as a requirement for graduation. While the details surrounding this ethnic studies class were still hazy, we all wondered how LAUSD would bring this class to scale. Who had the content and pedagogical expertise to do this well? Given the deep connection to the Roosevelt community, we discussed how one of the school's signature courses, "Boyle Heights and Me," would be a powerful context for pre-service learning and development of an ethnic studies pedagogy.

—Emma Hipólito, TEP Director

The Boyle Heights and Me course, taken by all ninth graders at both RHS and MSTMA, is grounded in an ethnic studies framework, positioning high school students as both learners and experts. Alberto, one of the authors of the course, described the pedagogical grounding of the class:

> We center our ethnic studies course . . . around the living history of the community and of the students and the stories of the students. We are not like ahistorical beings. . . . And so whatever happened in the past and what is happening in the present, there's a direct link. So [we are] also learning about our own personal histories and the histories of our families, the history as a community. It's just the constant connection of going back and forth and within.

Juana, another author of the Boyle Heights and Me course, shared that as she and her coauthors were working on the course curriculum, they came upon the statement that a "powerful ethnic studies class should honor and acknowledge and center community assets." The next step was to reach out to community members and organizations that already had a presence on the campus. One of the organizations was 826LA, a nonprofit organization that provides one-on-one creative and expository writing support to K–12 youth. Roosevelt educators had already been working with this organization. As part of this project, students interviewed "cultural treasures" within the community.

In the Boyle Heights and Me class, the partnership metamorphosed into a "book project focused on the themes of resistance, resilience, and/or reimagination," which would become one of the texts for future incarnations of the class. Alberto described the work as the class curriculum, as it encompassed the "stories and testimonials of our students . . . and documents the lived experiences and realities and the living history of the community." In this approach to curriculum, students become constructors of knowledge as they share their work through the printed word or public reading of their stories. Elexia R. McGovern and Tracy L. Buenavista urge educators to see communities of color as both holders and creators of knowledge and to seek ways to coconstruct empowering curricula with students. They encourage teachers to interrogate their own sources of knowledge by asking questions such as, "Whose truths do I value?"[13] Critical hope is another aspect of this pedagogy.[14] Students need to see examples of resilience and activism in their own community and consider themselves agents of change. As Alberto notes, the coursework that makes up Boyle Heights and Me "teaches our students that whatever they're doing in the class, it's going to not only transform the community, but it becomes a part of that living history of that legacy of the community as well."

Curricula that position students as both Boyle Heights experts and change makers occur in other classes as well. For example, during our interview, Gillian discussed a new project she was implementing in her eleventh-grade United States history courses; it explores how local industries have affected health in the community. It originated from a connection she made with an organization, East Yard Communities for Environmental Justice, that is fighting industrial contamination in this part of Los Angeles. Roosevelt students toured hazardous areas in the neighborhood and were also provided with a history of the Mothers of East Los Angeles, a grassroots organization that fought against the construction of a prison in East Los Angeles, and other examples of organizing for environmental justice. As part of this unit, students researched an issue facing their community and presented proposed solutions. Tom spoke to the development over time of a curriculum centered on the importance of students' rights, workers' rights, and individual rights. Sunny brought up a youth participatory action research (YPAR) project at MSTMA that culminated in the Eastside Stories Conference and student-led workshops:

> I always had a focus on creating a curriculum that reflected communities of color, even as a more traditional English teacher. I taught novels like *Always Running* or the poetry of the Harlem Renaissance. Developing critical researchers and activists has become more central to my specific work in the upper grades. It's exciting when students not only can identify problems but come up with solutions like advocating for personal finance courses to address predatory lending practices in a reverse-redlined neighborhood or calculate the feasibility of creating a business improvement district to support ethnic entrepreneurs in challenging gentrification.

Sunny referred to work presented by students in this project as "our own all-day teach-in."

These three curricular examples—industry impacts on community health, units focused on rights, and the MSTMA YPAR project—as well as the Boyle Heights and Me course began with the self-identified challenges facing the Roosevelt community. Educators built upon students' expertise in their community by engaging them in research and, in the Boyle Heights and Me course, through exploring writings by other RHS students. In these cases, students are situated as researchers capable of finding and articulating answers to the problems they face, and thus they become creators of knowledge and change agents. As Russell notes, "Students come with voice . . . I feel as if part of our job as educators is to put them in situations where they develop those qualities." This approach to content reflects the belief in elevating student voice and in a curriculum that is rooted in culturally responsive and sustaining teaching.[15]

RECONCEPTUALIZING SYSTEMS AND STRUCTURES OF SCHOOLING

On June 12, 2017, Mariana Ramirez, MSTMA teacher, and I helped organize a press conference and rally outside the gates of the Roosevelt campus to protest the Immigration and Customs Enforcement (ICE) detainment of Claudia Rueda, an MSTMA alum, college student, and immigrant rights activist. Participants included MSTMA and RHS teachers and students, representatives of United Teachers Los Angeles, Claudia's professors, and community activists. Roosevelt High School MEChA also played a leadership role—helping to plan the event, tweeting, making phone calls, asking Claudia's former teachers to write character letters, speaking at the rally, making banners, and organizing other students. We were demanding not only Claudia's release, but an end to the collaboration between the local police and ICE, as well as an end to ICE raids in Boyle Heights. While seemingly focused on the fate of one individual, the demands also spoke to broader issues facing the Roosevelt community.

—Gillian Russom, RHS teacher and
United Teachers Los Angeles activist

As noted earlier, activism beats in the heart of Roosevelt and Boyle Heights. This is another way that RHS and MSTMA align with the goals of Center X and TEP, which include engaging "prospective professionals in generative processes for implementing change that fundamentally challenges, reconceptualizes, and transforms [schools] into places of hope and opportunity for all students."[16] This call has been taken up by numerous TEP graduates over the last two decades; TEP alumni have helped us flesh out what it means for experienced educators to be change agents. They have raised examples of how they worked toward changing policy within Roosevelt, outside the school community, and in the broader policy arena. Gillian, who shared the story about the 2017 press conference and rally with us, spoke about her involvement with the Los Angeles Unified School District (LAUSD) teacher union, a cosponsor of the rally, as originating from a longer-term political commitment to unions and a place of frustration. As a new teacher, she saw "the limits of what you can impact in an individual classroom" and sought other ways to make change. She wondered about going beyond a social justice curriculum to "*doing* social justice work as an educator" (emphasis added). She remembered that unions were not discussed in TEP, so part of her journey as a social justice educator has been to explore the role they play in social justice movements.

Both Juana and Alberto also spoke to system-wide change when discussing their Boyle Heights and Me class. Their work in the field of K–12 ethnic studies is not only changing their district, the largest in the state; it has also shaped the teaching of ethnic studies statewide. While the initial goal of their curricular work was to transform RHS school culture to be "socially just, empowering, and healing," their approach has reverberated across the state, and they have generously shared their learning in multiple educator spaces with presentations and publications. Juana and Alberto's statewide advocacy for ethnic studies courses in K–12 settings has made Alberto ponder what the class will look like in other districts. He and Juana firmly believe that this curriculum needs to be responsive and localized. Alberto explains that the key to curriculum writing is to ensure the course is "responding to the community, to the history of the community, and the history of the people and families" within that community. The Boyle Heights and Me course serves as a model for other educators and administrators seeking to bring ethnic studies to their schools. Both Alberto and Juana serve on the LAUSD Ethnic Studies Leadership Team, a group that is shaping implementation of ethnic studies throughout LAUSD. Alberto is also a member of the California Teachers Association and the Stanford Instructional Leadership Corp's Ethnic Studies team, two organizations that support practitioner-driven professional development. The Boyle Heights and Me course has also played a weighty role in shaping TEP's ethnic studies pathway. Since the 2014 pilot program, five cohorts of students have been able to work alongside the teachers of Boyle Heights and Me as part of their student teaching experience.

Gabriela's thinking about change making brings us back to the Roosevelt campus. This experienced educator asserted that she is "constantly working toward change, or else I wouldn't be in this profession." When speaking about transformative work, Gabriela highlighted the effort to implement restorative justice at both RHS and MSTMA. Restorative justice builds a positive school culture and climate by reconsidering a school's approach to discipline. Specifically, for LAUSD, "restorative justice promotes trust and respect in relationships, setting the foundation for teaching and learning. In addition, the practices provide meaningful opportunities for students to develop self-discipline and positive behavior in a caring and supportive environment."[17] Initially, Gabriela perceived that there were no guidelines to support restorative justice work at Roosevelt. Still, she believed in the practice and was determined to bring it to campus. The result of her efforts was that Roosevelt employees became trained in nonviolent communication and on how to do restorative justice circles. Gabriela also pointed to an incentive program modeled after one at a neighboring school. Students received rewards for certain behaviors, as decided upon by RHS and MSTMA faculty, such as being "resilient, respectful, and responsible," as well as other, more traditional rewards for behaviors such as attendance. Gabriela described this and other schoolwide initiatives she had engaged in as both "beautiful" and "powerful."

It should be noted that Roosevelt teachers have been given significant curricular autonomy to create courses and shape assignments and have taken leadership roles at both schools. They serve as department chairs, pathway leads, restorative justice leads, and as a community outreach director, using their influence to build a school culture grounded in social justice. This level of independence does not happen in all schools, especially urban schools, and it has been a powerful force in shaping the practices we have shared here. As Juana noted, "I've had a lot of freedom but also I've seen people model what you can do with that freedom, and it's made a huge difference because I've been able to learn and then expand beyond what I got to see." The trust shown to the Roosevelt teachers and the spaces created for collaboration have been a powerful impetus for change; however, we also learned from teachers that this approach to curriculum and pedagogy took time to develop. Gabriela added to this thinking: "I knew I was social justice in my heart. . . . I don't think the activism . . . came out in my teaching . . . until much later, maybe in my third or fourth, fifth year." She elaborated that it was not until she connected with other like-minded educators that she began to envision a curriculum grounded in social justice and activism: "In the beginning, it feels really forced."

The reflective and collaborative nature of these teachers' work has propelled them to think more deeply about what it means to be a social justice educator. Now in her thirteenth year of teaching, Gabriela has had years to examine what it means to teach for social justice. She understands that teaching children to go on a march is activism, but teaching kids to read is also activism. Similarly, Rocio spoke of struggling to find a way to incorporate a "resistance piece" or an activism-inspired approach to her curriculum. However, she has come to realize that she wants her students to develop "a really strong math lens" as part of their journey toward being an advocate for themselves and their families. She also acknowledged that there is a great deal of instruction in math that has a traditional focus and says, "I'm trying to humanize it."

Working together, these like-minded allies support each other to take pedagogical risks and express views that may not be shared by the entire Roosevelt faculty. This experience contrasts with what some consider the norm for progressive teachers of color: toxic relationships with school leaders and colleagues that can cause teachers to contemplate leaving their school or the teaching profession altogether.[18]

CONTEXT AND PARTNERSHIPS MATTER

The ability to work with mentors who have a deep understanding of the mission and vision of Center X and who share that philosophy has allowed us to enhance coursework through the articulation of practice-based exemplars. This strong connection to the field is in keeping with recent reform efforts in teacher education that have focused on the impact of field-based learning on preservice teacher development. Linda Darling-Hammond, in a 2014 study of seven successful teacher preparation programs, referred to clinical practice as the "holy grail" of teacher education and called for a "major overhaul" of the relationship between universities and K–12 schools.[19] These calls for change are a response to research findings that traditional teacher education programs are often too detached from the school-based settings where new teachers will work.[20] In California we have several policies around field-based placements, including a specified number of hours teacher candidates must complete in schools, the types of field-based activities they should engage in, and the types of schools where they should student teach.

TEP has understood the importance of context and preservice teacher development for some time. TEP has purposely placed teacher candidates in the specific communities and schools that mirror the sites where these students will find employment in the second year of the program. TEP clinical faculty work to build relationships with teachers and administration at school sites. Additionally, teacher candidates are placed in small cohorts at schools, which ensures that TEP clinical faculty are a presence at the school and can observe classrooms regularly. This also provides TEP students with a built-in community to help develop their understanding of the placement. TEP classes are held in the late afternoons within partner schools throughout the city. All these practices have been found to strengthen clinical practice.[21]

Yet, despite these long-standing commitments, most experienced educators remember a disconnect between the theoretical foundations of TEP and their experiences as student teachers. One Roosevelt teacher spoke to feeling misaligned philosophically with her guiding teacher but not having the language to articulate the disconnect, as she was still developing her teacher identity. This disconnect is one reason some teachers decide to serve as mentors or guiding teachers; they wish to retain quality teachers by helping them develop a supportive community of peers and colleagues.

In recent years TEP has become more deliberate about supporting mentors who understand and share the social justice goals of the program. As noted by Lauren M. Anderson and Jamy A. Stillman, preservice teachers need more than a placement in an urban school. They need "to be apprenticed by adaptive experts who are successfully engaging in equity-minded practice."[22] The Roosevelt teachers serve as an exemplar of mentors who live the mission of the program—to transform public schools. The partnership with RHS and MSTMA educators enhances and builds upon the coursework of TEP students. At Roosevelt, preservice teachers can observe and be mentored by experienced educators who have collaboratively and collectively worked alongside community-based organizations for change. Cognizant of their positionality, these educators, even those with roots in the neighborhood, entered this community as learners. Rather than dismissing the cultural wealth and community knowledge of Boyle Heights, they raise it up in their curriculum to build connections with students and to facilitate skill development. These are among some of the strongest values TEP holds. In many ways, our participants exemplify the qualities of a community teacher as outlined by Peter Murrell in his framework for effective urban teaching.[23]

We know that the TEP partnership also benefits RHS and MSTMA faculty. Roosevelt educators continue to welcome these opportunities to maintain connections and relationships with TEP faculty in the program. They also feel a responsibility to expand their network of like-minded colleagues by supporting new teachers. They value the dialogue with teacher candidates regardless of whether they are discussing new readings, established theories, or implementation of new practices. One teacher referred to these conversations as "keeping me on my toes" and as a way to continue to grow. TEP is continually renewed by this strong connection to the field of education, to socially just pedagogy, and to alumni who share the vision of the program.

In Spring 2020, I was interviewing prospective science and math teachers for the upcoming school year. It had been a few years since we had had openings in these departments. I was particularly interested in hiring a TEP applicant who I knew would be a good fit, but that teacher had commitments to a neighboring community. I wondered what I might do to persuade this person to take the job at Roosevelt. I decided to ask TEP alumni at Roosevelt to contact the prospective teacher. Their response was immediate and the outreach effective. The candidate accepted the offer and will be joining this powerful community of teachers in the fall.

—Ben Gertner, RHS Principal

CHAPTER 9

UCLA Community School

*Creating a Workplace Culture that
Sustains Social Justice Educators*

*Karen Hunter Quartz, Leyda Garcia,
Queena Kim, and Marisa Saunders*

INTRODUCTION

On his way to visit César Chávez in 1968, Robert F. Kennedy decided
to run for president. He arrived in the rural California town of Delano
to help his friend break a twenty-five-day fast—a nonviolent protest
seeking to improve wages, education, housing, and legal protection
for migrant farm workers. Three months later, Kennedy addressed an
ecstatic crowd in the Embassy Ballroom of Los Angeles's famed Am-
bassador Hotel after winning the California Democratic presidential
primary. The tragedy that ensued is well documented, but few have
heard the remarkable story of hope and courage that lives today in the
same space. Now a stately library shared by six new public schools—

the Robert F. Kennedy (RFK) Community Schools—the former ball-room is anchored by a fifty-five-foot mural. Chávez and Kennedy, at their fateful meeting, now watch over the education of four thousand K–12 students, mostly immigrants from Mexico and Central America. Today, over half of California's young people are Latino, yet only 18 percent of the adults in their lives are college graduates. The civil rights struggle of 1968 lives on in the explosion of new schools aimed at preparing first-generation college-going students to succeed.

This chapter tells the story of the University of California, Los Angeles (UCLA) Community School—one of the six RFK Community Schools. From the groundwork to create the school in 2006 to the achievement of preparing all of its graduates for college in 2018, the school's success lies deep inside the people who have shaped it, the histories they have lived, and the shared virtues that propel them forward. The UCLA Community School was created to advance teaching, research, and service—merging the mission of the university with the core work of K–12 schooling. It is an example of a public cross-sector partnership that contributes resources to K–12 schooling to study and support innovative educational practices. These resources, however, in no way eclipse the challenges the school faces. In most respects, the UCLA Community School is a very typical public school, barraged by external reforms, inadequate funding, large class sizes, and the political instability of revolving district leadership. That's why it makes such an interesting school for collaborative study. In particular, we're interested in how educators navigate the challenges faced in today's urban schools—working within a system they are trying to change.

We know schools are powerful sites for reproducing the cultural and economic norms that marginalize low-income students of color. Being a social justice educator means tackling these norms head on— exercising agency over what and how students are taught in order to disrupt long-standing inequities.[1] We also know that being a community teacher committed to social justice means that you don't act alone. Teacher agency is part of a complex dynamic that shapes and is shaped by the structural and cultural features of the school, not merely a feature of individuals.[2] School structures and culture determine teachers' sense that they can innovate and make work-related decisions that are based on shared goals, interests, and beliefs—the extent to which teachers experience agency.[3] Agency—or more apt, collective agency—is not viewed as the capability of a teacher but rather is shaped by both the teacher and the school context in which the teacher acts.

Collective teacher agency is important for many reasons, including the preparation, career development, and retention of social justice educators. As documented throughout this volume, novice teachers learn to become powerful social justice educators when they are immersed in school communities that share their commitment to social justice. As teachers develop in their careers, they thrive and stay in schools that value and support their agency and create professional working conditions that allow them to do their best work.[4] To capture the collective agency of social justice educators at the UCLA Community School, we present five brief stories chronologically and conclude by situating these stories in the larger policy debates about urban teacher retention and community schooling.

2006: ENVISIONING COLLECTIVE AGENCY

The UCLA Community School was conceived in 2006, during a national reform moment defined by three related change efforts: expanding school choice, building small schools, and ensuring teacher autonomy.[5] Locally, the Los Angeles Unified School District (LAUSD) was in the midst of the nation's most ambitious school-building campaign, with 159 new construction projects—including 79 new schools—to relieve overcrowding and stop the inequitable practice of year-round schooling. The new school buildings offered the city a rare opportunity to re-envision its system of public schools. And as the largest public university in the city, UCLA was eager to play a role.

To begin, UCLA convened a study group of diverse stakeholders to assess the feasibility of creating a new school. Similar efforts by the University of California (UC) San Diego and UC Berkeley to start new charter schools informed the group's deliberations, yet the UCLA team was committed to finding an alternative to charter schools, given the movement's rapid expansion across the city and the group's collective worry that charters would drain resources from the district. The feasibility study, released in 2007, outlined a new school vision as well as an assessment of the costs, benefits, and potential risks related to school quality, governance, equity and admissions, and sustainability. Ultimately, the university decided to move forward with the new school, in partnership with LAUSD, United Teachers Los Angeles, and the local community.

Teacher autonomy and professionalism were foundational to the new school vision. Based on research, the study group recommended a small and decentralized school organization that would support professional autonomy and, with it, heightened retention and stability.[6] A longitudinal study of the career development of ten cohorts of UCLA-prepared teachers further informed the school vision with its findings that social justice educators struggle to both work within a system and change it at the same time. What propel and support this struggle are opportunities to exercise professional autonomy and judgment, participate in collaborative school-based and profession-wide social networks, and construct meaning and significance as members of a long-standing activist and intellectual tradition.[7] The challenge was to design a school where the collective agency of social justice educators would flourish.

For this reason, the new school proposal submitted to the district in 2007 cautioned that it was provisional and would come to life only when all community stakeholders could fully engage in the design process. The proposal described "a community-based, learner-centered, university-assisted school—a school where many different people come together, driven by the nation's long legacy of common schooling." Lead teachers were at the core of this design process, and the UCLA-led hiring committee recruited a principal and initial team of three lead teachers to turn the broad vision into a reality. Granted local autonomy over curricula, instruction, assessment, staffing, budget, and schedule, the new school was part of an original cohort of ten Belmont Pilot Schools, a reform model that traveled from Boston to Los Angeles in response to the growth of charter schools.[8] The

UCLA Community School was set to open alongside five other new pilot schools in a historic site—the first wall-to-wall complex of pilot schools in the city. The stakes were high, and the demand to get students off buses and year-round calendars necessitated opening K–5 one year and expanding through the high school the next. The inaugural faculty and partners welcomed students from more than sixty feeder schools throughout the city. Students were now able to walk to their neighborhood schools, and parents were eager to know that their children were in good hands.

2009: COLLECTIVE AGENCY AS SCHOLARSHIP

Parents filtered into the UCLA Community School's multipurpose room on October 8, 2009, the first back-to-school night, curious to learn more about the new school they had entrusted to teach their children. "Buenas noches y bienvenidos. I am the proud principal of the UCLA Community School." Founding principal Georgia Lazo exuded optimism, switching effortlessly from Spanish to English throughout an inspiring welcome address. Teachers lined the wall, wearing new white polo shirts with the school's blue Bruin logo. The lead teachers had been prepping for months, working with UCLA researchers to design a dual-language program that would honor the community's dominant home languages of Spanish and Korean. Brochures were printed with the bold claim that the school would prepare all children to graduate bilingual, biliterate, and multicultural.

UCLA professor and bilingual education researcher Patricia Gándara explained why parents at the school should waive their right to monolingual instruction, given California's "English-only" Proposition 227, and embrace the school's program to build on and maintain students' home language. Students entered the school with years of experience in programs designed to erase their home languages. In this context, the notion of implementing a "proven" program model struck everyone as naive. The problem-solving challenge went beyond instructional strategies and bilingual materials because teachers had to first know and respect what each and every child was bringing to their classrooms.

The school was aware of the concerns parents had about rapid English-language acquisition as well as their strongly held value that primary language should be honored because it is a part of students' connection to their culture and families. Teachers were also conscious of the dynamic of language ideology, and their experiences confirmed the overpowering nature of English, especially when it is the language of instruction. In response to the communities' priorities and research, the school created a program focused on three areas: bilingualism and biliteracy, academic achievement, and sociocultural competency. The program was designed to preserve home language, support English reading achievement, and develop a positive bicultural and ethnic identity. The decision to implement a target-language-dominant bilingual model was based on research that suggests it is more effective than other dual-immersion models at promoting overall bilingual proficiency.[9] Teachers envisioned that graduates of the school would read, write, listen, and speak in at least two languages, and be able to use those languages flexibly with different audiences in order to think critically about the world around them, to engage as agents of social change, and to promote democratic practices.

The first few years were a big transition for both students and teachers. The reform context in 2009 prescribed a strict reinforcement of a scripted phonics basal reading program, and, in opposition, teachers made a deliberate choice to institute a balanced biliteracy approach to language arts. They were developing this approach while still laying the foundation of a new school and training the staff. Many aspects of the bilingual program needed articulation and development. The program lacked cohesion, accountability, resources, and processes for evaluation. As students moved through the program, teachers and school leaders recognized the need for ongoing planning, reflection, and improvement. The school's partnership with university researchers supported this improvement process through a variety of collaborative inquiry cycles that included biliteracy data collection and analysis, the development of biliteracy teaching tools and rubrics, and a focus on translanguaging.

One particularly generative research-practice partnership involved elementary teachers partnering with a bilingual education researcher (and former bilingual teacher) to create the Reader Identity Self-Assessment (RISA). The RISA is a set of lesson plans and assessment routines that facilitate students' analysis of their own Spanish and English reading data. It was designed to provide both teachers and students with formative data to inform reading instruction and learning. Students set goals in two languages and monitor their progress, sharing their progress during student-led parent conferences. Since teachers began administering the RISA, the percentage of students reading at grade level in Spanish and English has steadily increased across student cohorts (grades K–5), and the collaborative inquiry continues to further support students' bilingual reading development through high school.[10]

This story of collective agency focuses on the role of social justice educators as scholars. Along with their research partners, teachers have presented findings about the RISA and other practices at professional conferences and in publications.[11] When surveyed about their professional identities, 95 percent of UCLA Community School educators agreed that it's important to read and discuss research, and 70 percent agreed that their professional identity includes being an educational researcher.

2012: THE POLITICS OF COLLECTIVE AGENCY

In 2012, *Vergara v. California* was focusing public attention on how to fire bad teachers. Alongside this acrimonious lawsuit, LAUSD was forced to make massive layoffs due to budget cuts. The year before the layoffs, in August 2010, the *Los Angeles Times* had recklessly published a database with thousands of teachers' names alongside a measure of how much "value" each had added to their students' standardized test scores. To say that it was a stressful time to be a teacher would be an understatement, yet the narrow and punitive focus on value-added test score measures of teaching quality ignited a teacher-led and university-supported effort to create an alternative, multiple-measures system of teacher evaluation at the UCLA Community School.

Teachers there eagerly adopted individual and collective responsibility to promote exemplary teaching practices, believing that using multiple measures to evaluate teaching practice would increase their knowledge and growth as teachers. They interrogated the measures under development to make sure those measures would help improve teaching. For instance, teachers added open-ended questions to student surveys, pressing students for ways in which teachers could improve. Students made helpful suggestions such as requesting additional explanation of math strategies. Teachers also received scores, broken down by student groups, in areas such as academic challenge and classroom engagement, allowing them to analyze their effectiveness at a granular level. For example, a simple bar graph allowed them to see whether struggling students felt as supported and challenged as high-achieving peers. One teacher, moved to tears by the results, remarked, "These are my students talking to me." Teachers deeply appreciated having feedback that was informed by trustworthy data.

Additionally, the school's principal and assistant principal spent hours observing the teachers in their classrooms, documenting their instructional moves and practices, and debriefing with them on what went well and what could be improved. Teachers also put together a portfolio containing an assignment they gave students, an explanation of how they taught that assignment, and samples of the work students produced. This portfolio was scored by educators trained at UCLA to assess teaching quality on several dimensions, including academic rigor and relevance. Finally, teachers completed a reflection on their scores, saying what they learned from the data and how they planned to improve their teaching.

After they received the student surveys, observations, and portfolio assessments, almost all the teachers reported, via a survey, that they appreciated being evaluated according to multiple measures. Most reported that the measures provided a fair assessment of the quality of their teaching and that the evaluation process helped them grow in their practice. But they also agreed that they needed more information to help them improve their scores. For example, some teachers wanted guidance on making assignments more relevant to students' lives; others asked for additional support reflecting on the observation transcripts. Perhaps most importantly, this new system restored teachers' trust in the evaluation process.[12]

The contributing teachers were enormously proud of this new system and gave upbeat guest lectures and conference presentations about their experiences. Yet, after three years, the workload to sustain this system no longer seemed worth it. The political tides had turned, the debate about value-added models had retreated, and the district had developed a process that seemed sufficient to most. Teachers made a collective decision to focus their finite reform energies elsewhere—illustrating how social justice educators are constantly strategizing about how best to challenge the status quo.

2014: COLLECTIVE AGENCY TO REIMAGINE SCHOOLING

The work of community schools calls for a commitment to the development of entire communities and the interrogation of hegemonic systems that marginalize students and their families. The UCLA Community School seeks to redefine and reimagine public schooling for students of color, for immigrant-origin youth, for LGBTQ+ youth, and for low-income families through a social justice orientation. Within a contextually responsive leadership framework, community schools like the UCLA Community School respond and adapt to the community.[13] The actions of the school community stem from a social justice orientation that embraces an *oppositional imagination* to guide transformative work in education.[14] Social justice leadership embraces specific themes that have been codified in the literature as proactive, transformative, committed, persistent, inclusive, democratic, relational, caring, reflective, and oriented toward a socially just pedagogy that seeks to create a counternarrative about marginalized students and their communities.[15] But what moves the work forward is the praxis of social justice leadership that involves both reflection and action in all the dimensions of the work. And all the dimensions of the work are nested within highly democratic, collaborative, and open spaces that build on the rich experiences of the school's members.

The development of the school's special education inclusion program illustrates how democratic infrastructures help support and advance the work to create affirming educational spaces for students. When the school opened, a significant number of students with disabilities spent the majority of their day in one classroom with one or two teachers. The students were isolated, and their constant behavioral disruptions let the school know the system was not working for them. Owning the school's role in the shortcomings of its special education program was the beginning of a journey to redefine the role of special education for students.

Educators embarked on a disciplined inquiry to test various changes to make special education truly work for students. The first step included professional development for the special education teachers through an instructional framework. But after months of meetings, everyone realized that it was time for something much more innovative. Thanks to the leadership of one special education teacher, the team began researching inclusion models and learning about different implementation options. At a time when inclusion was neither the goal nor the common practice in educational settings, the school decided to reimagine special education classrooms. Special education teachers were ready to embrace the new challenge because it was grounded in social justice and the needs of students. The change was monumental; the first phase of the inclusion program mainstreamed students in the school's English and science courses.

The initial challenges were numerous: insufficient common planning time, reallocation of resources, and facilitating coteaching in different settings. Teachers were given release days to plan together. To ensure buy-in and to allow collective agency to guide the process, teachers developed the agendas. Through the use of various protocols, the collaborative space resulted in the creation of working agreements and expectations. Slowly the coteaching relationship was taking shape. Students were still struggling in core academic classes, so teachers advocated for the creation of a Learning Lab, a space where students would receive additional content support and practice for building necessary skills to access all their academic courses. Another change was the selection of a special education lead teacher to represent the department and the needs of students, families, and teachers participating in the program. This example speaks to educators' ability to think outside existing conditions and reimagine spaces for students who are often marginalized through infrastructures and practices that tend to push them out, rather than include them and build on their strengths. The bumps in the road are ever present, but the collective commitment to developing affirming spaces for students with individualized education plans continues and spurs actions to remove obstacles. The school now hosts teams of teachers, paraprofessionals, and administrators from LAUSD and neighboring districts to share practices and the lessons about inclusion learned along the way. These visits help educators reflect on their trajectory and reinvigorate the school's commitment to emancipatory practices for all students.

2019: COLLECTIVE AGENCY AS ORGANIZING

On January 14, 2019, after months of unsuccessful negotiations between the teacher union and LAUSD, teachers joined hands with students, families, and community members on picket lines across the district. For teachers, the purpose of the six-day strike went beyond pushing for salary increases: they were calling attention to the need for better school funding and the resources that can improve the quality of students' education, including a range of needed social services.

At the UCLA Community School, the decision made by teachers to join their colleagues was about securing better conditions for teaching and learning for all students—not just the one thousand students they served on a daily basis. Based on their shared commitment to educational justice, the strike was an opportunity to emphasize issues of racial equity and the importance of building stronger communities. But for six days the strike disrupted the local community that teachers, administrators, students, and families had worked ten years to establish. For all stakeholders—the administrators who kept the doors of the school open, the teachers who picketed outside the school gates, and the students and families who made the difficult decision to either enter the school or remain outside—established practices tied to understandings of social justice worked to align the strike with the intentional and purposeful pursuit of the collective goals of the school. These schoolwide practices assisted the community in preparing for, experiencing, and healing from the strike.

In one second- and third-grade class, stories like *Click, Clack, Moo: Cows That Type* and *¡Sí, Se Puede! Yes, We Can!: Janitor Strike in L.A.* were used to introduce students to the concept of a strike and how individuals can unite to make change. Once the strike was confirmed, these age-appropriate stories enabled younger students to discuss what the upcoming strike meant for teachers, students, and families. In the upper school, the strike was situated within the context of students' everyday learning. Students shared how they had studied social movements in their government class and had been assigned a final project in which they described how a chosen movement had affected their lives. In their economics class, students had completed a lesson on the Longshore Strike. In their everyday practice, teachers aim to teach students about making positive change by connecting with them, discussing real-world problems, providing multiple perspectives, creating classroom community, and providing opportunities to address issues through social action research projects. The strike brought this learning to life, enabled students to view their teachers as active agents of change, and assisted them in processing the strike's significance. According to one student's reflections, "Expressing voice, bringing change, all these things are tough. [The teachers'] reason [for the strike] was to support others, especially their students. . . . They can bring [about] the difference and change and let the district listen to their voice. That's what I learned. It's not easy."

Community circles—an established practice used across the school—created an important space for students to ask difficult questions about the strike. In the upper grades, students facilitated community circles, exploring their own actions in light of the strike. In describing a student-facilitated community circle, a student shared how the discussion ranged from addressing questions such as "What happens if your parents say that you can't stay home?" to a deep conversation responding to "What does the strike mean, what is the goal, and what can we do?"

For many students in the upper grades, the strike provided an opportunity to exercise their own agency. In addition to the facilitation of community circles, students called lunchtime meetings to share information and dispel myths and mobilized students districtwide to rally alongside teachers to demand educational justice. According to students, their ability to play these active roles was nurtured by the school community: "It is the sense of community and the support from the teachers and the administration [that] plays a big role in students [feeling they] are able to speak up."

Throughout the six-day strike, administrators played the vital role of reminding the entire community that they were unified in their collective vision for educational justice. On the fifth day, as picketing persisted outside the school gates and students and families continued to wrestle with the decision to enter or not, administrators organized a brief respite. With a mariachi band serenading, those inside the gates joined those outside. Through hugs and tears, they were reminded of their shared goals. As one student shared, it takes "the sacrifice of a momentary pause to create a better community."

SUSTAINING SOCIAL JUSTICE EDUCATORS

These five stories of collective agency bring to life the everyday struggles of advancing educational justice in urban schools. First, the shared vision for social justice must be in the school's DNA and must be constantly revisited. For example, after the federal election in 2016, lead teachers developed a social justice checklist of instructional practices to reaffirm the school's commitment to equitable and inclusive teaching at a political moment that threatened the school's immigrant students and families. And two years after that, the UCLA Law School established an Immigrant Family Legal Clinic on campus to further advance the school's social justice vision. As the school has developed over the past decade, its social justice vision has served as a strong rudder to guide collective action.

The bilingual education story foregrounds collaborative inquiry and scholarship as essential to the identity of social justice educators. Standing back to reflect on and analyze practice has not only propelled innovations such as the RISA but also created a workplace culture that embraces the complexity of teaching and learning—countering efforts to script and control the work of teachers. The teacher evaluation story builds on this theme. Developing multiple measures of good teaching and using them to learn was a powerful political statement at a reform moment that threatened to reduce good teaching to a single test score. Similarly, the special education inclusion story foregrounds the oppositional imagination needed to go beyond the status quo—exercising collective agency to imagine a new way to counter the marginalization of students with disabilities. The final story, about the Los Angeles teachers' strike, is a more typical narrative about collective agency and the power of social movements. Yet embedded in this and the other stories is also a powerful narrative about community and the importance of sustaining one another to continue the fight.

The annual teacher turnover rate at the UCLA Community School is lower than the national average for Title I schools (11 percent versus 16 percent).[16] In the early days, it was much lower, as the founding staff immersed themselves in the work of starting a new school. Despite the high retention rate, however, about half of the school's educators, when asked whether the workload is sustainable, report either that they are not sure or that it is not sustainable. This contrast between high retention and unsustainability sparks thoughtful conversation at the school. Most recently, the discourse has included the growing community schools movement and its focus on the range of supports marginalized students need to succeed in school. The work feels unsustainable, in part, because the challenges facing students and their families can feel insurmountable at times. By distributing and coordinating the work of addressing deep societal inequities, community schools—as the 2019 Los Angeles strike poster says—build democracy.

BUILDING DEMOCRACY THROUGH COMMUNITY SCHOOLS

In 1927, John Dewey wrote, "Democracy must begin at home, and its home is the neighborly community."[17] The century-old community schools movement sparked by Jane Addams, Dewey, and many others is experiencing a renaissance tied to collective impact reforms, such as the Harlem Children's Zone and federal Promise Neighborhood initiatives, as well as mounting research evidence that the community schools strategy is effective at connecting enriched academic learning with supports for social and emotional development. The four pillars of community schools are integrated student supports, expanded and enriched learning time and opportunities, family and community engagement, and collaborative leadership and practice.[18] As a framework, these four mutually reinforcing pillars help us see how the work of schools involves the work of many. Though educators—as community teachers—are at the heart of community schools, the movement recognizes that disrupting the deeply entrenched inequities that define life in America for urban youth requires mobilizing the collective agency of social workers, psychologists, lawyers, nurses, librarians, food service workers, artists, and many others.

An important question for the community schools movement is how it can expand the work of teaching while also attending to the problem of sustainability. For example, Matthew A. Kraft and his coauthors examined how teachers and administrators in high-poverty urban schools orient the work of their school as an open system, expanding teaching work to include serving on student support teams, engaging with parents, and interacting with the many uncertainties related to the complex social, health, and economic factors facing students living in poverty.[19] The authors found that teachers' ability to manage work in this environment depended on systematic organizational responses for supporting teachers. This chapter has tried to capture how one organization, the UCLA Community School, developed a workplace culture that supports teachers' collective agency to make a difference in the local community—alongside parents, students, university partners, and many others. This culture is defined by respectful, supported, and productive collaboration to solve problems, such as how to educate in two languages, evaluate teachers, or mainstream students with disabilities. The culture is deeply democratic and reflexive. It's routine to ask, "Does this advance social justice?" It's also a culture with a powerful and particular history that continues to define and sustain all members of the school community.

On March 5, 2018, the children and grandchildren of César Chávez and Robert F. Kennedy joined students, parents, and teachers in the school's Cocoanut Grove auditorium. They had all come together to commemorate the fiftieth anniversary of Chávez's historic twenty-five-day fast in Delano. The event is memorialized in the school's library mural, Kennedy sharing a piece of bread with Chávez, honoring the solidarity of the United Farm Workers (UFW) and other struggles for civil rights. Between the two men in the mural stands UFW cofounder Dolores Huerta, who was by Chávez's side when he broke the fast in Delano and by Kennedy's side at the podium in the Embassy Ballroom, now the school's library, three months later, on June 5, 1968, the night he was assassinated. On that spring day in 2018, to a packed and hushed audience, Ms. Huerta shared her experience working with both Chávez and Kennedy for the rights of farm workers and for social justice. She ended with a chant that felt suspended in time. Repeat after me, "Sí Se Puede!"

CHAPTER 10

Mann UCLA Community School

Reimagining and Restoring a Neighborhood Public School

Carrie Usui Johnson, Orlando Johnson, Ung-Sang Lee, Christine Shen, and Carla Estes

HORACE MANN JUNIOR HIGH SCHOOL opened in 1926 as a pioneer in community schooling, offering expanded services such as meals and afterschool programs to neighborhood youth. Named after a founder of American public education, the school has anchored our South Los Angeles community for nearly a century—providing hope, in Mann's words, that education is "the great equalizer of the conditions of men."[1]

In this chapter, we share the school's recent history, a familiar story in communities of color across the nation who are struggling to keep their historic neighborhood schools open. The backdrop is declining enrollment and public divestment in an era of expanding school choices and market-based reforms. In 2016, Mann's enrollment had fallen to 330 students and faced heavy competition from the thirty-seven charter schools within a 2.5-mile radius of the school. As a result of these trends, the University of California, Los Angeles (UCLA), partnered with the school and neighborhood community to reimagine and restore the school.

Our story has three parts. We set the stage by sharing how the neighborhood's history informed the partnership's social justice vision. We then describe the process of building trust across our institutions. We conclude the chapter with a discussion of the structures and democratic processes we helped create over three years, in hope that our narrative can help others engaged in the collaborative revitalization of urban neighborhood schools.

BUILDING ON COMMUNITY HISTORY

The Mann-UCLA partnership was formed during one of the school's most challenging periods, with historically low enrollment, unstable staffing, and threat of being closed. It was also built in response to a long history of public neglect of the neighborhood, both in its educational resources and its broader public infrastructure. Below is a brief history of the school to center our partnership vision.

Our school is located in the Chesterfield Square neighborhood of South Los Angeles—a neighborhood that resembles other segregated urban neighborhoods across the country. Such neighborhoods are characterized by diverse and varied cultural assets and histories of political and civic engagement that contrast with the many forms of inequity and systemic violence the communities have experienced and continue to contend with. Since its opening in 1926, Horace Mann Junior High School has been shaped by its community's history. In the 1930s, racially restrictive housing covenants led to a predominantly White student population that peaked in enrollment in the 1940s, when students were bused to Mann from other communities. During the 1960s, discontent and anger at the inequities and racism levied against Black communities through housing discrimination and low-paying jobs erupted in nearby Watts and communities just east of Mann. At the same time, with housing restrictions loosening, White flight from the neighborhood led to an increase in Black students, and in the 1970s, Latinx students.[2]

In the late 1970s, in response to the court-ordered requirement to desegregate schools, the Los Angeles Unified School District started programs to desegregate schools like Mann, introducing magnets and a permit-with-transfer program. The permit-with-transfer program put students on buses from places like South Los Angeles to more affluent schools across the city. While intended to solve the inequities in education in Los Angeles, it also took resources, both monetary and human, out of the neighborhood schools. While there were many attempts to revitalize schools like Mann during the 1980s and 1990s, such as changing from a grades 7–9 junior high school to a grades 6–8 middle school, for many families the draw of sending their children to other schools in "safer" neighborhoods proved to be too great, leading to a consistent decline in enrollment that continued until 2017.

The Los Angeles uprising in 1992 brought police violence against Black people to the forefront when four Los Angeles police officers caught violently assaulting Rodney King on video were acquitted. While media and reporting focused on this injustice as an isolated incident that exploded into violence for three days across South Los Angeles and all the way north into Koreatown, the reality is the Los Angeles uprising was a response to generations of racism and inequities in the Black community.[3] The slow-burning resentment of decades became a blaze fueled by the public dismissal of police violence. Mann, which is near significant sites of the uprising, has suffered from public association of the area with the "LA riots" and the underlying history of inequities that led to the uprisings in the first place. As a result, the school was stigmatized as unsafe, which drove down enrollment.

In the fall of 1992, less than five months after the Los Angeles uprising, the California State Legislature passed the Charter Schools Act of 1992. For the community surrounding Mann, this legislation accelerated the decline in enrollment already spurred by busing. Between

2000 and 2017, thirty-seven charter schools opened within a 2.5-mile radius of the school and enrollment plummeted from 1,800 students to 330. Multiple top-down reforms were enacted to keep the school alive, including reconstitution. The situation was further exacerbated by the passage of Proposition 39 in 2000, legislation that allowed charter schools to apply for and receive space on public school campuses if classrooms there went unused on a daily basis. There were multiple bids to share the physical space at Mann, including a successful one in 2017 that lasted one year and caused additional turmoil on campus. It was at the end of this harrowing progression toward near-complete divestment and school closure that school stakeholders, district leaders, and university researchers began the gradual process of collaborative revitalization in 2014.

REPAIRING TRUST ACROSS THE SCHOOL, UNIVERSITY, AND COMMUNITY

Inheriting Eroded Trust

When the school and UCLA initiated discussions to form a partnership to revitalize public education in the neighborhood, it was evident that trust between the neighborhood community and the school had eroded considerably over the years. We recognized that the considerable decline in enrollment at Mann was a sign that the community, particularly students and parents, had lost faith in their neighborhood school. Reimagining Horace Mann Middle School into the Mann UCLA Community School, which would be both middle school and high school, would require rebuilding trust within the community, including students, parents, longtime community members, and the teachers and staff who had seen a revolving door of reform efforts start at the school and peter out. Instead of making assumptions about why families were choosing not to attend Mann, we conducted surveys and focus groups with community members to learn why they were choosing other schools. The responses from the surveys and small focus groups illustrated the community's mistrust of the school. One parent who had generations of family attend Mann stated, "You can't fix Mann. Why don't you just blow it up and start over?" Students said, "Mann is a school for the leftover kids" and "no one cares about me at this school." It was clear that to build a truly just and equitable community school, we had to regain the trust of the community.

Teachers at Mann also shared feelings of skepticism and mistrust of what seemed to them just one more reform movement to try to "fix Mann" and of the power imbalance between the school and the university. Early feedback from the staff included a wide variety of responses, from hopeful to "I've been through this before." One response in particular highlighted the challenge of building bridges between a university represented by mainly White and Asian leadership and a school with a predominantly Black and Latinx staff:

> Ms. Bailey was hesitant to develop a partnership with another organization out of fear of becoming a "Pocahontas" story, where University would be viewed as coming in and "saving" the school. Ms. Bailey explained that she did not want it to have been a situation "where [the university], a school that doesn't accept a whole lot of 'us,' coming in and trying to be the White savior for these Black people that they're still not letting in their school."[4]

Ms. Bailey's words highlight the multiple levels of power imbalance that school-university partnerships must grapple with.

We saw in the surveys and interviews some common threads related to establishing trusting relationships in the partnership. There was a tension between the sense of community and belonging at Mann and the lack of a sense of safety there. Community members who had gone through earlier changes and top-down reforms expressed a lack of confidence that efforts to improve the school would persist. They also expressed an assumption that a high-quality education could not be obtained in their own community and suspicion about the motivations behind a university partnership.

Building a Foundation for Trust: Collaborative Governance

Reimagining and reinvesting in a community where promises had often been made and broken required a high level of commitment to listening, challenging assumptions and beliefs, visibility, and follow-through.[5] While all the stakeholders involved in reimagining Mann into a community school (the district, local district, school staff, community members, and UCLA) had a common revitalization goal, our individual understandings of how that goal would be attained varied widely. Building trusting relationships across all levels of the partnership and trust in the process needed to be at the center of the work.[6]

The teachers' and community's skepticism toward the school and the school-university partnership spurred us to take immediate steps to show that efforts to revitalize public schooling in the neighborhood would be responsive to community needs and committed to ongoing improvements and would deliver concrete benefits to students and the community. Trust building in the partnership started at the highest levels, among district, school, and university leadership. Challenges to building trust at higher levels stemmed from the starts and stops in the conversations about establishing the partnership, which started in 2014 and continued until 2016 because of changes in institutional regimes and policies.

At the district level, there were other challenges. Mann had been part of the district's Intensive Support and Innovation Center (ISIC), an office created to support low-performing schools and small, innovative schools. ISIC had some autonomy to engage in partnership building. But ISIC was disbanded, and Mann was reintegrated into its original local district, with new district leadership and priorities.

Slowly, we refined our vision of the partnership to meet the needs of institutional leaders and to align it with the pillars of community schooling.[7] These pillars include collaborative leadership, integrated student supports, expanded learning time and opportunities, and family and community engagement. To build trust, it was necessary to create democratic structures for collaboration and decision-making. The partners formed a design team with representation from both the school (administrators, teachers, and students) and UCLA (staff, researchers, and faculty). This team was tasked with initial problem-solving, data collection, and creation of proposals for the larger Mann community to approve. Creating processes for community members to participate in the partnership design was another key step in initial trust building. The UCLA leadership continued to attend difficult meetings and recruited key members of the Mann community to participate in planning the partnership.

Much of the initial trust building occurred while the school and university stakeholders were still developing a blueprint document for the partnership, through the successful joint implementation of partnership programs that met the school's immediate needs. To facilitate these programs, it was essential to have a direct liaison who knew the university well and could work closely with Mann leadership on a daily basis. Listening to the school stakeholders' needs and goals allowed the liaison to connect the school with appropriate university resources. This visible, on-the-ground work built an essential bridge between the school and university.

For example, during the summer of 2016—before the official start of the partnership—we offered the first Mann UCLA Community School summer institute, a seven-week program that was an extension of the district-offered summer school. Through the summer institute, one hundred Mann students attended an enrichment program with both Mann and UCLA teacher leaders that culminated with a weeklong trip to UniCamp, a sleepaway camp in Big Bear run by UCLA students. This first student experience showed the current students and their families why they should continue at Mann, especially as Mann expanded to include high school. The summer institute and UniCamp showed students what the full Mann UCLA Community School experience would be like—hands-on and relevant instruction that would be useful beyond the classroom and engage students in fun experiences and activities.

While we were negotiating the trust-building structures, the work of creating the plan also had to move forward. We collected data from the different stakeholders about what they hoped to see happen as a result of the partnership with UCLA, and the Mann design team synthesized that data to create a governance structure that would model the democratic practices needed to respond as a community school. The team felt that the existing governance model and collective bargaining agreement between the teachers and the district were not sufficient to allow autonomies that would reverse the years of divestment from the school and community. After careful review of all the governance models available to district schools, the team decided to use a Local Initiative School (LIS) governance model, which would enable the staff, students, families, and leadership to determine ideal policies to improve the school, maximize student learning, and construct broader school governance structures. The LIS governance model offered the ability to determine local policy in areas including governance, staffing, professional development, instruction, and school organization.

With this decision made and with input from all stakeholders, the design team crafted the following school vision: "Mann UCLA Community School will be a cornerstone for high-quality education in Chesterfield Square. Our students will enter the adult world as confident and capable human beings, prepared to succeed in college, pursue meaningful careers, participate in our democracy, and become agents of change for our community." To make this vision a reality at Mann UCLA Community School, we then began to undertake the work of restoring the school community through staffing, recruitment, and sustained professional learning: the next challenge in reimagining a more democratic and responsive community school.

In reflecting on these efforts, the lessons of this initial partnership work are clear. The process of transformation must contend with stakeholder mistrust built over decades of community divestment and traditional governance structures that are not conducive to community participation. The school design team was able to win the community's trust only by listening fully to stakeholders and delivering positive outcomes well before the partnership was formalized. As we moved from reimagining and crafting the plan to implementing and sustaining the plan, the challenge of maintaining trust continued to be a balancing act.

COLLABORATIONS THAT SUSTAIN COMMUNITY SCHOOLING

As the design team was finalizing the school vision, the work of rebuilding the school had begun. This process was initiated without the luxury of a planning year or pilot testing, and while attending to the school's daily operations. Additionally, while the university partnership did receive some grant funding, it was not nearly enough to implement all of the plans. To address these challenges, we identified three initial priorities based on staff and community voices. These included staffing and professional development, student and community enrichment and services, and the implementation of democratic governance. In this section, we discuss how sustained collaboration among school stakeholders drove improvements in these three key areas.

Staffing and Professional Development

Can we just get a qualified teacher to be with my child? Why has she had subs the entire year?

—Parent

Can we find better teachers?

—Student

During the 2015–2016 school year, when the formal partnership plans were initiated, nearly half the teaching staff were substitute teachers, and in a particularly egregious case, all seventh-grade teachers were substitutes. This was a chronic problem at Mann. Staffing Mann with highly effective instructors that believed in the school was, to say the least, challenging.[8] Mann had developed a reputation as an undesirable work environment, making it difficult to hire teachers who were committed to working in the community. With several positions unfilled every year, Mann needed to accept "must-place" teachers (individuals who had been in a pool of displaced teachers for more than a year because of declining enrollment or poor performance, or because they had returned from a leave and had yet to be hired by a school). Not only did that leave Mann with some teachers who were disgruntled because of their forced placement, in many cases must-place teachers would just not show up on the first day of school. If Mann was to fulfill the vision set forth by the partnership, sustained staffing needed to be a core component of the process.

The LIS governance plan and the UCLA partnership helped break this cycle of understaffing. The LIS governance plan allowed the school to interrupt the reliance on must-place and substitute teachers, while the university's Teacher Education Program director and faculty advisors helped identify high-quality candidates. They recruited teachers who were invested in working at Mann and willing and able to engage in rebuilding the school, which required them to build trust with the community, work in challenging classroom environments, and lead the development of innovative curricula and instructional practices as a new teacher.

The UCLA Teacher Education Program (UCLA TEP) helped provide high-quality instruction for all students, especially given its focus on social justice and placing teachers in schools with vulnerable student populations. In the first full year of the partnership, UCLA TEP was able to help Mann fill most of the vacant positions so that for the first time in five years there were no vacant positions at the start of the school year in 2017. However, filling the positions was only the first step in restoring a collective staff of highly skilled and effective instructors at Mann. With large variations in teacher skills, expertise, and practices, supporting the whole staff to unite under one instructional vision while also recognizing their diverse assets was challenging. It required constant reflection, revision, and differentiation for all of us who were planning and providing professional development.

Creating a responsive, inclusive, and effective professional learning plan was critical if Mann UCLA Community School's faculty were to fully embrace the mission and vision of the school. In the partnership proposal, the school had articulated an instructional model called Learn-See-Do. This model, based on project-based learning and culturally relevant pedagogy, was a huge departure from existing instructional frameworks, and it required collaborative learning and planning by the staff that had not previously been the norm. The school responded by developing an alternative professional development schedule that would give teachers more time to collaborate. Together, the staff agreed to a new block schedule that would allow two mornings a week to be used for professional development. In addition, funds were allocated to provide summer retreats focused on planning to implement the school instructional vision, with content-area coaches and other UCLA staff.

While the opportunities to engage in collaborative learning and planning as a staff increased, the simultaneous focus on the instructional vision and the current instructional reality for both the leadership and the teachers made it difficult to meet everyone's professional learning needs. In initial interviews with the teachers about the importance of an engaging, culturally relevant, and challenging curriculum, all of those interviewed saw implementing that kind of curriculum as very important. Many teachers who were interviewed also discussed the challenge of developing a rigorous curriculum based on the new instructional framework. It was not until the summer, when they were given full days of department learning and planning with a UCLA content coach, that teachers reported feeling more supported in this vision.[9]

The summer retreats served two main purposes: first, to bring the staff together around the idea of Learn-See-Do through collaboration to get everyone on the same instructional page, and second, to provide opportunities for team and relationship building. While overall we received positive feedback from the staff, it was complex and challenging to create a professional learning plan that would support the diverse needs of a school in transformation. On the one hand, many teachers felt the summer retreats provided needed quality time to collaboratively plan for the new instructional vision and develop relationships, especially with the new teachers. On the other hand, some teachers questioned the focus on instructional planning, feeling that schoolwide routines and classroom management should have been the focus. The expansive learning needs were especially overwhelming for new teachers, one of whom said, laughing, "We were floundering; we were just like 'what do we do?' We had no idea how to do anything; we were gasping for air."[10] This tension required us to be more flexible and fluid with the professional development plan, adding different support structures that included targeted supports for new teachers, in-class support through UCLA instructional coaches, and more of a focus on departmental collaboration time.

Supporting the professional learning of the staff greatly improved the stability in staffing. Each year, fewer teachers needed to be hired, and the school was able to attract more experienced teachers wanting to teach at a school like Mann UCLA Community School. At a school that had struggled to keep teachers from leaving throughout the school year, the first year of the partnership saw no teachers leave midyear. Now, three years into the partnership, six out of the nine original new teachers remain, and each year fewer teachers are hired to fill vacancies (some new hires are a result of the addition of the high school). Collaborative and responsive professional learning helped the school attract and retain high-quality teachers.

As the faculty became more stable—with full-time permanent staff instead of an influx of long-term substitutes—and more cohesive through relationship building, the school focused on a comprehensive, integrated professional development plan that

- aligned all curriculum with the unified mission and vision;
- created meaningful assessments to determine the mastery level of the students and the effectiveness of instructional and school-wide strategies;
- built the instructional leadership capacity of all stakeholders;
- developed and supported culturally relevant curriculum; and
- strengthened the content knowledge and pedagogical skills of the faculty.

Collaborative partnerships that develop and empower all members of the community in continuous improvement is a critical element for the sustainability of the mission of the school. Focused on relationship building, instructional collaborative partnerships not only strengthen teachers' content and pedagogical knowledge, they also develop teachers' individual and collective efficacy and interdependence. The instructional collaborative partnerships that the Mann UCLA Community School teachers engaged in, such as instructional coaching and teacher improvement science networks, created safe spaces to push their thinking and uncover best practices for teaching and learning at Mann.

For example, Mann UCLA Community School math and science teachers were members of the UCLA Partner School Network, a collaborative professional development network informed by improvement science,[11] in which local teachers critically explore their instructional practices, using student work and assessments as a guide. Of this experience, one Mann UCLA Community School math teacher stated, "In our partnership to improve math instruction, we ask questions like 'how will we revolutionize the way we teach?' There's no such thing as going back to the way it was." This opportunity to transform their own instruction created a level of participatory action for sustained and continuous learning communities and continuity with the overall mission and vision of the school.

Student and Family Enrichment and Services

A sustained commitment to social justice, achievable with a stable teaching staff, allowed us to focus on student experience. It was evident that if the school wanted to restore and rebuild the student population at Mann, it needed to provide engaging, equity-producing educational experiences and services for the students and broader neighborhood community. While student enrollment, which nearly doubled in the first three years of the partnership, served as one indicator of improved relationships between the school and the community, the new opportunities for enrichment and services would serve as a measure of the school's successful implementation of its vision. Therefore, the school–university partnership was leveraged to develop enrichment activities and expand on critical services for students and their families.

We saw enrichment beyond traditional academic outcomes as a key component of the school's social justice–focused mission, so we sought to deepen and expand student learning opportunities that privileged the assets and experiences of students. Collaborative partnerships with departments at UCLA gave students additional opportunities to see themselves in real-life applications of learning that were relevant and personal.

When Mann UCLA Community School students engaged with the UCLA School of Theatre, Film, and Television (TFT) for a ten-day summer workshop, "Finding Your Voice, Telling Your Story," the students transformed their personal stories into a fictional genre, such as horror or romantic comedy, while also learning the craft of filmmaking through screenwriting, lighting, and cinematography. This collaborative partnership helped students see that their personal stories have value and see themselves working in the entertainment industry: "TFT heightened my interest and gave me a pathway to pursue my dream job in movie production," said student Xavier Alejo. The experience opened the students' eyes to future possibilities and empowered them to pursue opportunities at the school. One student volunteered to write a screenplay for the middle school students at Mann, and another started a creative writing club.[12] The experience with TFT demonstrates how schooling can be reimagined for students at a school like Mann by investing in their personal experiences to empower them in their education and beyond. It put the power of learning back into the hands of the students.

Democratic Governance

As Mann UCLA Community School implemented its blueprint for community schooling, we considered it vital to engage all stakeholders in practicing democratic governance to privilege student and community assets. While the original partnership plan included a democratic governance structure, some stakeholders engaged in the considerable work of building the organizational infrastructure, culture, and routines that brought the democratic governance vision to life.

The governance subcommittees included a diverse set of stakeholders that would lead key school initiatives. These subcommittees included, among others, the Data and Research Committee, which tracked key school improvement measures through surveys and interviews; the Integrated Student Services Committee, which was tasked with developing critical services for students such as mental health supports; and the Community Outreach Committee, which was tasked with bringing family and community members into broader school initiatives.

When the work first started in these subcommittees, they were still made up mostly of teachers and UCLA partners, and work was rarely coordinated across committees. This was effective in getting some of the foundational work for the school off the ground, as each subcommittee carried out urgent tasks that served the immediate needs of the school. However, knowing that we needed to bring synergy, relevance, and broader participation to the subcommittees, the school engaged in a number of steps to refine the democratic governance structure.

The first step was to better define each subcommittee in relation to the broader school vision. During one end-of-year schoolwide meeting, members of subcommittees were asked to reflect upon their work and goals in relation to each other and the larger school mission and initiatives. Then the subcommittees were asked to choose a superhero or mascot to represent each committee. As the subcommittees shared their work and goals, they asked each other questions and made connections between their work. The session ended with each subcommittee creating a visual representation of their committee's goals and identity.

We all cheered when the Student Experience Committee shared that their mascot, "We Are Mann!" or "WAM!," was an auditory mascot—a cheer—because it captured the feeling of what the Student Experience Committee wanted to create for students at Mann. Each subcommittee developed an explicit, outward-facing identity and clarified who they were within Mann's democratic governance structure. The session culminated with the development of individual subcommittee webpages that stated their overall mission, goals for the school year, key data points from previous school years, and latest updates. These details and updates were accessible to all stakeholders across the subcommittees on a shared website to encourage ongoing communication and alignment.

We have been learning that the type of democratic governance that we hoped to build requires ongoing refinement to the structure of governance and its mission. While we tried to synergize the work of the subcommittees to advance the school's vision, the subcommittee members in the early stages were predominantly school and UCLA staff struggling to recruit families and students into the collaborative work. Furthermore, despite the efforts mentioned above, the subcommittees still needed considerable work to strike a balance between being efficiently and effectively aligned with one another's work and privileging the leadership and judgment of its members.

The ground-up organizing by teachers, students, parents, and UCLA researchers, in response to the racialized tragedies of the COVID-19 outbreak and police violence, served as the next significant impetus to revamp the democratic governance structure. Over the summer of 2020, a group of nearly thirty teachers, students, families, and UCLA researchers from both UCLA Community School in Koreatown and Mann UCLA Community School campuses volunteered to meet weekly to strategize about how the school could push its antiracist social justice agenda further during the upcoming academic school year. The group, self-named the UCLA Community School Anti-Racist Committee (ARC), had identified key areas of school practice, including restorative justice, student activism, family engagement, and culturally relevant curricula and instruction, as priority areas where the school could refine its practices to advance the school vision. As those participating in the summer meetings brainstormed how to pursue local antiracist goals in the school, we determined that the subcommittees were well positioned to put some of the ideas developing in ARC into practice.

At the beginning of the school year, we proposed a new structure for democratic governance to teachers and administrators in a presentation to all school staff members. ARC would serve as an intermediary between the broad school vision and the work of the subcommittees, steering the governance work to more explicitly center antiracism and social justice by planning and facilitating deeper collaboration between the committees. Furthermore, ARC and the subcommittees would commit to and prioritize recruiting students and families into subcommittees. The school staff was receptive to the proposal, and at the time of this writing, the ARC team is planning a large community gathering that introduces the work of ARC, with the goal of recruiting students and families as deep partners in articulating and implementing antiracist work at the school. By doing so, we hope to further embed our school's social justice mission into the neighborhood community and ensure that the success of the school mirrors the empowerment of the neighborhood.

LESSONS LEARNED AND QUESTIONS FOR THE FUTURE

Improving the student experience at Mann required balancing feedback from the students, families, and community and having the resources, both monetary and human, to execute better experiences in response. From bringing in more human resources to increase a sense of safety on campus to laying out the plan for a California Interscholastic Federation–approved athletics program to starting student clubs and enrichment programs, each step required making decisions based on what's available now and what we will be able to build for the future. We had a wish list for grant, foundation, and UCLA funders to send students to UniCamp, donate sports equipment, and sponsor student activities—initiatives that, in other schools, booster clubs, PTAs, and the district might have undertaken. Further, with each new grade added to the high school, the activities and needs grow, pushing us to envision new ways of partnering in order to keep growing the reimagined vision for Mann UCLA Community School.

Reimagining and reinvesting in public schooling at Mann UCLA Community School is an ongoing learning process that requires creativity, flexibility, and reflexivity. In three short years of reinvesting in the school and community, we are seeing changes in the culture and community take root. We see the staff stability leading to more collaboration and openness to instructional changes that are relevant, responsive, and rigorous for the students. We see more community resources located on campus, making the school a community hub for healing, empowerment, and action. We see the students taking ownership of their learning and seeing themselves in careers. We have learned so much and continue to have questions as we move into the future, especially one that has become full of uncertainties and change.

We have learned that reversing a history of injustice is more challenging than we could have ever imagined and requires clear and consistent action for effective communication and building trust. It has been a challenge to create the level of transparency needed for all stakeholders to feel meaningfully involved, especially while collaboratively reinvesting in a school reeling from the effects of historical public divestment. What's most important is that we continue to communicate, in multiple ways, the ultimate goals of the partnership, why those goals are important to the community and the school, and how as leaders of the school we will involve the community in reaching those goals and then move forward with actions that match that communication.

We have also learned that partnering across multiple organizations requires being open to conflict, mistakes, and setbacks. Keeping everyone focused on the goal of the partnership is important; there will always be differences of opinion about how to implement the goal. Working within a system means facing its policy, funding, and relational limitations. Each partner must work within their own system and with their partners' systems. Sometimes the systems are aligned—for instance, the university and the district had the shared goal of supporting community schooling. Sometimes they aren't—for instance, when stakeholders differ significantly on how to make decisions or allocate resources. These differences, while they can slow down the work and cause conflict, force us to be more creative in solving problems when there are roadblocks and limited resources.

As we look to the future of community schooling at Mann UCLA Community School, we will continue to ask ourselves the following questions:

- With the world changing so quickly, how will we continue to reinvest in the community and adapt to these changes, which go far beyond the school walls?
- What are some of the ways we will continue to create sustainable structures for leadership across stakeholders in the school?
- As we prepare for our first graduating class of seniors at Mann UCLA Community School, how will we keep graduates con-

nected to the school and community to create a cycle of investment that will span generations?

The work of Mann UCLA Community School is rewarding, humbling, and, at its core, the embodiment of what it means to transform urban public schooling to create a more just, equitable, and humane society. We can see the future at Mann UCLA Community School, and the future is bright.

CHAPTER 11

We Asked for Trouble

Jeannie Oakes

THIS BOOK BEGAN WITH "Making the Rhetoric Real," the piece I wrote twenty-five years ago to document UCLA's Center X and its roots in the uprising that followed the not-guilty verdict in the Los Angeles police beating of Rodney King. Our aspiration, audacity, and, I hope, our humility are all on display in the conclusion of that piece:

> Using our powerful symbolism of the university and the extraordinary talent of the educators in the university and the schools, the staff at Center X have committed to the view—however idealistic—that schools and teaching for low-income, racially, culturally, and linguistically diverse children can change. We've also asked for a whole lot of trouble, and in fact, we've gotten lots. As I read what I've written here, I realize that sentences and paragraphs strung together make our efforts sound far tidier than they are. We're struggling to do something we really don't know how to do. We're asking questions we don't know how to answer. We frustrate many of our partnering educators who want more clarity and definition of our

program than we can provide. We worry some of our colleagues who think we're too ideological. We anger some of our students when we won't give them a safety net of classroom management strategies and structured lesson-planning procedures that we think will create more problems than they will solve. We ask everyone to tolerate our ambiguity. We're not being realistic. We work too hard. We work our students too hard. We expect too much.

Frankly, we wouldn't have it any other way. We don't expect to stop the fires from coming again to Los Angeles. But next time, we'll know that we tried.

For almost thirty years, UCLA educators have followed an ambitious social and educational agenda. Together, we dismantled a highly rated traditional teacher-preparation program whose student teachers and graduates were recruited by the most highly regarded schools in Los Angeles and across the country. We rebuilt the curriculum and pedagogy, and we redrew our geographic and demographic boundaries. We raised the banner of social justice at a time when the concept seemed dangerously radical. Over the years, the Center X community has worked with thousands of educators—novices and veterans—to bring outstanding teaching to young people across a much-expanded spectrum of public schools.

As the Center X team was finishing the chapters of this book in the summer of 2020, the anguish of the racial reckoning made us examine what we have done to disrupt the racial injustice that still pervades our society. In creating Center X, we set out to change public education—not only in the common parlance of "improvement," but structurally, systemically, and equitably. We believed that our job was to make our national rhetoric of justice and equality real. But all these years later, public education in Los Angeles still perpetuates inequities that underlie the enraged plea that Black Lives Matter. Our children of color enter a school system on unequal footing; they experience unequal schooling; and this inequality is manifest in their schooling outcomes and in the life chances that schooling helps to shape. Even so, the narratives in this book allow us, in the anguish of this moment, to retain our aspirations and audacity alongside our much-deepened humility.

A COMMITMENT TO TROUBLE

When congressman and civil rights icon John Lewis died in July 2020, his words—repeated everywhere—brought strange comfort. In particular, five short sentences encapsulate the force that drove conversations that led to Center X, even as we looked out the windows at a burning Los Angeles:[1]

> We have been too quiet for too long. There comes a time when you have to say something. You have to make a little noise. You have to move your feet. This is the time.

Lewis asked the *New York Times* to publish an inspiring essay on the day he was buried—his words there speak to both our initial ambition and our current determination to continue in the face of disappointment in the persistence of injustice. Reflecting on what he had learned from Dr. King, Lewis wrote:[2]

> [W]e are all complicit when we tolerate injustice. He said it is not enough to say it will get better by and by. He said each of us has a moral obligation to stand up, speak up and speak out. When you see something that is not right, you must say something. You must do something. Democracy is not a state. It is an act, and each generation must do its part to help build what we called the Beloved Community, a nation and world society at peace with itself. . . . Ordinary people with extraordinary vision can redeem the soul of America by getting in what I call good trouble, necessary trouble.

"Good trouble, necessary trouble": I won't pretend that Center X measures up to Lewis's full meaning, but I am sure that our work has been in its spirit. The brilliant and inspiring UCLA educators in the chapters here show how they continue to seize moments when, in the words of Lewis, it is time to "say something," "make a little noise," and they move their feet.

What makes "trouble" good and necessary (and productive) instead of infuriating and divisive? In the introduction to this volume, Annamarie Francois and Karen Hunter Quartz trace the idea of "beloved community" from Royce to King, and we again meet the idea here in Lewis's formulation. We might admirably face our individual troubles, but the struggle for justice in education cannot be borne without a beloved community. The day-to-day acts (moving one's feet) of helping teachers struggle to become transformative professionals in schools serving students who are racially, culturally, linguistically marginalized and often poor requires the nurturing of a beloved community. Center X educators become caring advocates for all students, reflective inquiry-based practitioners, community builders, and generative change agents. That can happen only because Center X makes its rhetoric real by being itself caring, ethical, racially harmonious, and socially just. Although, to be sure, that too is a struggle.

Because it has been a dozen years since I left UCLA, I asked each of the authors to reflect on whether and how they see the Center X work as an example of ordinary people trying to get into the kind of trouble Lewis meant—trying to achieve racial justice in education. One, who's been with Center X from the beginning, responded that John Lewis's concept truly captures what we have tried to do. She noted that, while there have been ups and downs—hits and misses— overall we kept our focus on disrupting the pervasive injustices in our schools. In fact, we wanted not simply to disrupt, but to truly transform. Another affirmation came from an author who started as a Center X student and teacher candidate in 1998 and, after fifteen years of teaching, returned as a faculty member to support the next generation. She shared that rereading "Making the Rhetoric Real" was emotional because it is true today—we are still asking for trouble. Others' reflections are peppered throughout this essay. I share them with great pride.

PRINCIPLES THAT LEAD TO GOOD TROUBLE

I think we were right when we decided to withstand the trouble we were making by establishing a set of nonnegotiable and public principles. Rather than avoiding trouble, these principles invited challenges and strengthened our commitments. We wanted more than a set of best practices; we were uncertain of what those practices might be; and we knew that, whatever we thought they were then, they would change. So, rather than beginning with a program design, we identified a set of values to guide our decisions and glue our work together.

In addition to the usual indicators of the quality of teacher and leader education—knowledgeable and skilled practitioners who remain in the field—we would use these principles to assess our progress and our reach. In what follows I revisit these principles, providing examples of how they are reflected in today's practices—as articulated by today's Center X educators—and how they have guided "good trouble, necessary trouble."

Embody a Social Justice Agenda

At first, we defined this simply, as turning policy makers' attention, teachers' talents, and resources toward those in our city who have the least outside of school. We limited our programs to those choosing to teach and lead in schools located in underserved neighborhoods of color. As only Angelenos would, we specified neighborhoods with reference to freeways: schools south of the 10 and east of the 405. This was definitely seen as trouble by some university administrators ("You'll destroy the program"), by some colleagues in suburban schools ("Don't white students need social justice as well?"), and by some prospective teacher candidates ("My mom doesn't think it's safe for me to be in those schools").

Over time, we added substance to our social justice agenda, fusing a critical stance on racism and inequality with an insistence that all children have rigorous, authentic learning experiences. As we elaborated in the textbook we wrote for the program in 1998, *Teaching to Change the World*, we wanted to prepare teachers and leaders to look beneath the surface of structures and practices and consider the values and politics that pervade education, even as they mastered the technical aspects of teaching and organizing schools.[3] We wanted them to question how conventional thinking and practice came to be, and who in society benefits from them. We wanted them to note inequalities associated with race, social class, language, gender, and other social categories and seek alternatives to those inequalities.

Our critical stance has evolved over time. In chapter 2, the authors share the most recent articulation of our antiracist, abolitionist practices: reflecting on positionality, developing cultural knowledge, engaging in critical inquiry, and learning critical pedagogical knowledge and skills. But a critical stance, while necessary, is not sufficient. Social justice education also requires *rigorous, authentic learning experiences* that engage teachers and schools in using curricula, teaching practices, and assessments that promote intellectual development and prepare students to be knowledgeable participants in twenty-first century life and capable agents of change. This, we argued, meant engaging students in *constructing knowledge*—whereby they actively integrate new knowledge with their prior learning and experiences. Completing the circle, constructing new knowledge may also mean *deconstructing* other knowledge and cherished traditions. And oh, the troubles that wrought! At the heart of a constructivist approach to learning lies a challenge to seeing teachers as knowledge transmitters and students as passive recipients of facts their teachers give to them.

The teacher evaluation and learning framework described in chapter 3 instantiates both a critical approach and rigorous, authentic learning. The framework—focused on content rigor, content discourse, classroom ecology, and equitable access to content—signals to preservice teachers, mentors, teacher educators, and partners what competencies are core to rigorous and authentic learning experiences. The framework includes tools and concrete examples that guide teachers' progress toward mastering competencies; for example, using classroom talk to support content rigor. However, tools and concrete examples are of limited value unless melded with principles of learning and social justice. In that spirit, chapter 3 shares how to think about teacher evaluation and learning, as much as how to do it.

Treat Professional Education as "Cradle to Grave"

Our second nonnegotiable value is that Center X must simultaneously attract young people to teaching, provide learning experiences for teacher candidates and novice teachers, and scaffold seasoned professionals, including leaders. Structurally, that meant bringing together distinct programs from separate locations in the university and with quite different opinions about how the work would be done. It took a full year of deep conversations about the meaning of (and at times the value of) social justice and learning before we could even begin imagining working together. We used the moniker "Center X" as a placeholder, since we couldn't even agree on what to call this place we were inventing.

It turned out that blending critical social justice values with authentic and rigorous content instruction drew these separate enterprises together. Over time, the impact of engaging educators throughout their careers has been extraordinary. The agenda that we advanced with our teacher candidates came to characterize Center X's work with seasoned educators as well. For example, the professional learning strategies described in chapters 5 and 6 aim at replacing pedagogies of poverty, which have been the norm in so many schools of color and poverty, with transformative practices in which students engage in inquiry, construct knowledge, and solve problems in their communities and the world. Such practices have typically been limited to more advantaged or "gifted" students. Overcoming skepticism about making them the standard approach in every classroom is good and necessary trouble.

This approach also drives UCLA's Principal Leadership Institute (PLI) program—the Center X coursework and clinical experiences that satisfy the state's administrator credentialing requirement. For example, in chapter 7, Letitia Davis, principal at Baldwin Hills Elementary, credited her PLI experience for "fortifying" her actions to integrate social justice values and authentic learning at her school. PLI, she reports, encouraged her to join with "social justice and change agents" committed to connecting the school with the culture and experience of the surrounding neighborhood. She describes the result in a blog post:[4]

> Culturally responsive pedagogical practices, paired with engaging [student] scholars in 21st century skills and competencies, is the frame upon which we build our curriculum. Our students read texts, explore histories, and see reflections of who they are culturally as their first teaching—and as the foundation upon which all other learning is set. This level of relevance shows the level of value we place on our students, recognizing their worth and value as children

of color, and it is a means not just to bring about affirmation and validation but to push the level of rigor.

Notably, Baldwin Hills was named a California Distinguished School in 2020—an honor accorded only to schools that demonstrate exemplary achievement.

High school principal Mauro Bautista, a former Center X teacher and PLI alum, sees making good trouble as simply part of the job. His successful pushback against random student-search policies initiated by the district included meeting with his school board member, talking with parents, and expressing his views on local cable television. Mauro knows well that principals are supposed to defer to and enact line authority. But Mauro sees himself as accountable to his community and principles of justice as well as to his superiors. The result? A board resolution to end random searches, triggering districtwide attention to restorative practices.

Because PLI will "not let you go," it has become a community of practice that includes not only novices entering the program but also alumni who have served as principals for several years. This community is profoundly different from the "old boy networks" historically enabled by administrator-credentialing institutions. Consequently, over the years, many cohorts of PLI students have heard Mauro (and many others) talk about how they have responded to unjust mandates. When experienced principals themselves speak of the ways they make good trouble—telling how and why they take the risks they do—they shape the practice of principals who are just learning to be social justice leaders.

Engaging educators throughout their careers has been powerful, in part, by extending the social justice agenda beyond preservice teacher candidates who may be vulnerable to "real-world," "realistic" views of educating low-income students of color. Some schools have powerful cultures that unstintingly suppress divergent views about both justice and learning. Over time, new Center X teachers have taken jobs in schools where Center X alumni share their perspectives, in schools where Center X professional development is helping seasoned educators, and increasingly in schools that are now co-run by UCLA. Center X principals (many of whom are former Center X teachers) embed these commitments in the school culture and beyond. Throughout their careers, Center X alumni help one another to become caring advocates, reflective inquiry based practitioners, community builders, and generative change agents.

Collaborate Across Institutions and Communities

A third founding principle is to build long-term, positive, interdependent connections and equal-status partnerships among UCLA, K–12 schools, and the diverse communities of Los Angeles. In the beginning, we were strong on theory, clear on our social justice values and goals, and widely varied in our experiences, but foggy on how and where to begin transforming schooling for the city's most underserved young people. We needed like-minded partners in schools and communities to coconstruct our programs. And like teacher educators everywhere, come September, we needed classrooms to place preservice teachers for clinical practice. Clearly, in addition to our internal expertise, we needed institutional and individual relationships that were outside our university and different from typical teacher-training settings.

A pressing first task was to identify and engage schools where Center X teacher candidates could do observations, student teaching, and so on. Because we were the "best" university with the "best" students," we had many long-standing relationships with the "best" schools, where the "best" practices could be found. Not surprisingly, these schools were not typically in the traditionally underserved neighborhoods we were committed to. We knew that our conventional placement arrangements wouldn't do. Happily, schools within our preferred boundaries were delighted to welcome our teacher candidates. Not so happily, few of these schools modeled the practices of social justice and authentic learning we wanted our students to learn. (Of course, this was also the case in the schools where we had placed students before.)

Over time, we realized that this was fundamentally a learning problem—that our collaborations must focus on learning, not just cooperation. And, as described in chapter 5, our theory of learning placed relationships at the core of our mission: "Learning occurs as people participate together, as their rich histories shape how they participate together, where the structures of schooling and society shape how they participate together." We did not fully understand (but quickly turned our attention to) the depth of the relationships that transformative collaboration both fosters and requires. In the face of entrenched schooling habits and traditions, collaboration with practitioners to prepare teachers to make good trouble goes far beyond polite cooperation.

Center X's twenty-five-year partnership with Roosevelt High School in Boyle Heights illustrates how learning relationships can become a long-lasting norm and an institutional identity. We are people who engage; we learn from each other; we call out hurtful speech; we help newcomers; we seek out (rather than avoid) members of the community. The list of attributes is much longer because such positive qualities multiply in an environment where the question "Is it just and fair?" accompanies even the most routine decisions and behaviors. As described in chapter 8, relationships between UCLA, Roosevelt High School, and Boyle Heights residents enabled this school community to develop collective knowledge grounded in the rich history and activist legacies that define the school and neighborhood. Make no mistake, the school faces abundant challenges and setbacks, but it carries on, and each year becomes stronger.

In many respects Roosevelt resembles a multigenerational school family with norms, values, and relationships that run deep. Center X placed teacher candidates at the school in cohorts, and they, along with Center X faculty and Roosevelt teachers, became a supportive community. Over time, Center X graduates joined the Roosevelt faculty and mentored new cohorts of candidates. Roosevelt teachers, some themselves Center X graduates, became students in PLI. Some Roosevelt faculty began teaching methods courses at UCLA. As the relationships deepened, candidates increasingly experienced compatibility between their own social justice commitments and those of the school. Some teachers with no prior contacts with UCLA were drawn to what seemed like a better way of teaching school while living their own professional values.

Over the years, compelling evidence has mounted that ethnic studies curricula serve a multitude of learning goals, including melding a social justice perspective with traditional course content. As of this writing, an ethnic studies course is likely to become a standard part of California's high school curricula. In no small part, this movement has been supported by a Center X pathway focused on ethnic studies, developed collaboratively with the Roosevelt faculty. Roosevelt's innovative Boyle Heights and Me course, with its student-centered, activist pedagogy, has played a weighty role. Five cohorts of Center X students have now worked alongside Roosevelt faculty as part of their student teaching. But, in Center X fashion, the influence goes further. Roosevelt faculty serve on an Ethnic Studies Leadership Team, which is shaping implementation of ethnic studies districtwide. One is a member of a statewide organization, supporting practitioner-driven professional development in ethnic studies. Professor Theresa Montaño, a former Center X faculty member now with the California State University system, is leading a curriculum-writing team for the ethnic studies course referred to above.

Many other Center X practices are possible only because of deep and trusting relationships among teacher candidates, mentor teachers, and Center X faculty. The Reciprocal Learning Partnerships for Equity (described in chapter 4) that teacher candidates and their "partner teachers" (our term for "supervising teachers") use as part of their novice–expert dialogues illustrate how trusting relationships both build from and blur rigid distinctions between teaching and learning. Center X students enter schools expecting partner teachers to model exemplary practices that foster authentic learning in socially just classrooms. When that is not the case in the mind of the student (as happens in every school), nothing in the traditional student-teaching relationship permits either partner to wrestle with it respectfully or productively. After collaborating with trusted school partners, Center X introduced the reciprocal learning practice, which positions Center X teacher candidates as partners with, rather than only apprentices to, their guiding teachers. That way, they can address difficult classroom challenges together.

As one author recounts, we wanted to nudge traditional paradigms of mentorship to include explicit conversations about identity and positionality that can uncover beliefs that lie behind inequitable practice. The deep relationships built over time have allowed even the most experienced teachers to be receptive. Some feel relieved by the permission to be a learner and to reject the expectation that they have every answer. Mentor teachers report valuing the dialogue with teacher candidates—regardless of whether they are discussing new readings, established theories, or new practices—as a way of keeping them on their toes and continuing to grow. One author reflects that, although this reciprocity can result in troubling interactions, it is "good and necessary trouble."

Deep and lasting relationships also became the foundation of Center X's ongoing, school-based professional learning approach. This approach is a far cry from most professional development summer workshops, as articulated in chapter 5:

> We have found that it is about collective action. Collective action requires working across the siloed spaces in universities and districts in ways that create new relationships, new ways of working together, new work to do together.

Valuing collaboration, Center X no longer relies on transmission of best practices as the primary mode of professional development. Some learning just requires sustained conversations and sharing spread over daily work rather than exposing participants to a chunk of knowledge in a time-limited "training" and expecting deep understanding to follow. Ongoing relationships and collaboration are especially salient when pursuing a social justice agenda, which requires the sensitive addressing of resistance and misinformation in settings where it is safe to reflect and dispute—not often the case in a room full of "attendees." One chapter author who serves as a coach to seasoned teachers in a partner school reflects on the good but disruptive trouble that the approach makes possible when the culture itself supports racism, misogyny, homophobia, and so forth. Now, when a lesson he is observing reinforces racist perceptions, he reflects, he must say something, as silence is an act of oppression.

Such generative relationships led in 2006 to the UCLA Community School—one of six small schools newly built at the site of the assassination of Robert F. Kennedy, in what has become Los Angeles's Korean community. They also led Center X more recently to take on and operate a school less than four miles from the site of the Rodney King beating—Mann UCLA Community School. The latter, especially, was clearly an act of good and necessary trouble. One Center Xer recalled that Mann was so neglected and underserved that a community member told us that we were crazy and that we should "blow it up" rather than partner with them. Even some UCLA colleagues warned that it was hopeless and not worth the battle.

Bring Together Educators' and Students' Need for Depth of Content Knowledge, Powerful Pedagogies, and School Cultures That Enable Serious and Sustained Engagement in Teaching and Learning

Because the three domains of teaching and learning—depth of content knowledge, powerful pedagogies, and school cultures that enable serious and sustained engagement—are mutually reinforcing, we set out to design our programs accordingly. Easy to say, but hard to do.

Here, too, the evolution in professional development from summer workshops to the whole-school learning partnerships described in chapters 5 and 6 shows the blending of these three domains. The science project, for example, works in classrooms with some of the city's most disadvantaged students. Cadres of science teachers learn how to teach students using hands-on, experiential pedagogies suited to the Next Generation Science Standards—pedagogies usually reserved for affluent schools or classes of gifted students. Together with Center X partners, they engage students in legitimate versions of science practice—designing and doing experiments, developing and refining models and explanations, analyzing evidence, making arguments to learn foundational science concepts. Oriented toward real-world phenomena, teachers encourage students to study what they see in their communities, including how the laws of motion operate in car crashes and how climate change contributes to frequent and extreme wildfires, topics of great relevance to young people in Los Angeles.

Do these shifts represent good and necessary trouble? One author reflects that, although society says that science is unbiased, the fields within it have few marginalized people of color. Preservice and in-service teachers need to explore how traditional science teaching continues this oppression. Ideally, teaching and learning science takes place in a community (classroom) where students craft science identities that honor their culture and experiences. They do not need to change or assimilate to be a part of science, but they do need to disrupt antiscience practices and norms with outspoken advocacy—good trouble for sure.

Focus Simultaneously on Professional Education, School Reform, and Reinventing the University's Role in K–12 Schooling

We knew we had to change ourselves if we wanted to help others change. The trouble is that university faculties and administrations don't embrace change any more enthusiastically than other sectors of society. One common way to try to shape attitudes and practices is to hector others about their social "responsibility." Because that doesn't work, we rolled up our institutional sleeves and plunged into collaborative relationships.

According to a UCLA administrator who helped start the partnership between UCLA, Horace Mann Middle School, and the Los Angeles Unified School District, "lots of people said we were crazy, don't bother, let the school quietly disappear." In fact, the school was in dire straits. As chapter 10 details, Mann's enrollment had fallen from 1,800 to 330 students, and thirty-seven charter schools had opened within a 2.5-mile radius of the school. Many Mann teachers came from the district's "must-place" list and wanted to be anywhere but there. For an entire year, seventh graders had long-term substitutes in all of their core classes. These conditions didn't "just happen"; they were largely the result of public policy.

The partnership reveals how joint work on challenging problems (learning together, as described above) both exposes flaws in thinking and practice and forces change to become more than an institutional imperative; it gets personal. And, once begun, building trusting relationships and engaging in this challenging work as a community can become enormously satisfying. That has been our experience.

Still in its early years, the UCLA-Mann partnership is making great strides flouting prevailing views about what's possible in failing urban schools. Governance has become more inclusive, with committees cochaired by a Mann representative and a UCLA representative and including Mann teachers, administrators, Center X faculty, and, on some occasions, students. Today, most Mann teachers are Center X alumni; most report feeling privileged to fight for students while being scaffolded with Center X professional development and coaching. Teaching students in this historically ignored and disrespected community, Mann teachers still face challenges; but most would agree they are good troubles.

As the structures of inequity (such as teacher assignment policies) are dismantled, students are beginning to thrive. During a recent visit to the school by the Accrediting Commission for Schools, Western Association of Schools and Colleges (ACS WASC), teachers, students, and parents all talked about the amazing place Mann UCLA Community School has become. Students told the officials about high expectations and rigorous classes in which teachers push them so hard that they can compete with anyone. They also talked about caring teachers who are supportive and available. Students said their teachers make them feel that they are getting an education that rich kids get.

How has the university's role changed? The Mann partnership is a commitment to using community resources and building the school from within, rather than presuming it needs UCLA to bring value. One author emphasizes that it is also about taking a stand in the face of powerful policies that perpetuate racism and inequity. It is about listening first, being patient, and creating spaces for relationship-based partnerships across all stakeholders in the school. This is not how universities typically behave.

It is hard, hard work. According to one author, Mann is a place that can "put one on the edge of burnout on most days. And yet, the work is necessary trouble, and serving the Mann community is a call-ing more than a job." The UCLA administrator shares her pride and gratitude that Center X has persisted:

> It can be easy to get lost in a sea of despair at Mann—especially if you consider the historical racial injustices of the community. I hope that the work of the partnership to become the Mann UCLA Community School is an example of a daily, weekly, monthly, yearly struggle to make the good trouble the students and community of Mann deserve.

Blend Research and Practice

Center X set out to combine professional education, research aimed at creating new knowledge, and the practical application of that knowl-edge in schools. One goal was to support UCLA scholars to formulate and conduct their research and teaching in ways that reflect the reali-ties of children, educators, schools, and communities. Another was to help school professionals learn to guide their practice by a process of critical inquiry, reflection, and social responsibility.

The yearlong Master's Inquiry Project—the culminating assign-ment in the two-year teacher preparation program described in chap-ter 2—is a good example of how Center X teacher candidates are expected to work at the intersection of practice and research. The assignment provides novices, now working as full-time teachers of record (residents), a structured opportunity to continue their develop-ment as reflective antiracist practitioners working to transform urban schools. At the same time, it engages them in a systematic, intentional study of their own professional practice—inquiry into a researchable question about student learning from a social justice perspective aris-ing from their first few months of classroom teaching. The project requires teachers to design an action-research plan, informed by re-search and grounded in a social justice theory of learning and change. After eight weeks of collecting and analyzing data from student work, interviews, surveys, and ethnographic notes, they write up their find-ings and the implications for their own practice. Their scholarly proj-ects are shared in community presentations and archived as resources for novice teachers who come after them.

More challenging—because it runs counter to usual practice—has been engaging faculty in research that can inform other researchers, teacher educators, and teachers about making underserved city schools rigorous, socially just, and caring. Led by faculty researcher Karen Hunter Quartz, Center X and other UCLA faculty have produced longitudinal statistical analyses of the retention of Center X teachers in the educator workforce and in hard-to-staff schools, classroom-based studies of students' mathematical and science development, large-scale surveys of how school leaders advance social justice goals in a time of national crises, and rich case studies of the struggle to transform urban schools.[5] Many of UCLA's most senior faculty have contributed to this growing body of research.

Combining professional education, research creating new knowledge, and the practical application of that knowledge has been the focus of the UCLA Community School—one of six small schools at the Robert F. Kennedy site. As described by Quartz and her coauthors in chapter 9, the school was created to merge the research mission of the university (as well as its teaching and service mission) with the core work of K–12 schooling. The university both studies and supports innovative educational practices in a very typical public school, barraged by external reforms, inadequate funding, large class sizes, and the political instability of revolving district leadership. These challenges make the UCLA Community School distinctive. Together, researchers and educators examine how educators navigate the challenges faced in today's urban schools—working within a system they are trying to change.

This work has shaped practice at the more recent and more challenging Mann UCLA Community School, and it helps Mann itself to blend research and practice.

Remain Self-Renewing

The principle of remaining self-renewing required us to view change and problems as normal conditions that require a flexible and responsive learning organization. We were intent on remaining a commitment-driven entity that organizes people around important problems, interests, and goals.

As the authors of chapter 2 recount, the field of teacher preparation for urban schools has rapidly evolved in the past 30 years. That means "we are always in a state of reflection and inquiry about how we operationalize our beliefs. Our language and practice have become more refined, textured, and nuanced over the years, informed by the research of critical scholars and the work of critical practitioners."

This whole book speaks to self-renewing, principle-driven practices. For me, one is particularly meaningful and embraces the ethos of all of Center X—how Center X responded to the ban on affirmative action by overhauling the way it admits students, using indicators of merit closely aligned with the knowledge and skills required for success as an urban educator. Traditionally, admission to "highly selective" graduate programs like UCLA's relies almost exclusively on exam scores, GPA, and the quality or ranking of the schools where students received their bachelor's degrees. Center X kept these criteria but added highly relevant nontraditional ones such as experience in working-class communities of color, mastery of languages spoken by Los Angeles's families, experience with school-aged children, and knowledge of social justice issues. These nontraditional criteria are revealed in applicants' written statements of purpose, their life and work experiences, and their academic and professional references. Applicants visit campus for interviews, during which they read a critical social justice text, engage with four or five other applicants in a Socratic dialogue about it, and provide written reflections on the process. After years of refinement, this process allows Center X faculty to admit students with the greatest potential for growth and success. The resulting student body also reflects the diversity of Los Angeles.

AN ONGOING STRUGGLE

Embodying a social justice agenda and adhering to the principles that define Center X's work haven't been easy. But the work has endured. We watched with great relief as Center X programs were flooded with applications and the program thrived. We watched with amazement when teacher educators around the country were emboldened by our example, saying that if UCLA can take on this agenda, so can we. We noted with pride when our students strode into justice reforms where their more experienced colleagues feared to tread. And they survived and thrived. Of course, like nearly everyone in the education profession, they grumble and struggle with lesson planning, classroom and time management, paperwork, school bureaucracy, and so on. But what is remarkable isn't that they struggle with the ordinary; it's the quality and persistence of their struggle with extraordinary problems.

Center X began in the aftermath of Rodney King's beating; it continues in the aftermath of the killings of Breonna Taylor, George Floyd, Ahmaud Arbery, and so many others. It began with fires in Los Angeles; it continues as fires erupt in cities across the nation. And schools are full of children who are hungry for knowledge and a hot meal. Center X has not made the world safe, healthy, and decent; but it continues to teach and nurture those who would make it so. Some day.

Thank you, John Lewis, for this fitting conclusion to our story of a community of people trying hard to disrupt educational injustice and knowing that there is so much more to do:[6]

> Do not get lost in a sea of despair. Be hopeful, be optimistic. Our struggle is not the struggle of a day, a week, a month, or a year, it is the struggle of a lifetime. Never, ever be afraid to make some noise and get in good trouble, necessary trouble.

Notes

Introduction

1. Josiah Royce, *The Problem of Christianity* (Washington, DC: Catholic University of America Press, 1913), 357.
2. Martin Luther King Jr., "Statement to the Press at the Beginning of the Youth Leadership Conference," in *The Papers of Martin Luther King, Jr.*, ed. Carson Clayborne, vol. 5, *Threshold of a New Decade, January 1959–December 1960*, ed. Carson Clayborne et al. (Berkeley: University of California Press, 2005).
3. bell hooks, *Killing Rage: Ending Racism* (New York: H. Holt & Company, 1996).
4. "UCLA: Our Stories, Our Impact. A Centennial Initiative," ourstoriesour impact.irle.ucla.edu/patrisse-cullors/.
5. Marian Wright Edelman, "Ask What You Can Do for Your Country," *Minnesota Spokesman-Recorder*, December 4, 2013, https://spokesman -recorder.com/2013/12/04/ask-what-you-can-do-for-your-country/.

Chapter 1

1. Henry A. Giroux, *Schooling and the Struggle for Public Life: Critical Pedagogy in the Modern Age* (Minneapolis: University of Minnesota Press, 1988), 215.
2. James Macdonald and Susan Colberg Macdonald, "Gender, Values, and Curriculum," in *Contemporary Curriculum Discourses*, ed. William F. Pinar (Scottsdale, AZ: Gorsuch Scarisbrick, 1988), 480.
3. Paul Heckman, *The Courage to Change* (Newbury Park, CA: Corwin, 1996).
4. Kenneth A. Sirotnik, "Critical Inquiry: A Paradigm for Praxis," in *Forms of Curriculum Inquiry*, ed. Edmund C. Short (Albany, NY: State University of New York Press, 1991), 243–49; Kenneth A. Sirotnik and Jeannie Oakes, "Evaluation as Critical Inquiry: School Improvement as a Case in Point," *Evaluation and Social Justice* 45 (1990): 37–59; Earnest T. Stringer, "Socially Responsive Educational Research: Linking Theory and Practice," in *Theory*

and Concepts in Qualitative Research: Perspectives from the Field, ed. David J. Flinders and Geoffrey E. Miles (New York and London: Teachers College Press, 1993): 141–62.

Chapter 2

1. All interviews were edited for length and clarity.
2. Jeffrey Duncan-Andrade, "Note to Educators: Hope Required When Growing Roses in Concrete," *Harvard Educational Review* 79, no. 2 (2009); bell hooks, *Feminist Theory: From Margin to Center* (Boston: Pluto Press, 2000).
3. Melanie Acosta, Michelle Foster, and Diedre Houchen, "Why Seek the Living Among the Dead? African American Pedagogical Excellence: Exemplar Practice for Teacher Education," *Journal of Teacher Education* 69, no. 4 (2018): 341–53.
4. Jeannie Oakes, "Making the Rhetoric Real," *Multicultural Education* 4, no. 2 (1996). Reprinted as chapter 1 of this book.
5. Peter Murrell, *The Community Teacher: A New Framework for Effective Urban Teaching* (New York: Teachers College Press, 2001).
6. Bettina L. Love, *We Want to Do More Than Survive: Abolitionist Teaching and the Pursuit of Educational Freedom* (Boston: Beacon Press, 2019).
7. David Takacs, "How Does your Positionality Bias your Epistemology?," *Thought & Action* 19, no. 1 (2003): 27–38.
8. Acosta, Foster, and Houchen, "Why Seek the Living."
9. Murrell, *The Community Teacher.*
10. Tara Yosso, "Whose Culture Has Capital? A Critical Race Theory Discussion of Community Cultural Wealth," *Race Ethnicity and Education* 8, no. 1 (2005): 69–91.
11. Love, *We Want to Do More*, 128.
12. Christine E. Sleeter, *The Academic and Social Value of Ethnic Studies: A Research Review* (Washington, DC: National Education Association, 2011).
13. Love, *We Want to Do More*; Allyson Tintiangco-Cubales et al., "Toward an Ethnic Studies Pedagogy: Implications for K–12 Schools from the Research," *The Urban Review* 47, no. 1 (2015): 104–25; Duncan-Andrade, "Note to Educators."
14. Murrell, *The Community Teacher*, 52.
15. Lilia Bartolome, "Beyond the Methods Fetish: Toward a Humanizing Pedagogy," *Harvard Educational Review* 64, no. 2 (1994): 173–94; Yosso, "Whose Culture Has Capital?"
16. Acosta, Foster, and Houchen, "Why Seek the Living."
17. Douglas Kellner and Jeff Share, "Critical Media Literacy, Democracy, and the Reconstruction of Education," in *Media Literacy: A Reader*, ed. Donaldo Macedo and Shirley R. Steinberg (New York: Peter Lang Publishing, 2007), 3–23.
18. Oakes, "Making the Rhetoric Real," 14.
19. Paulo Freire, *Education for Critical Consciousness* (New York: Continuum, 1973), 1.
20. Jahaan Chandler, "Confronting Colorism: An Examination into the Social and Psychological Aspects of Colorism," in *Color Struck*, ed. Lori Latrice Martin et al. (Rotterdam: Sense Publishers, 2017), 143–56.

Chapter 3

1. Jeff Duncan-Andrade, "Gangstas, Wankstas, and Ridas: Defining, Developing, and Supporting Effective Teachers in Urban Schools," *International Journal of Qualitative Studies in Education* 20, no. 6 (2007): 635, doi:10.1080/09518390 701630767.

2. Jason Felch, Jason Song, and Doug Smith, "Who's Teaching LA's Kids? A *Times* Analysis, Using Data Largely Ignored by LAUSD, Looks at Which Educators Help Students Learn, and Which Hold Them Back," *Los Angeles Times*, August 14, 2010, https://www.latimes.com/archives/la-xpm-2010-aug-14-la -me-teachers-value-2010 0815-story.html; "Los Angeles Teacher Ratings," *Los Angeles Times*, http://projects.latimes.com/value-added/.

3. Thomas Kane and Douglas O. Staiger, *Gathering Feedback for Teaching: Combining High-Quality Observations with Student Surveys and Achievement Gains*, Research paper, MET project (Seattle, WA: Bill & Melinda Gates Foundation, 2012).

4. Jesse Rothstein, *Review of "Learning About Teaching: Initial Findings from the Measures of Effective Teaching Project"* (Boulder, CO: National Education Policy Center, January 2011).

5. Karen Hunter Quartz, Jose Felipe Martinez, and Jarod Kawasaki, "Using Multiple Measures of Teaching Quality to Improve the Preparation of Urban Teachers," *Education Policy Analysis Archives* 28 (2020): 128, doi: 10.14507 /epaa.28.5011.

6. Imelda Nava, Jaime Park, and Mollie Appelgate, *Observation Rubric for Secondary Science,*The Center XChange series no. IPMS024-X046-2011 (Los Angeles: UC Regents, 2011); Jaime Park, Imelda Nava, and Mollie Appelgate, *Observation Rubric for Secondary Mathematics*, The Center XChange series no. IPMS025-X047-2011 (Los Angeles: UC Regents, 2011), https://cxarchive .gseis.ucla.edu/xchange/images-and-media/MathObservationRubric.pdf.

7. Imelda Nava et al., "Measuring Teaching Quality of Secondary Mathematics and Science Residents: A Classroom Observation Framework," *Journal of Teacher Education* 70, no. 2 (2019): 139–54.

8. Pam Grossman, *Teaching Core Practices in Teacher Education* (Cambridge, MA: Harvard Education Press, 2018).

9. Robert Berry, "Opportunity to Learn Mathematics: Time, Task, & Talk," *ARISE: Advancing Research and Innovation in the STEM Education of Preservice Teachers in High-Need School Districts* (blog), 2019, https://aaas-arise .org/2019/10/09/opportunity-to-learn-mathematics-time-task-talk/.

10. Martin Haberman, "Pedagogies of Poverty Versus Good Teaching," *Phi Delta Kappan* 73, no. 4 (1991): 290–94; Jean Anyon, "Social Class and the Hidden Curriculum of Work," *Childhood Socialization* 162 (2011): 369.

11. Mary Kay Stein et al., "Algebra: A Challenge at the Crossroads of Policy and Practice," *Review of Educational Research* 81, no. 4 (2011): 453–92.

12. Mark Windschitl, Jessica Thompson, and Melissa Braaten, *Ambitious Science Teaching* (Boston: Harvard Education Press, 2018), 878–903.

13. Alan H. Schoenfeld, "What Makes for Powerful Classrooms, and How Can We Support Teachers in Creating Them? A Story of Research and Practice, Productively Intertwined," *Educational Researcher* 43, no. 8 (2014): 404–12, doi:10.3102/0013189 X14554450.

14. Fran Arbaugh and Catherine A. Brown, "Analyzing Mathematical Tasks: A Catalyst for Change?" *Journal of Mathematics Teacher Education* 8, no. 6 (2005): 499–536.
15. Frederick L. Dillon et al., *The Common Core Mathematics Companion: The Standards Decoded, High School. What They Say, What They Mean, How to Teach Them* (Thousand Oaks, CA: Corwin Press and NCTM, 2017).
16. National Research Council, *Next Generation Science Standards: For States, by States* (Washington, DC: The National Academies Press, 2013), doi:10.17226/18290.
17. Charlotte Danielson and Elizabeth Marquez, *A Collection of Performance Tasks and Rubrics: High School Mathematics* (New York: Routledge, 2014); Kaitlin Landon, "The Use of Graphing CERs (Claim, Evidence, Reasoning) to Improve Scientific Literacy" (UWP Seminar Papers, University of Wisconsin–Platteville, 2019), http://digital.library.wisc.edu/1793/79085.
18. Joseph D. Novak and Alberto J. Cañas, *The Theory Underlying Concept Maps and How to Construct and Use Them*, Technical Report IHMC CmapTools 2006-01 (Pensacola, FL: Institute for Human and Machine Cognition, updated January 2008).
19. Carol Ann Tomlinson, Tonya Moon, and Marcia B. Imbeau, *Assessment and Student Success in a Differentiated Classroom* (Alexandria, VA: Association for Supervision & Curriculum Development, 2013).
20. Paulo Freire, *Pedagogy of the Oppressed*, 30th anniversary ed. (New York: Bloomsbury, 2000).
21. Randi Engle and Faith R. Conant, "Guiding Principles for Fostering Productive Disciplinary Engagement: Explaining an Emergent Argument in a Community of Learners Classroom," *Cognition and Instruction* 20, no. 4 (2002): 399–483; Michael J. Ford and Ellice A. Forman, "Chapter 1: Redefining Disciplinary Learning in Classroom Contexts," *Review of Research in Education* 30, no. 1 (2006): 1–32; Okhee Lee, Helen Quinn, and Guadalupe Valdés, "Science and Language for English Language Learners in Relation to Next Generation Science Standards and with Implications for Common Core State Standards for English Language Arts and Mathematics," *Educational Researcher* 42, no. 4 (2013): 223–33.
22. Hosun Kang and Charles W. Anderson, "Supporting Preservice Science Teachers' Ability to Attend and Respond to Student Thinking by Design," *Science Education* 99, no. 5 (2015): 863–95; Elizabeth A. Van Es and Miriam Gamoran Sherin, "Mathematics Teachers' 'Learning to Notice' in the Context of a Video Club," *Teaching and Teacher Education* 24, no. 2 (2008): 244–76.
23. Megan L. Franke, Elham Kazemi, and Daniel Battey, "Mathematics Teaching and Classroom Practice," *Second Handbook of Research on Mathematics Teaching and Learning* 1, no. 1 (2007): 225–56; Sarah Michaels and Cathy O'Connor, *Talk Science Primer* (Cambridge, MA: TERC, 2012).
24. Hilda Borko and Jonathan Osbourne, "How Can Elementary Teachers Improve Their Ability to Run Productive Science Discussions?" *ARISE: Advancing Research and Innovation in the STEM Education of Pre-service Teachers in High-Need School Districts* (blog), 2019, https://aaas-arise.org/2019/10/28/how-can-elementary-teachers-improve-their-ability-to-run-productive-science-discussions/.

25. Masitah Shahrill, "Review of Effective Teacher Questioning in Mathematics Classrooms," *International Journal of Humanities and Social Science* 3, no. 17 (2013): 224–31; Peter Sullivan and Pat Lilburn, *Good Questions for Math Teaching: Why Ask Them and What to Ask, K–6* (Sausalito, CA: Math Solutions, 2002).

26. Ontario Ministry of Education, *A Guide to Effective Literacy Instruction, Grades 4 to 6* (Toronto, ON: Queen's Printer for Ontario, 2006), vol. 1.

27. Benjamin Bloom, *Taxonomy of Educational Objectives* (New York: McKay, 1956), 1:20–24.

28. Deborah Loewenberg Ball, "With an Eye on the Mathematical Horizon: Dilemmas of Teaching Elementary School Mathematics," *The Elementary School Journal* 93, no. 4 (1993): 373–97; Gaea Leinhardt and Michael D. Steele, "Seeing the Complexity of Standing to the Side: Instructional Dialogues," *Cognition and Instruction* 23, no. 1 (2005): 87–163; Alan H. Schoenfeld, "Toward a Theory of Teaching-in-Context," *Issues in Education* 4, no. 1 (1998): 1–95, doi:10.1016/S1080-9724(99)80076-7; Miriam Gamoran Sherin, "When Teaching Becomes Learning," *Cognition and Instruction* 20, no. 2 (2002): 119–50, doi:10.1207/S1532690XCI2002_1.

29. Suzanne Chapin, Catherine O'Connor, and Nancy Canavan Anderson, *Classroom Discussions: Using Math Talk to Help Students Learn, Grades K–6* (Sausalito, CA: Math Solutions, 2009).

30. Angie Su, "Standards, Classroom Mathematics Strategies That Work!" (Faculty Presentations 992, National Council of Supervisors of Mathematics, San Francisco, CA, April 1999), https://nsuworks.nova.edu/fse_facpres/992.

31. Berry, "Opportunity to Learn Mathematics."

32. *Principles and Standards for School Mathematics* (Reston, VA: The National Council of Teachers of Mathematics, 2000).

33. Bryan A. Brown, "'It Isn't No Slang That Can Be Said About This Stuff': Language, Identity, and Appropriating Science Discourse," *Journal of Research in Science Teaching* 43, no. 1 (2006): 96–126.

34. Angela Carrasquillo, Stephen B. Kucer, and Ruth Abrams, *Beyond the Beginnings: Literacy Interventions for Upper Elementary English Language Learners* (Buffalo, NY: Multilingual Matters, 2004); Jamal Abedi, "Issues and Consequences for English Language Learners," in *Uses and Misuses of Data for Educational Accountability and Improvement*, 104th Yearbook of the National Society for the Study of Education, pt. 2, ed. Joan Herman and Edward Haertel (Malden, MA: Blackwell, 2005).

35. Pauline Gibbons, *Scaffolding Language, Scaffolding Learning* (Portsmouth, NH: Heinemann, 2002); Luciano Mariani, "Teacher Support and Teacher Challenge in Promoting Learner Autonomy," *Perspectives: A Journal of TESOL Italy* 23, no. 2 (1997), http://www.learningpaths.org/papers/paper support.htm; Carol A. Tomlinson, *How to Differentiate Instruction in Mixed-Ability Classrooms* (Alexandria, VA: ASCD, 2001).

36. Ibid.

37. Inmaculada M. García-Sánchez and Marjorie Faulstich Orellana, eds., *Language and Cultural Practices in Communities and Schools: Bridging Learning for Students from Non-dominant Groups* (New York: Routledge, 2019).

38. Eric Gutstein, *Reading and Writing the World with Mathematics: Toward a Pedagogy for Social Justice* (Taylor & Francis, 2006); Cathery Yeh and Brande M. Otis, "Mathematics for Whom: Reframing and Humanizing Mathematics," *Occasional Paper Series* 2019, no. 41 (2019), https://educate.bankstreet.edu /occasional-paperseries/vol2019/iss41/8; National Research Council, *Next Generation Science Standards.*

39. Dominique Smith, Douglas Fisher, and Nancy Frey, *Better Than Carrots or Sticks: Restorative Practices for Positive Classroom Management* (Alexandria, VA: ASCD, 2015).

40. Barbara Rogoff, "Developing Understanding of the Idea of Communities of Learners," *Mind, Culture and Activity* 1, no. 4 (1994): 209–29.

41. Linda Christensen, *Reading, Writing, and Rising Up* (Milwaukee, WI: Rethinking Schools, 2000).

42. Kathleen Cushman, *Fires in the Bathroom: Advice for Teachers from High School Students* (New York: New Press, 2003); Shawn Ginwright, *Hope and Healing in Urban Education: How Urban Activists and Teachers Are Reclaiming Matters of the Heart* (New York: Routledge, 2015); Bettina L. Love, *We Want to Do More Than Survive: Abolitionist Teaching and the Pursuit of Educational Freedom* (Boston: Beacon Press, 2019); Smith, Fisher, and Frey, *Better Than Carrots or Sticks.*

43. Freire, *Pedagogy of the Oppressed*; Tony Knight, "Longitudinal Development of Educational Theory: Democracy and the Classroom," *Journal of Education Policy* 16, no. 3 (2001): 249–63.

44. Maggie B. McGatha and Peg Darcy, "Rubrics at Play," *Mathematics Teaching in the Middle School* 15, no. 6 (2010): 328–36.

45. Mollie Appelgate, "Connecting Math Methods and Student Teaching Through Practice-Based Strategies: A Study of Pre-Service Teachers' Math Instruction" (PhD diss., UCLA, 2012).

46. Jaime Park, Imelda Nava, and Jarod Kawasaki, "Supporting Pre-service Teachers Actualize Theories of Student-Centered Disciplinary Discourse Practices Using Video Instructional Rounds" (paper presented at the annual meeting of the American Educational Research Association, San Francisco, California, April 20, 2020).

47. Jaime Park and Imelda Nava, "How Can Pre-service STEM Teachers Enact Project-Based Learning for Authentic Community Engagement?" *ARISE: Advancing Research and Innovation in the STEM Education of Pre-service Teachers in High-Need School Districts* (blog), 2019, https://aaas-arise.org /2019/12/30/how-can-pre-service-stem-teachers-enact-project-based-learning -for-authentic-community-engagement/.

48. Charlotte Danielson, *Enhancing Professional Practice: A Framework for Teaching* (Alexandria: VA: ASCD, 2007).

Chapter 4

1. Tyrone C. Howard, "Culturally Relevant Pedagogy: Ingredients for Critical Teacher Reflection," *Theory into Practice* 42, no. 3 (2003): 195; Jeannie Oakes, *Keeping Track: How Schools Structure Inequality* (Birmingham, NY: Vail-Ballou Press, 1985).

2. Simon Veenman and Eddie Denessen, "The Coaching of Teachers: Results of Five Training Studies," *Educational Research and Evaluation* 7, no. 4 (2001): 385–417, doi: 10.1076/ edre.7.4.385.8936.

3. Barbara Rogoff, *Apprenticeship in Thinking* (New York: Oxford University Press, 1990).

4. Charles Palus and John McGuire, "Mediated Dialogue in Action Research," in *Sage Handbook of Action Research* (Thousand Oaks, CA: SAGE Publications, 2015), doi:10.4135/9781473921290.n72.

5. Gayatri C. Spivak, *The Post-Colonial Critic* (New York: Routledge, 1990).

6. Paolo Freire, *Pedagogy of the Oppressed* (New York: Seabury Press, 1973).

7. Anthony Bryk and Barbara Schneider, "Trust in Schools: A Core Resource for School Reform," *Educational Leadership* 60 (2003): 40–44.

8. Kris D. Gutiérrez, "Developing a Sociocultural Literacy in the Third Space," *Reading Research Quarterly* 43 (2008): 148–64.

Chapter 5

1. Martin Haberman, "Can Cultural Awareness Be Taught in Teacher Education Programs?" *Teaching Education* 4, no. 1 (1991): 25–32; A. Kohn, "The Case Against Grades," *Educational Leadership* 69, no. 3 (2011): 28–33.

2. Emily Klein and Meg Riordan Meg, "Putting Professional Development into Practice: A Framework for How Teachers in Expeditionary Learning Schools Implement Professional Development," *Teacher Education Quarterly* 36, no. 4 (2009): 61–80.

3. Linda Darling-Hammond, Marie E. Hyler, and Madelyn Gardner, *Effective Teacher Professional Development* (Palo Alto, CA: Learning Policy Institute, 2017); V. Darlene Opfer and David Pedder, "Conceptualizing Teacher Professional Learning," *Review of Educational Research* 81, no. 3 (2011): 376–407.

4. Jeannie Oakes, "Making the Rhetoric Real," *Multicultural Education* 4, no. 2 (1996): 4–10. Reprinted as chapter 1 of this book.

5. Jean Lave, *Cognition in Practice: Mind, Mathematics and Culture in Everyday Life* (New York: Cambridge University Press, 1988).

6. Ann Brown and Joseph Campione, "Psychological Theory and the Design of Innovative Learning Environments: On Procedures, Principles, and Systems," in *Innovations in Learning*, ed. Leona Schauble and Robert Glaser (Hillsdale, NJ: Erlbaum, 1996), 289–326; Jean Lave and Etienne Wenger, *Situated Learning: Legitimate Peripheral Participation* (Cambridge: Cambridge University Press, 1991); Jean Lave, "The Practice of Learning," in *Understanding Practice: Perspectives on Activity and Context*, ed. Seth Chaiklin and Jean Lave (New York: Cambridge University Press, 1993), 3–32.

7. Jeannie Oakes and John Rogers, *Learning Power: Organizing for Education and Justice* (New York: Teachers College Press, 2006).

8. Jody Priselac and Carol Truscott, "A School University Partnership: Working Together to Increase Academic Achievement Through Content Literacy" (presentation at the annual meeting of the American Education Research Association, Chicago, April 10, 2007).

9. Sylvia Rousseau, "A Bold Beginning," *Center X Forum* 2, no. 2 (2002): 1–15.

10. Pedro Noguera, "Toward the Development of School and University Partnerships Based upon Mutual Benefit and Respect," *In Motion Magazine*, July 9, 1998, http://www.inmotionmagazine.com/pnsup1.html.

11. Jeannie Oakes et al., "Research for High-Quality Urban Teaching: Defining It, Developing It, Assessing It," *Journal of Teacher Education* 53 (2002): 228–34.

12. Thomas Carpenter et al., "Using Knowledge of Children's Mathematics Thinking in Classroom Teaching: An Experimental Study," *American Educational Research Journal* 26 (1989): 499–531; Victoria Jacobs et al., "Exploring the Impact of Large Scale Professional Development Focused on Children's Algebraic Reasoning," *Journal for Research in Mathematics Education* 38, no. 3 (2007): 258–88; Megan L. Franke et al., "Capturing Teachers' Generative Growth: A Follow-Up Study of Professional Development in Mathematics," *American Educational Research Journal* 38 (2001): 653–89.

13. Lave and Wenger, *Situated Learning*; Na'ilah S. Nasir, Victoria Hand, and Edd V. Taylor, "Culture and Mathematics in School: Boundaries Between 'Cultural' and 'Domain' Knowledge in the Mathematics Classroom and Beyond," *Review of Research in Education* 32, no. 1 (2008): 187–240; Barbara Rogoff, *Apprenticeship in Thinking: Cognitive Development in Social Context* (New York: Oxford University Press, 1990).

Chapter 6

1. Jim Ryder, "Identifying Science Understanding for Functional Scientific Literacy," *Studies in Science Education* 36 (2001): 1–44.

2. National Research Council, *A Framework for K–12 Science Education: Practices, Crosscutting Concepts, and Core Ideas* (Washington, DC: National Academy Press, 2012).

3. John L. Rudolph, *How We Teach Science: What's Changed, and Why It Matters* (Cambridge, MA: Harvard University Press, 2019).

4. Jarod Kawasaki and William A. Sandoval, "The Role of Teacher Framing in Producing Coherent NGSS-Aligned Teaching," *Journal of Science Teacher Education* 30, no. 8 (2019): 906–22; William A. Sandoval, Jarod Kawasaki, and Heather F. Clark, "Characterizing Science Classroom Discourse Across Scales," *Research in Science Education* (2020): doi:10.1007/s11165-020 -09953-7.

5. Eve Manz, "Representing Student Argumentation as Functionally Emergent from Scientific Activity," *Review of Educational Research* 85, no. 4 (2015): 553–90.

6. Sarah Michaels, C. O'Connor, and Lauren B. Resnick, "Deliberative Discourse Idealized and Realized: Accountable Talk in the Classroom and in Civic Life," *Studies in Philosophy and Education* 27 (2008): 283–97.

7. Brian J. Reiser, Michael Fumagalli, and Michael Novak, "NGSS Storylines: How to Construct Coherent Instruction Sequences Driven by Phenomena and Motivated by Student Questions" (presentation at the Illinois Science Education Conference, Tinley Park, Illinois, October 23, 2015).

8. Richard A. Duschl, "Science Education in Three-Part Harmony: Balancing Conceptual, Epistemic and Social Goals," *Review of Research in Education* 32 (2008): 268–91.

Chapter 7

1. This case study of PLI draws on interviews and correspondence with PLI alumni during 2019 and 2020.
2. Jean Lave, "Teaching, as Learning, in Practice," *Mind, Culture, and Activity* 3, no. 3 (1996): 149–64; Jean Lave and Etienne Wenger, *Situated Learning: Legitimate Peripheral Participation* (Cambridge: Cambridge University Press, 1991); Etienne Wenger, *Communities of Practice: Learning, Meaning, and Identity* (New York: Cambridge University Press, 1998).
3. Jean Lave, "Teaching, as Learning, in Practice," 157.
4. Letitia Johnson-Davis, "Teacher Reflections on Being Culturally Responsive," *Education Evolving* (blog), June 28, 2019, https://www.educationevolving.org /blog/2019/06/teacher-reflections-on-being-culturally-responsive.

Chapter 8

1. Jeannie Oakes, "Making the Rhetoric Real," *Multicultural Education* 4, no. 2 (Winter 1996): 4–10. Reprinted as chapter 1 of this book.
2. Viv Ellis and Jane McNichol, *Transforming Teacher Education: Reconfiguring Academic Work* (London: Bloomsbury, 2015).
3. Pam Grossman, *Learning to Practice: The Design of Clinical Experience in Teacher Preparation* (Washington, DC: American Association of Colleges for Teacher Education and National Education Association, 2010).
4. Lauren M. Anderson and Jamy A. Stillman, "Student Teaching's Contribution to Pre-service Teacher Development: A Review of Research Focused on the Preparation of Teachers for Urban and High-Needs Contexts," *Review of Educational Research* 83, no. 1 (March 2013): 3–69.
5. George Sanchez, "'What's Good for Boyle Heights is Good for the Jews': Creating Multiculturalism on the Eastside During the 1950s," *American Quarterly* 56, no. 3 (September 2004): 635.
6. Caroline E. Luce, *Visions of a Jewish Future: The Jewish Bakers Union and Yiddish Culture in East Los Angeles, 1908–1942* (PhD diss., UCLA, 2013), https://escholarship.org/uc/item/2z3643xz.
7. Shana Bernstein, "Interracial Activism in the Los Angeles Community Service Organization: Linking the World War II and Civil Rights Eras," *Pacific Historical Review* 80, no. 2 (2011): 231–67.
8. Rita Kohli, "Behind School Doors: The Impact of Hostile Racial Climates on Urban Teachers of Color," *Urban Education* 53, no. 3 (March 2018): 307–33.
9. Patricia E. Halagao, "Liberating Filipino Americans through Decolonizing Curriculum," *Race, Ethnicity and Education* 13, no. 4 (2010): 495–512; Marinda K. Harrell-Levy and Jennifer L. Kerpelman, "Identity Process and Transformative Pedagogy: Teachers as Agents of Identity Formation," *Identity* 10, no. 2 (2010): 76–91; Elexia R. McGovern and Tracy L. Buenavista, *Ethnic Studies with K–12 Students, Families, and Communities: The Role of Teacher Education in Preparing Educators to Serve the People* (Los Angeles: UCLA XChange, 2016), https://ucla. app.box.com/v/Ethnic-Studies -Role-Teacher-Ed; Oakes, "Making the Rhetoric Real."
10. Tara J. Yosso, "Whose Culture Has Capital? A Critical Race Theory Discussion of Community Cultural Wealth," *Race, Ethnicity and Education* 8, no. 1 (2005): 69–91.

11. Zaretta Hammond, "Looking at SoLD Through an Equity Lens: Will the Science of Learning and Development Be Used to Advance Critical Pedagogy or Will It Be Used to Maintain Inequity by Design?," *Applied Developmental Science* 24, no. 2 (2019): 151–58.

12. Karen H. Quartz, "'Too Angry to Leave': Supporting New Teachers' Commitment to Transform Urban Schools," *Journal of Teacher Education* 54, no. 2 (March 2003): 99–111.

13. McGovern-Reyes and Buenavista, *Ethnic Studies with K–12 Students, Families, and Communities*, 8.

14. Jeff Duncan-Andrade, "Note to Educators: Hope Required When Growing Roses in Concrete," *Harvard Educational Review* 79, no. 2 (July 2009): 181–94.

15. Django Paris, "Culturally Sustaining Pedagogy: A Needed Change in Stance, Terminology, and Practice," *Educational Researcher* 41, no. 3 (April 2012): 93–97.

16. Oakes, "Making the Rhetoric Real," 14.

17. Los Angeles Unified School District, *Restorative Justice in LAUSD*, May 2013, https://achieve.lausd.net/site/handlers/filedownload.ashx?moduleinsta nceid=34066&dataid=64943&FileName=Restorative%20Justice%20in%20 LAUSD%20-%20Flyer-5-24-18.pdf.

18. Dorinda J. Carter Andrews et al., "Changing the Narrative on Diversifying the Teaching Workforce: A Look at Historical and Contemporary Factors That Inform Recruitment and Retention of Teachers of Color," *Journal of Teacher Education* 70, no. 1 (January 2019): 6–12.

19. Linda Darling-Hammond, "Strengthening Clinical Preparation: The Holy Grail of Teacher Education," *Peabody Journal of Education* 89, no. 4 (2014): 547–61.

20. Arthur Levine, *Educating School Teachers* (Washington, DC: The Education Schools Project, 2006), http://www.edschools.org/pdf/Educating_Teachers _Report.pdf; Ken Zeichner, "Rethinking the Connections Between Campus Courses and Field Experiences in College- and University-Based Teacher Education," *Journal of Teacher Education* 61, no. 1–2 (January 2010): 89–99.

21. Linda Darling-Hammond and Jeannie Oakes, *Preparing Teachers for Deeper Learning* (Cambridge, MA: Harvard Education Press, 2019).

22. Anderson and Stillman, "Student Teaching's Contribution."

23. Peter Murrell, *The Community Teacher: A New Framework for Effective Urban Teaching* (New York: Teachers College, Columbia University, 2001).

Chapter 9

1. Jeannie Oakes et al., *Teaching to Change the World* (New York: Routledge, 2015); Marilyn Cochran-Smith, "Learning to Teach Against the Grain," *Harvard Educational Review* 61, no. 3 (1991): 279–311.

2. Amanda Datnow, Lea Hubbard, and Hugh Mehan, *Extending Educational Reform* (New York: Taylor & Francis, 2002).

3. Evelien Ketelaar et al., "Teachers' Positioning Towards an Educational Innovation in the Light of Ownership, Sense-Making and Agency," *Teaching and Teacher Education* 28, no. 2 (2012): 273–82.

4. Susan Moore Johnson, "The Workplace Matters: Teacher Quality, Retention, and Effectiveness" (working paper, National Education Association Research Department, Washington DC, 2006); Nicole S. Simon and Susan Moore Johnson, "Teacher Turnover in High-Poverty Schools: What We Know and Can Do," *Teachers College Record* 117, no. 3 (2015): 1–36.

5. Ramon Antonio Martinez and Karen Hunter Quartz, "Zoned for Change: A Historical Case Study of the Belmont Zone of Choice," *Teachers College Record* 114, no. 10 (2012): 10–50.

6. Lois Weiner, "Research in the 90s: Implications for Urban Teacher Preparation," *Review of Educational Research* 70, no. 3 (2000): 369–406; Karen Seashore Louis, Helen M. Marks, and Sharon Kruse, "Teachers' Professional Community in Restructuring Schools," *American Educational Research Journal* 33, no. 4 (1996): 757–98.

7. Karen Hunter Quartz et al., *Making a Difference: Developing Meaningful Careers in Education* (New York: Routledge, 2010).

8. Martinez and Quartz, "Zoned for Change," 10–50.

9. Kathryn J. Lindholm-Leary, *Dual Language Education* (Buffalo, NY: Multilingual Matters, 2001).

10. Janet Cerda et al., *The Power of Self-Assessment: Using Community-Based Measures to Advance Biliteracy* (Los Angeles: UCLA Center for Community Schooling, 2019), https://communityschooling.gseis.ucla.edu/the-power-of-self-assessment/.

11. For example, Cerda et al., *The Power of Self-Assessment*; Janelle Franco and Gabriella Pérez-Swanson, *Nurturing Play: How Schools Can Provide Powerful Opportunities for Children to Learn* (Los Angeles: UCLA Center for Community Schooling, 2019), https://communityschooling.gseis.ucla.edu/nurturing-play/; Karen Hunter Quartz et al., "Framing, Supporting, and Tracking College-for-All Reform: A Local Case of Public Scholarship," *The High School Journal* 102, no. 2 (2019): 159–82.

12. Karen Hunter Quartz, "How Do You Measure a Teacher's Worth?" *Zocalo Public Square,* May 21, 2015, http://www.zocalopublicsquare.org/2015/05/21/how-do-you-measure-a-teachers-worth/ideas/nexus/. Reprinted in *Time*, May 26, 2015, http://time.com/3896073/education-teacher-evaluation/.

13. Latish C. Reed and Raji Swaminathan, "An Urban School Leader's Approach to School Improvement: Toward Contextually Responsive Leadership," *Urban Education* 51, no. 9 (2016): 1096–125.

14. Gail Furman, "Social Justice Leadership as Praxis: Developing Capacities Through Preparation Programs," *Educational Administration Quarterly* 48, no. 2 (2012): 191–229.

15. Furman, "Social Justice"; George Theoharis, "Social Justice Educational Leaders and Resistance: Toward a Theory of Social Justice Leadership," *Educational Administration Quarterly* 43, no. 2 (2007): 221–58.

16. Information based on 2011–2012 data. See Desiree Carver-Thomas and Linda Darling-Hammond, "Teacher Turnover: Why It Matters and What We Can Do About It" (Palo Alto, CA: Learning Policy Institute, 2017).

17. John Dewey, *The Public and Its Problems* (Chicago, IL: Gateway, 1927), 213.

18. Anna Maier et al., *Community Schools as an Effective School Improvement Strategy: A Review of the Evidence* (Palo Alto, CA: Learning Policy Institute, 2017).
19. Matthew A. Kraft et al., "Educating Amid Uncertainty: The Organizational Supports Teachers Need to Serve Students in High-Poverty, Urban Schools," *Educational Administration Quarterly* 51, no. 5 (2015): 753–90.

Chapter 10

1. Horace Mann, *Report No. 12 of the Massachusetts School Board* (1848).
2. Richard Rothstein, "The Racial Achievement Gap, Segregated Schools, and Segregated Neighborhoods: A Constitutional Insult," *Race and Social Problems* 7, no. 1 (2015): 21–30.
3. James H. Johnson Jr., C. K. Jones, W. C. Farrell Jr., and M. L. Oliver, "The Los Angeles Rebellion: A Retrospective View," *Economic Development Quarterly* 6, no. 4 (1992): 356–72.
4. Shante K. Stuart McQueen, "Becoming a Community School: Teacher Perspectives Through the Transition from Traditional Public to Public Community School" (PhD diss., UCLA, 2018).
5. John Kretzman and J. L. McKnight, *Building Communities from the Inside Out* (Chicago: ACTA, 1993).
6. Anthony S. Bryk and Barbara Schneider, "Trust in Schools: A Core Resource for School Reform." *Educational Leadership* 60, no. 6 (2003): 40–45.
7. Jeannie Oakes, Anna Maier, and Julia Daniel, *Community Schools: An Evidence-Based Strategy for Equitable School Improvement* (Palo Alto, CA: Learning Policy Institute, 2017).
8. Betty Achinstein et al., "Retaining Teachers of Color: A Pressing Problem and a Potential Strategy for 'Hard-to-Staff' Schools," *Review of Educational Research* 80, no. 1 (2010): 71–107.
9. Stuart McQueen, "Becoming a Community School."
10. Ibid., 131.
11. Anthony S. Bryk et al., *Learning to Improve: How America's Schools Can Get Better at Getting Better* (Cambridge, MA: Harvard Education Press, 2015).
12. Akiva Gottlieb, "Horace Mann UCLA Community School Offers Summer Workshop," *Variety*, May 17, 2019, https://variety.com/2019/film/festivals/horace-man-ucla-community-school-summer-workshop-1203213335/.

Chapter 11

1. John Lewis in 2016 at the House sit-in after the Pulse shooting in Orlando.
2. John Lewis, "Together, You Can Redeem the Soul Of Our Nation," *New York Times*, July 30, 2020, section A, page 23.
3. Jeannie Oakes et al., *Teaching to Change the World*, 5th ed. (New York: Routledge, 2018).
4. Letitia Johnson-Davis, "Teacher Reflections on Being Culturally Responsive," *Education Evolving* (blog), June 28, 2019, https://www.educationevolving.org/blog/2019/06/teacher-reflections-on-being-culturally-responsive.
5. See, for example, Karen Hunter Quartz et al., *Making a Difference: Developing Meaningful Careers in Education* (New York: Routledge, 2010); Karen Hunter Quartz, Jody Priselac, and Megan Franke, "Transforming Public

Schools: A Synthesis of Research Findings from UCLA's Center X," *Equity & Excellence in Education: The University of Massachusetts Amherst School of Education Journal* 42, no. 3 (2009): 313–26; Jarod Kawasaki and William A. Sandoval, "The Role of Teacher Framing in Producing Coherent NGSS-Aligned Teaching," *Journal of Science Teacher Education* 30, no. 8 (2019), https://www.tandfonline.com/doi/full/10.1080/1046560X.2019.1657765; John Rogers et al., *School and Society in the Age of Trump* (Los Angeles, CA: UCLA Institute for Democracy, Education, and Access, 2019).

6. John Lewis, tweet from June 27, 2018.

About the Editors

Annamarie Francois is the executive director of UCLA's Center X, where she guides the work of equity-driven educator preparation, development, and support for urban school communities, and is a faculty member in the UCLA Teacher Education Program. She has over thirty years of teaching, teacher leadership, and administrative leadership in the Los Angeles Unified School District, the charter school community, and UCLA's Department of Education. Francois is currently the University of California representative on the California Commission on Teacher Credentialing, advisor to the California State University Center to Close the Opportunity Gap, and board president of the Center for Powerful Public Schools. She is an active contributor to national, state, and local networks working to develop models for equity-driven, student-centered, antiracist practices within educator preparation programs. Her public scholarship, teaching, and service support educator development, critical multicultural education and culturally responsive literacies, and transformative school-university collaboration. She received her BA from UCLA; her MA in higher education, administration, and supervision from California State University, Northridge; and her EdD in Educational Leadership from UCLA.

Karen Hunter Quartz directs the UCLA Center for Community Schooling and is a faculty member in the UCLA Graduate School of Education and Information Studies. Her research, teaching, and service support community school development, teacher autonomy and retention, and educational reform. Quartz led the design team in 2007 to create the UCLA Community School and served in 2017 on the design team for a second site, the Mann UCLA Community School. She currently oversees a portfolio of research-practice partnerships at both schools, designed to advance democracy, inquiry, and change. She is recipient of the 2001 Outstanding Book Award from the American Educational Research Association, the 2004 Outstanding Writing Award from the American Association of Colleges for Teacher Education, the 2017 national Teacher-Powered Schools Initiative's Advancement in Research Award, and the 2017 Outstanding Professional Teaching Award from the UCLA Department of Education. She received her BA from Huron College, MA in philosophy from the University of Western Ontario, and her PhD in education from UCLA.

About the Contributors

Melissa S. Arias is a faculty advisor for multiple-subject teacher candidates in the Teacher Education Program at UCLA. In addition to supporting candidates in the field, she teaches mathematics methods, writing methods, and a three-part course focused on identity and community in urban schools.

Heather F. Clark is a doctoral student in the Urban Schooling division of the Graduate School of Education and Information Studies at UCLA. Her research focuses on the teaching and learning of climate change. Using a participatory design approach, Clark collaborates with science teachers to design and study equity-oriented and community-based climate science learning opportunities with the aim of empowering youth to imagine and create a more just socioecological future.

Carla Estes is a dynamic high school administrator who has seventeen years of experience in education. She is an assistant principal at Mann UCLA Community School, entrusted with managing the partnership between Horace Mann and UCLA since its inception. Carla governs the high school expansion, community partnerships, and college and career pathways.

Megan L. Franke is a professor of education at UCLA. Franke and her colleagues support and study teachers as they make use of research-based information about the development of children's mathematical thinking (CGI) and consider how attention to students' mathematical thinking can help challenge existing school structures and create opportunities for marginalized students to learn with understanding. Her research work to support teachers, schools, and communities was recognized with the American Educational Research Association's Research into Practice Award, and she was elected to the National Academy of Education.

Leyda Garcia is principal of the UCLA Community School in central Los Angeles. She feels honored to work in her community, alongside families with shared stories of migration and perseverance. Garcia graduated from Stanford University (BA/MA) and UCLA's Principal Leadership Institute (MEd). She is a doctoral student at LMU. She is the recipient of Ettore Majorana's Erice prize honoring "science for peace," as well as the 2019 UCLA Howard Welinsky Advocate of the Year Award.

Ben Gertner is principal of Theodore Roosevelt High School in the Boyle Heights neighborhood of Los Angeles. He earned his BA from UC Berkeley, MA in folklore from UCLA, and an MEd and administrative credential from UCLA's Principal Leadership Institute; he is currently pursuing his EdD from UCLA's Educational Leadership Program. Gertner taught high school English and journalism for eight years and has been an administrator for ten. He is honored to lead a school that celebrates its traditions while striving to provide every student with an excellent education.

Emma Hipólito is the director of the UCLA Teacher Education Program in the Graduate School of Education and Information Studies. She specializes in teacher preparation and development with a focus on justice-focused social studies curriculum and instruction. Hipólito has over twenty-five years of experience serving as a history and social science educator, a leader in the field of teacher professional learning, and a teacher educator.

Jo Ann Isken is a faculty member of the Principal Leadership Institute at UCLA. As the director of the IMPACT UCLA urban teacher residency program, she coordinated teacher preparation efforts for elementary and secondary STEM preservice teachers. She served as the interim director of the Teacher Education Program from 2014 to 2017. She is a former teacher, principal, and assistant superintendent. As a principal, she served as a faculty advisor for the UCLA Teacher Education Program, leading preservice teacher teams based in her school.

Lynn Kim-John is the director of the UCLA Educational Leadership Program. In this role, she focuses on the development of socially just executive leaders in K–12, community colleges, and higher education spaces. Earlier, she was the director of science programs at UCLA Center X and the site director for the California Science Project. Her passion for education stems from the more than ten years she served as a high school science teacher in Los Angeles Unified School District. She obtained her BA in psychobiology, MA in education, and PhD in education from UCLA.

Carrie Usui Johnson is the director of professional development and partnerships at UCLA Center X. Usui Johnson supports the development of a highly regarded coaching community and partners with urban schools and districts to support coaching, leadership development, and whole-school transformation efforts focused on equity. She works nationally as a training associate for Thinking Collaborative in Adaptive Schools, a seminar that supports participants in developing and facilitating collaborative groups, and is also an agency trainer for Center X in Cognitive Coaching^{SM}.

Orlando Johnson is the founding principal of the Mann UCLA Community School and has committed his career to supporting families in

South Los Angeles. He served as a teacher leader and administrator at Markham Middle School in Watts, Drew Middle School, Gompers Middle School, and Dorsey High School, his alma mater. He was awarded the 2019 UCLA Howard Welinsky Advocate of the Year award for his commitment to improving the lives of students by helping them become critical thinkers with the skills necessary to become agents of change.

Jarod Kawasaki is an assistant professor at California State University, Dominguez Hills, and a former faculty member in the UCLA Teacher Education Program. His research focuses on supporting science teacher learning with an emphasis on promoting equity and social justice through productive student discourse. He received his BS in applied health from Azusa Pacific University, MA in educational technology from California State University, Northridge, and PhD in education from UCLA.

Queena Kim is an assistant principal and founding member of the RFK UCLA Community School in central Los Angeles. She is a graduate of the UCLA Teacher Education Program (MEd) and Principal Leadership Institute (MEd). Kim began teaching in central Los Angeles in 2003, primarily as an elementary Spanish bilingual teacher. She guides the development of the TK–12 dual language program and collaborates closely with teachers and researchers to study and advance an innovative and culturally sustaining approach to language learning.

Jon Kovach is the director of the UCLA Science Project at UCLA Center X and has worked in education for almost twenty years in Los Angeles. During this time he has been a middle school and high school science teacher, department chair, and science instructional coach, and he has designed and facilitated professional learning for over thirty school districts in and around Los Angeles. He is also a training associate for Thinking Collaborative in Adaptive Schools, a seminar that supports group development and collaboration.

Ung-Sang Lee is a postdoctoral scholar at UCLA's Graduate School of Education and Information Studies. He facilitates institutional design partnerships and studies how such partnerships can be leveraged to produce equity in school communities. In his current role at Mann UCLA Community School, he studies and supports learning infrastructures that respond to community schooling models. He received his BA in international relations and philosophy from Claremont McKenna College; teaching credential from University of Michigan, Ann Arbor; and PhD in education from UCLA.

Imelda L. Nava is a faculty member of the Teacher Education Program at UCLA in the Graduate School of Education and Information Studies. As a part of the Urban Teacher Residency Program at UCLA (IMPACT—Inspiring Minds through a Professional Alliance of Community Teachers), her research focuses on using multiple pedagogical instruments to promote teacher growth. In addition, her research interests include humanizing STEM pedagogy, urban STEM teacher development, and equity.

Jeannie Oakes is Presidential Professor Emeritus at UCLA and a senior fellow at the Learning Policy Institute. Oakes's research examines inequalities in US schools and follows the progress of equity reform, including efforts by policy makers, educators, and grassroots organizations to build democratic school communities. Her awards include the American Educational Research Association (AERA)'s Early Career Award, Outstanding Research Article Award, Outstanding Book Award, and Social Justice in Education Research Award. She is a fellow of AERA, former AERA president, and member of the National Academy of Education.

Tonikiaa Orange serves as the director for the Culture and Equity Project (CEP) and is the assistant director for the Principal Leadership Institute (PLI) at UCLA Center X. Her work focuses on preparing the next generation of social justice leaders to transform and create equitable and culturally responsive educational spaces for all students.

Nancy Parachini is director of the UCLA Principal Leadership Institute. She specializes in leadership development, teacher learning, language acquisition, bilingual/dual immersion education, and international education for teachers and leaders. Parachini is passionate about preparing social justice educators to transform inequitable conditions in urban public schools. She collaborates with international agencies in Argentina, Kenya, Taiwan, China, and Mexico to provide professional learning for educational leaders.

Jaime J. Park is a faculty member of the UCLA Teacher Education Program. Park's teaching and research interests focus on secondary mathematics education grounded in equity, deep sensemaking, community, and relevance.

Leticia Perez is director of curriculum for the STEMC3+ project within the UCLA Graduate School of Education and Information Studies as well as the professional learning lead with the UCLA Science Project. Her work focuses on bringing equity and access to K–12 science classrooms through teacher professional development and curricula.

Jody Z. Priselac is the associate dean for community programs in the UCLA School of Education and Information Studies. Priselac has thirty years of experience as a mathematics educator, high school teacher, professional development leader, teacher educator, and educational researcher whose work focuses on access and equity in teaching and learning and school-university partnerships. She received her BA in mathematics and her PhD in education from UCLA.

John Rogers is a professor of education at UCLA and serves as the faculty director of Center X and director of the Institute for Democracy, Education, and Access. Rogers studies issues at the intersection of education, democracy, and inequality. He earned his BA in public policy and African American studies from Princeton University and his PhD in education from Stanford University.

William A. Sandoval is a professor of education at UCLA. He is especially interested in how science learning in school can promote a deep understanding of scientific argument that supports productive engagement with science in public life. He earned his BS in computer science from the University of New Mexico and his PhD in learning sciences from Northwestern University.

Marisa Saunders is associate director for research at UCLA's Center for Community Schooling. Her primary areas of research focus on K–12 transformation efforts aimed to address long-standing educational inequalities. Marisa has coauthored a number of publications and books, including *Beyond Tracking: Multiple Pathways to College, Career, and Civic Participation* (Harvard Education Press, 2008) and *Learning Time: In Pursuit of Educational Equity* (Harvard Education Press, 2017).

Christine Shen is the director of the UCLA Community School Initiatives and has over twenty years of experience leading large-scale school transformations in Los Angeles. Shen was a founding member of the first start-up public charter middle school in Los Angeles. She served as a senior advisor for LA Mayor Antonio Villaraigosa, helping to secure and manage fifteen urban schools, and collaborated with the Los Angeles Police Department and other city departments to ensure safe school passages for over one hundred schools in the Los Angeles Unified School District.

Index

academic language, 54, 62–64
achievement gap, 6, 43, 77
Addams, Jane, 177
advocacy
  by Center X, 201–202
  by teachers, 17–19
affirmative action, 216
African American students,
    32–33, 36, 94, 129
agency
  collective, 165–175, 177
  student, 6, 43, 45, 107–108,
      111, 116–117, 175
  teacher, 164–175
Alinsky, Saul, 13
alumni
  Center X, 206–207
  PLI, 127–128, 131–140
  TEP, 35, 93, 94, 99–103,
      146–149, 156
Anti-Racist Committee (ARC),
    194–195
antiracist pedagogy, 5, 32, 34, 42
Appelgate, Mollie, 66
Arbery, Ahmaud, 31, 217
Arias, Melissa S., 5, 49–71
Assembly Bill 2, 126
assessment
  formative, 50, 54, 59, 67–68

of teachers, 50–53, 169–171,
    204
autonomy
  curricular, 158
  teacher, 166

Baldwin Hills Elementary, 138–
    139, 205–206
Banks, Jim, 13
Bautista, Mauro, 132, 136–137,
    140, 206
Beck, Lynn, 13
Belmont Pilot Schools, 166
beloved community, 3, 201–202
Berry, Robert, 58, 61
best practices, 77–78, 90, 207,
    210
biases, 6, 78
Bilingual Cross-cultural Language
    and Academic Develop-
    ment (BCLAD), 14, 28
bilingual instruction, 22, 167–
    169, 176
Black Lives Matter, 3, 127
Bloom, Benjamin, 60
Boyle Heights, 144–146, 150–
    152, 156, 208
Boyle Heights and Me course,
    152–157

Buenvista, Tracy L., 153

California English Language
    Development Standards, 53
California Subject Matter Projects,
    14
California Teacher Credentialing
    Commission, 22
caring advocacy, 17–19
case studies, 28–29
centering relationships, 92
Center X, 3–7, 12, 13, 200
    advocacy by, 201–202
    affirmative action and, 216
    alumni, 206–207
    collaborations by, 207–211
    ethnic studies and, 209
    guiding principles of, 15–16, 33,
        35, 52–53, 201
    mentors and, 159
    ongoing learning and, 92–103
    ongoing struggle for, 216–217
    partnerships, 24–25
    partnership with Los Angeles
        Unified School District,
        94–99
    PLI program and, 205–206
    purpose of, 13–14, 156
    racial injustice and, 31–32
    research program, 25–29
    teacher education and, 16–25
    UCLA Mathematics Project,
        99–100
challenges
    as opportunities, 101
    to student-centered teaching,
        111–115
change agents, 154, 156
    teachers as, 21, 44–45, 156
charter schools, 165–166, 180,
    181–182
Chávez, César, 163, 164, 178
chemistry, 108

Chesterfield Square neighborhood,
    180–182
Chicano Movement, 145
Cisneros, Sandra, 137
civil rights movement, 164, 178
civil unrest, 7, 11–12, 31–32
CLAD (Cross-cultural, Language,
    and Academic Develop-
    ment) Emphasis credential,
    22, 28
CLAD/BCLAD (Cross-cultural
    Language and Academic
    Development / Bilingual
    Cross-cultural Language
    and Academic Develop-
    ment), 14
Claim, Evidence, Reasoning
    (CER) strategy, 59
Clark, Heather F., 105–124
class discussions, 60–62
classroom ecology, 54, 56, 64–
    66
classroom observation, social
    justice rubric, 5
classroom routines, 54, 64–66
classrooms, culture of equity in,
    115–117
coaching, 5–6, 77
    reconceptualizing, 78–80
    traditional paradigms, 77–78,
        83
Cochran-Smith, Marilyn, 13
cognitively guided instruction
    (CGI), 99–102
coherent instruction, 116–118
cohorts, 23–24
collaboration, 15, 148–149,
        152–155, 158, 207–211
    See also partnerships
collaborative governance,
    183–186
collective action, 93
collective agency, 165–175, 177

envisioning, at UCLA Community School, 165–167
as organizing, 173–175
politics of, 169–171
to reimagine schooling, 171–173
as scholarship, 167–169
colorism, 45
Common Core State Standards, 53
communities, collaboration with, 207–211
community activism, 153–155
community builders, teachers as, 20–21
community circles, 174–175
community connections, 150–152
community engagement, 184–185
Community Inquiry Project, 38–39, 41
community members, 29021
community of learners, 54, 64–66
community of practice, 206
PLI as, 131–133
Community School (UCLA). *See* UCLA Community School
community schools, 171–173, 176–178
Mann UCLA Community School, 179–197
UCLA Community School, 163–178, 215
community science, technology, engineering, and mathematics project-based learning (C-STEM-PBL) assignment, 69–70
Community Service Organization (CSO), 146
community teachers, 5, 31–47, 160, 164
about, 32–33
as change agents, 44–45

critical inquiry by, 40–42
critical pedagogical knowledge and skills of, 42–44
cultural knowledge of, 37–40
developing, 32, 34–46
racial injustice and, 33–34
reflecting on positionality by, 36–37
concept maps, 59
constructivist approach, 204
content discourse, 54, 56, 59–62
content knowledge, 16, 42, 62, 211–212
content relevance, 54, 62–64
content rigor, 54, 56, 57–59
continued learning, 91–103
core values, 2
COVID-19 pandemic, 2, 127, 132, 194
critical consciousness, 45
critical hope, 153
critical inquiry, 19–20, 40–42
Critical Media Literacy course, 44
critical pedagogical knowledge, 42–44
critical race theory, 80
critical reflection, 82, 84, 88
critical social justice, 130
critical third space theory, 80–81
Cullors, Patrisse, 3–4
cultural community wealth, 150–151
cultural competence, 110
cultural congruence, 18–19
cultural knowledge, 37–40, 80
culturally democratic pedagogy, 18–19
culturally relevant pedagogies, 108
culturally responsive pedagogy, 151, 205–206
cultural norms, 164–165
cultural relevance, 42

cultural studies, 44
Cummins, Jim, 13
curricular autonomy, 158
curriculum, 152–155

Darder, Antonia, 13
Darling-Hammond, Linda, 159
Davis, Letitia, 134, 138–139, 205
deficit perspectives, 43, 77, 79,
      85–86, 151
democracy
   building, 176–178
   schools as center of, 2
democratic classrooms, 54, 64–66
democratic governance, 192–195
democratic leadership, 130, 132
democratic theory, 130
desegregation, 181
Dewey, John, 13, 32, 129, 177
dialogue
   reflective, 140
   student-to-student, 119–120
differentiation, 54, 62–64
discrimination, 13
discipline, 130, 157–158
district partnerships, 123
diversity, student, 18, 90
Duncan-Andrade, Jeff, 50

Edelman, Marian Wright, 7
educational inequality, 2, 12–13,
      200
educational justice, 174–175
educational reform, 15–16, 21,
      106, 212–214
educational standards, equity and,
      106–108
education policy research, 51,
      182
emergent bilinguals, 129
English language learners, 94
"English-Only" Proposition 227,
      167

equitable access to content, 54,
      56, 62–64
equity, 46, 52, 62, 129
   gap, 6, 42
   in instruction, 115–122
   issues, naming, 81, 87
   questions, 83
   reciprocal learning partnerships
      for, 75–90, 78
   in science education, 105–124
   standards and, 106–108
   work, 84–89
equity actions, 82, 84, 87–89
Estes, Carla, 7, 179–197
ethnic studies, 39–40, 46, 152–
      154, 156–157, 209
exclusion, 129
experimentation, 121
experts, 86

families
   discouraged, 20
   engagement of, 184
   enrichment and services for,
      191–192
feedback, 58–59, 170
fellows, 81, 86
field-based learning, 159
Floyd, George, 3, 31, 217
formative assessment, 50, 54, 59,
      67–68
framing
   purpose of instruction, 118–119
   questions, 83–84
Francois, Annamarie, 31–47, 201
Francois, Annamarie M., 5
Franke, Megan L,, 6, 91–103
Freire, Paulo, 32, 129

Gallimore, Ron, 13
Gándara, Patricia, 167
Garcia, Leyda, 6, 163–178
Gertner, Ben, 6, 143–161

Gibbons, Pauline, 63
Giroux, Henry, 13, 17
global pandemic, 2, 127, 132, 194
Gonzalez, Cynthia, 132
Goodlad, John, 27
"good trouble," 7, 201–216
Graduate School of Education
    and Information Studies
    (UCLA), 11–12
Grant, Carl, 13
Gutierrez, Kris, 13

Haberman, Martin, 58
Hanson, Patricia, 134
Harlem Children's Zone, 177
high-level tasks, 58–59
Hipólito, Emma, 6, 143–161
hooks, bell, 3, 13
Horace Mann Junior High School,
    179
    See also Mann UCLA Commu-
    nity School
Huerta, Dolores, 178

identity, 82, 86, 88, 210
identity questions, 83
Immigrant Family Legal Clinic,
    175
IMPACT Classroom Observation
    Rubric (ICOR), 50, 52–66
    community science, technology,
    engineering, and math-
    ematics project-based
    learning (C-STEM-PBL)
    assignment, 69–70
    development of, 53–55
    domain 1: content rigor, 57–59
    domain 2: content discourse,
    59–62
    domain 3: equitable access to
    content, 62–64
    domain 4: classroom ecology,
    64–66

ensuring reliability of, 55–57
measurement and accountabil-
    ity, 70–71
planning, instructing, assessing,
    and reflection (PIAR)
    assignment, 67–68
subdomains, 56
using to support teaching,
    66–70
Video Instructional Rounds
    Cycle (VIRC) assign-
    ment, 68–69
inclusion, 3, 129, 172–173
inequality, 12
inequity, 85–86, 129
inquiry, 19–20, 40–42, 58,
    214–215
Inspiring Minds through a Profes-
    sional Alliance of Commu-
    nity Teachers (IMPACT),
    34, 50–51
instruction
    coherent, 116–118
    framing purpose of, 118–119
instructional equity, 115–122
Instructional Logs, 52
instructional practices, 129–130
Instructional Quality Assessment,
    52
Intensive Support and Innovation
    Center (ISIC), 184
Isken, Jo Ann, 6, 75–90

Johnson, Carrie Usui, 7, 179–197
Johnson, Orlando, 6, 179–197

K-12 cultures, 97–98
K-12 education, university's role
    in, 212–214
Kawasaki, Jarod, 31–47, 105–124
Kawasaki, Jarrod, 5
Kennedy, Robert F., 163, 164,
    178, 211

Kim, Queena, 6, 163–178
Kim-John, Lynn, 105–124
King, Martin Luther, Jr., 3
King, Rodney, 3, 11–12, 181, 199, 211, 217
Know, Want to Know, Learn (KWL) activity, 64
knowledge production, 152–155
known-answer questions, 112
Kovach, Jon, 105–124
Kraft, Matthew A., 177

Ladson-Billings, Gloria, 13
language, 62–63
LA riots, 181, 217
Latino students, 94
Lave, Jean, 127
Lazo, Georgia, 167
leaders, 7
leadership
  democratic, 130, 132
  preparation of, 128–130
  social justice, 125–140
learning
  See also professional development
  centrality of student dialogue to, 119–120
  constructivist approach to, 204
  defined, 92–93
  field-based, 159
  ongoing, 91–103
  problem-based, 53
  project-based, 42–43, 53, 69–70
  reciprocal, 209
  as social process, 80
  sustained engagement in, 211–212
  through collaboration, 207–208
  together, 101–102
learning community, 4
learning environments, 43
Learn-See-Do, 189

Lee, Ung-Sang, 7, 179–197
legal structures, 130
leveled questions, 60–61
Lewis, John, 7, 201, 202, 217
LGBTQ+ youth, 129
liberatory pedagogy, 45
Linked Learning, 53
literacy, 95–96
Local District 7, 94–99, 102
Local School Initiative (LSI) governance model, 186, 188
Los Angeles Unified School District (LAUSD), 94–99, 102–103
  CGI partnerships, 99–102
  desegregation of, 181
  Ethnic Studies Leadership Team, 157
  PLI alumni leadership in, 135
  school-building by, 165–167
  teacher union, 156, 173–175
love, 3

Macdonald, James B., 17
Macdonald, Susan Colberg, 17
Mann, Horace, 179
Mann UCLA Community School, 7, 179–197, 211–215
  Anti-Racist Committee (ARC), 194–195
  collaborations, 186–195
  collaborative governance at, 183–186
  community history of, 180–182
  democratic governance of, 192–195
  enrollment at, 180, 181–182
  future of, 196–197
  lessons learned from, 195–197
  staffing and professional development, 187–191
  student and family enrichment and services, 191–192

summer institute, 185
trust building at, 182–186
vision for, 186
marginalization, 128–130, 132,
    164, 176
Martinez-Gertner, Maria, 125
Master's Inquiry Project, 41–42,
    214–215
Math, Science, and Technol-
    ogy Magnet Academy at
    Roosevelt (MSTMA), 145,
    152–156, 160–161
    See also Roosevelt High School
mathematics, 58, 63, 64, 99–102,
    158
McGovern, Elexia R., 153
McLaren, Peter, 13
Measures of Effective Teaching
    (MET) project, 51
mentor teachers, 23–25, 43, 46,
    51, 76–77, 144, 210
    disconnect between preservice
        teachers and, 160
    novice teachers and, 76–81, 160
    preparing to do equity work,
        84–89
    reconceptualizing coaching and,
        78–80
    TEP and, 146–148, 159,
        160–161
    traditional coaching paradigms
        by, 77–78
models, 121
Moll, Luis, 13
Montaño, Theresa, 209
multiculturalism, 13, 151
Murrell, Peter, 32, 34, 40, 160
"must-place" teachers, 187, 212

National Council on Teacher
    Quality, 51
Nava, Imelda L., 5, 49–71
Navarro, Jose, 133

Next Generation Science Stan-
    dards, 53, 59, 106–111,
    115–122, 124, 211
NGSS First Five, 121–122
Noddings, Nel, 13
novice teachers, 23–26
    See also preservice teachers
    advice for, 49
    critical inquiry by, 40–42
    developing cultural knowledge
        in, 37–40
    mentor teachers and, 76–81,
        160
    preparing to do equity work,
        84–89
    recruitment of, 35
    reflection by, 36–37
    social justice and, 165

Oakes, Jeannie, 5, 7, 11–29, 32,
    92, 199–217
Observation Rubric, 52
ongoing learning, 91–103
    CGI-LAUSD partnerships,
        99–102
    school-university partnerships
        for, 94–99
open-ended questions, 120, 170
opportunities, challenges as, 101
oppositional imagination, 171
Orange, Tonikiaa, 6, 75–90

Parachini, Nancy, 6, 125–140
Parent, Family, and Caregiver
    Engagement Project, 38, 39
parents, 20
    See also families
Park, Jaime J., 5, 49–71
Park, Jay, 63
participation structures, 54, 60–62
participatory inquiry, 81–82
partnerships, 24–25
    goals of, 196

partnerships (*continued*)
  importance of, 159–161
  reciprocal, 75–90, 209
  research-practice, 6, 16,
        110–115, 123–124, 169,
        214–215
  school-university, 3, 5, 15–16,
        24–25, 94–99, 110–115,
        143–161, 212–214
Partners in Practice meetings, 86
partner teachers, 81, 86, 209
pedagogies, 16
  antiracist, 5, 32, 34, 42
  critical, 42–44
  culturally democratic, 18–19
  culturally relevant, 108
  culturally responsive, 151,
        205–206
  liberatory, 45
  powerful, 211–212
pedagogy of poverty, 58
peer groups, 20
Perez, Leticia, 105–124
planning, instructing, assess-
        ing, and reflection (PIAR)
        assignment, 67–68
police violence, 31–32, 181, 194
political activism, 145–146, 155,
        156, 158
political community, 3–4
portfolio defenses, 28
portfolios, 28
positionality, 36–37, 78, 82, 84,
        86, 88, 210
poverty, 12, 13
  pedagogy of, 58
preservice teacher learning, 49–71
  context and, 159–161
  teacher residencies and, 50–53
preservice teachers, 144, 209–210
  cohorts, 23–24
Principal Leadership Institute
        (PLI), 6, 92, 125–140,
        205–206

alumni, 127–128, 131–140
  as community of practice,
        131–133
  creation of, 126
  as leadership preparation
        program, 128–130
  prospective students, 131
  social justice and, 127–128
  work of, 126–127
Priselac, Jody Z., 6, 91–103
problem-based learning, 53
problem-solving, real world, 20
professional development, 6, 13,
        14, 95–96
  "cradle-to-grave," 15, 204–207
  equity-oriented science,
        105–124
  First Five, 121–122
  at Mann UCLA Community
        School, 187–191
  ongoing, 91–103
  research-practice partnership
        for, 110–115
  school-based, 210, 211–212
  school reform and, 212–214
  in science teaching, 108–109
  structuring for sustainable
        change, 110–111
professionalism, 166
professional learning partnerships,
        5–6
project-based learning (PBL),
        42–43, 53, 69–70
Promise Neighborhood initiatives,
        177
Proposition 39, 182

Quartz, Karen Hunter, 6, 163–
        178, 201, 215
questions
  critical reflection, 84
  equity, 83
  equity action, 84
  identity, 83

known-answer, 112
leveled, 60–61
open-ended, 120
positionality, 84
reciprocity, 83
relational trust, 83
that prompt dialogue, 83–84

race
  critical race theory, 80
  social justice and, 127
Race to the Top policy, 50
racial equity, 46
racial inequality, 92
racial injustice, 200
  reframing teacher education as
    response to, 33–34
racial justice, 3–4, 130, 202
racial violence, 2, 7, 12, 31–32,
    217
racism, 85, 102
radical change, 44–45
Ramirez, Mariana, 155
Reader Identity Self-Assessment
  (RISA), 169
reciprocal learning partnerships
  (RLPs), 75–90, 209
  in action, 81–82
  coaching and, 78–80
  equity work and, 84–89
  example, 87–89
  facilitators, 87
  framework, 80–81
  framing questions in, 83–84
  relational trust and, 82
reciprocity, 82, 86, 88
reciprocity questions, 83
reflection, 19–20, 36–37
  critical, 82, 84, 88
  ongoing, 140
relational trust, 82, 83, 86, 89
relationship building, 93–94
relationships
  centering, 92

importance of, 95–97, 100
  ongoing, for professional devel-
    opment, 210
research-practice partnerships, 6,
    16, 110–115, 123–124,
    169, 214–215
research program, of Center X,
    25–29
resilience, 153–154
respect, 3
restorative justice, 130, 157–158
rigorous tasks, 58–59
Robert F. Kennedy (RFK) Com-
    munity Schools, 164
  See also UCLA Community
    School
Rogers, John, 6, 125–140
Roosevelt High School, 6, 208
  community connections with,
    150–152
  community of like-minded
    educators at, 148–149
  context of, 145–146
  curriculum, 152–155
  ethnic studies at, 209
  preservice teachers at, 160–161
  reconceptualizing systems and
    structures at, 155–159
  TEP partnership with, 143–161
  transformative practices at,
    149–159
Roybal, Edward, 146
Royce, Josiah, 3
Royce Hall, 3
Rueda, Claudia, 155
Russom, Gillian, 155

Sandoval, William A., 105–124
Saunders, Marisa, 6, 163–178
scheduling, 130
Schoenfeld, Alan H., 58
scholarship, 167–169
school cultures, 16, 97–98,
    164–165, 211–212

school desegregation, 181
schooling, reimagining, 171–173
school reform, 15–16, 21, 106,
        212–214
schools
    as center of democracy, 2
    historical context of, 90
school-university partnerships,
        3, 5, 15–16, 24–25,
        94–99, 110–115, 143–161,
        212–214
science, 58
science education, 59, 105–106,
        211–212
    challenges in, 111–115
    equity in instruction in,
        115–122
    equity-oriented professional
        development, 105–124
    NGSS and, 115–122
    professional learning and,
        108–109
    research-practice partnership
        for, 110–115, 123–124
    scaling social justice, 122–124
    standards and equity in,
        106–108
    student-centered, 106–109,
        121–122
science talk, 119–120
scientific practices, 120–121
scripted curricula, 4
segregation, 129
self-renewal, 16, 215–216
Shen, Christine, 7, 179–197
Sleeter, Christie, 13
social capital, 12
social class, 127
social contract, 2
Social Foundations and Cul-
        tural Diversity in American
        Schools course, 41
social justice, 5, 13, 46, 52, 77

ongoing learning and, 91–103
science teaching, scaling,
        122–124
TEP commitment to, 76
social justice agenda, 15, 203–
        204, 206–207
social justice classroom obser-
        vation rubric, 5
Social Justice Community Nights,
        21
social justice leadership, 125–140
    practice of, 127–128, 132–133,
        135–140
    reimagining schooling and, 171
social justice teachers
    preparation of, 33–34, 70–71
    as scholars, 169
    sustaining, 175–176
    workplace culture to support,
        163–178
social norms, 65
social supports, 19
sociocultural learning theory, 13,
        129
sociocultural theory, 80
special education, 172–173, 176
standardized tests, 4, 50, 51,
        106–108
state subject matter projects, 109
STEM pedagogies, 34
story lines, 118
stratification, 129
structural racism, 102
student achievement, 51
student agency, 6, 43, 45, 107–
        108, 111, 116–117, 175
student-centered teaching, 106–
        115, 121–122, 204
student content discourse, 54,
        60–62
students
    of color, 32–33, 36, 94, 129,
        164, 200

critical consciousness in, 45
disadvantaged, 12–13
diversity of, 18, 90
empowerment of, 45
enrichment and services for, 191–192
feedback from, 170
marginalized, 78, 128–129, 130, 132, 164, 173, 176
with special needs, 129
student teachers. *See* preservice teachers
student teaching, 23
student-to-student dialogue, 119–120
student voice, 65–66
Study of Education of Educators, 27
substitute teachers, 187
success, defining, 49–50
surveys, 27–28
sustainable change, 110–111, 177–178
systems and structures of schooling, 155–159

talk, centrality of, 119–120
Taylor, Breonna, 3, 31, 217
teacher education/preparation, 5, 13
  abolitionist practices in, 5
  for agents of radical change, 44–45
  context of, 159–161
  fast-track, 4
  new culture of, 16–21
  new structure of, 21–25
  ongoing learning, 91–103
  practice-based, 57
  reform of, 144, 159
  reframing as response to racial injustice, 33–34
  social justice and, 33–35

to support development of community teachers, 34–35
  traditional coaching paradigms in, 77–78
  university-based, 51
Teacher Education Program (TEP), 5, 13–14, 33, 35, 53, 75–76, 92–94
  alumni, 35, 93, 94, 99–103, 146–149, 156
  community-focused pedagogy of, 152
  gials of, 156
  knowledge production and, 152–155
  Mann UCLA Community School and, 188
  mentor teachers and, 146–148, 159–161
  mission of, 143
  partnership with Theodore Roosevelt Senior High School, 143–161
  transformative practices of, 149–159
teacher quality, 5, 50–53
teacher questioning, 60–62
teacher residencies, 50–53
teachers
  agency of, 164–175
  autonomy of, 158, 166
  biases of, 6
  as caring advocates, 17–19
  as change agents, 21, 44–45, 156
  collaboration by, 148–149
  community, 5, 31–47, 160, 164
  as community builders, 20–21
  deskilling, 4
  effectiveness of, 49–50
  evaluation of, 50–53, 169–171, 204
  layoffs of, 169

teachers (*continued*)
  at Mann UCLA Community
      School, 187–191
  mentor. *See* mentor teachers
  "must-place," 187, 212
  novice. *See* novice teachers
  partner, 81, 86, 209
  questioning by, 54
  as reflective, inquiry-based
      practitioners, 19–20
  retention of, 90, 215
  social justice. *See* social justice
      teachers
  substitute, 187
  turnover of, 96
teachers' strike, 173–175, 176
teacher unions, 156, 173–175
teaching
  equity in, 115–122
  science, 105–124
  student-centered, 106–115,
      121–122, 204
  sustained engagement in,
      211–212
  using ICOR to support, 66–70
teaching quality, 43, 169–171
TEP Core Practices, 56–59, 67
test scores, 50, 51, 169
Thalkar, Dan, 125
Tharp, Roland, 13
Theodore Roosevelt Senior High
      School. *See* Roosevelt High
      School
Tieu, Darlene, 65
transformative intellectuals, 17
transparency, 196
trust, relational, 82
trust building, 182–186

UCLA. *See* University of Califor-
      nia, Los Angeles (UCLA)
UCLA Community School, 6,
      163–178, 215

beginnings of, 165–167, 211
bilingual instruction at, 167–
      169, 176
collective agency and, 165–175
introduction to, 163–165
reimagining schooling at,
      171–173
special education program,
      172–173, 176
teacher evaluation at, 169–171
teachers' strike and, 173–175
teacher turnover rate, 176
UCLA Mathematics Project
      (UCLAMP), 99–100
UCLA Science Project (UCLASP),
      109, 110, 115–116,
      122–124
understanding, checking for,
      58–59
UniCamp, 185, 195
United Farm Workers (UFW), 178
university cultures, 97–98,
      212–214
University of California (UC)
      Regents, 126
University of California, Los
      Angeles (UCLA), 3
  Graduate School of Education
      and Information Studies,
      11–12
  Mann UCLA Community
      School, 7, 179–197, 211
  Partner School Network, 191
  Principal Leadership Institute, 6,
      92, 125–140, 205–206
  Principals' Center, 14
  Teacher Education Program,
      5, 13–14, 33, 35, 53,
      75–76, 92–94, 143–161,
      188
university-school partnerships.
      See school-university
      partnerships

urban schools, 76
   partnership between universities
      and, 143–161
   sustainable change in, 177–178
   transformation of, 149–159

Vergara v. California, 169
Video Instructional Rounds Cycle
   (VIRC) assignment, 68–69

Wang, Deborah, 66
whole-group discussions, 120
workplace culture, 163–178

Yosso, Tara, 32, 150

Zeichner, Ken, 13